# OXFORD PHOTO DICTIONARY

## INGLÉS–ESPAÑOL

Oxford University Press

Oxford University Press
Great Clarendon Street, Oxford OX2 6DP

Oxford New York
Athens Auckland Bangkok Bogotá Buenos Aires
Calcutta Cape Town Chennai Dar es Salaam
Delhi Florence Hong Kong Istanbul Karachi
Kuala Lumpur Madrid Melbourne Mexico City
Mumbai Nairobi Paris São Paulo Singapore
Taipei Tokyo Toronto Warsaw

and associated companies in
Berlin Ibadan

Oxford and Oxford English are trade marks of
Oxford University Press

ISBN 0 19 431375 1



First published 1992
Fifth impression 2000

Produced for OUP España



Editor: Jane Taylor

Printed in Hong Kong

# Acknowledgements

**Location and studio photography by:** Graham Alder, Chris Andrews, Martyn Chillmaid, Nigel Cull, Nick Fogden, Paul Freestone, Gareth Jones, Mark Mason.

**The publishers would like to thank the following for permission to reproduce photographs:** ABI Caravans Ltd; Allsport (UK) Ltd/B Asset, S Bruty, R Cheyne, T Duffy, S Dunn, J Gichigi, J Hayt, B Hazelton, H Heiderman, J Loubat, A Murrell, J Nicholson, M Powell, P Rondeau, H Stein; Animal Photography/S Thompson, R Willbie; Ardea London Ltd/D Avon, I Beames, L Beames, J Clegg, E Dragesco, M England, J Ferrero, K Fink, D Greenslade, A Lindau, J Mason, E Mickleburgh, P Morris, S Roberts, R & V Taylor, A Weaving, W Weisser; Art Directors Photo Library/S Grant; Associated Sports Photography; Clive Barda; Barnaby's Picture Library; J Allan Cash Ltd; Bruce Coleman Ltd/J Anthony, E & B Bauer, J Burton, M Dohrn, J Foot, N Fox-Davies, M Kahl, G Langsbury, W Layer, G McCarthy, M Price, A Purcell, H Reinhard, K Taylor, N Tomalin, R Wilmshurst; Colorsport/Compoint; Cotswold Wildlife Park; Cunard Line Ltd; Mary Evans Picture Library; Fiat Fork Lift Trucks; Michael Fogden; Ford Motor Company Ltd; Robert Harding Picture Library/Griffiths, G Renner; Eric Hoskin/W Pitt; Hovertravel Ltd; Libby Howells; The Hutchison Library/M Scorer; Rob Judges; Landscape Only; Frank Lane Picture Agency/A Albinger, R Jones, Silvestris, M Thomas, L West; Leyland Daf; London Tourist Board; Mazda Cars (UK) Ltd; Metropolitan Police; National Motor Museum, Beaulieu; Oxford Scientific Films Stills/S Dalton, L Lauber, M Leach, Partridge Films Ltd, Presstige Pictures, R Redfern, F Skibbe, G Wren; Planet Earth Pictures/Seaphot/M Clay, W Deas, D George, J George, K Lucas, J Lythgoe, N Middleton, J Scott, J Watt; Renault UK Ltd; Rex Features Ltd/N Jorgensen, J Tarrant; Rover Cars; RSPB/G Downey, P Perfect, M Richards; Science Photo Library/T Beddow, M Bond, Dr J Burgess, D Campione, M Dohrn, T Fearon-Jones, V Fleming, NASA, S Patel, R Royer, St Bartholomew's Hospital, J Sanford, S Stammers, J Stevenson, S Terry; Shell UK Ltd; Spectrum Colour Library; Swift Picture Library/T Dressler, M Mockler; Toleman Automotive Ltd; Trust House Forte; Wedgewood; World Pictures; Zefa/D Cattani, Damm, D Davies, Goebel, C Krebs, R Maylander, K Oster, J Pfaff, A Roberts, Rosenfeld, Selitsch.

**The publishers would like to thank the following for their help and assistance:** Abingdon Hospital; Abingdon Surgery; Russell Acott Ltd; Apollo Theatre; B & L Mechanical Services, Eynsham; Douglas Bader Sports Centre, St Edward's School; Barclays Bank; BBC Radio Oxford; The Bear & Ragged Staff, Cumnor; H C Biggers, Eynsham; Boswells of Oxford; Bournemouth International Airport; British Rail; Cassington Builders Ltd; Cheney School; Cherwell School; City Camera Exchange, Brighton; Comet; Daisies, Oxford; Early Learning Centre; Education & Sci Products Ltd; Elmer Cotton Sports, Oxford; Eynsham Car Repairs; Faulkner & Sons Ltd; For Eyes; Phylis Goodman Ltd, Eynsham; Habitat Designs Ltd; W R Hammond & Son Ltd, Eynsham; Hartford Motors Ltd; Headington Sports; Heather's Delicatessen, Hove; Hove Delicatessen; Inshape Body Studios Ltd; Johnsons of Oxford; Littlewoods PLC; London Underground Ltd; Malin Farms, Eynsham; P J Meagher, Eynsham; John Menzies Ltd; North Kidlington Primary School; Ocean Village Marina, Marina Developments PLC; Nigel Olesen BDS; Options Hair Studio, Eynsham; Oxford Despatch; Oxford Royal Mail & Post Office Counters; Paramount Sewing Machines; Parkwood Veterinary Group; Payless DIY; Phoenix One & Two; Qualifruit; Red Funnel Isle of Wight Ferries; SS Mary & John School; Southampton Eastleigh Airport; Stanhope Wilkinson Associates, Eynsham; Summertown Travel; Texas Homecare, Oxford; Paul Thomas; Richard Walton, Eynsham; Warlands, Cycle Agents; Welsh National Opera; Western Newsagents, Hove; Chris Yapp Consultants Ltd.

# Indice


1 Parentescos
3 El Cuerpo Humano
5 Descripción Física
6 ¿Qué pasa?
7 El Cuidado de la Salud
9 Describiendo Ropa
10 Ropa
12 Disfrazarse
13 Edificios
15 El Comedor
16 El Cuarto de Estar
17 El Cuarto de Baño
18 El Dormitorio
19 El Lavadero y Cuarto de Plancha
20 La Cocina
21 Herramientas
22 El Jardín
23 En el Mercado
25 En la Floristería
26 En la Tienda de Periódicos
27 En la Charcutería
28 En el Restaurante
29 En la Tienda de Fotografía
30 En la Tienda de Sonido
31 Servicios de Correos
33 Números/La Fecha
34 En el Banco
35 Dinero Americano
36 Dinero Británico
37 La Hora
38 Servicios de Urgencia
39 Trabajos
41 Rutina Diaria
43 Verbos en la Oficina
44 La Oficina
45 Un Laboratorio de Ciencias
47 Formas y Líneas
48 Pesos y Medidas
49 La Clase
50 El Espacio
51 El Tiempo
52 La Temperatura/Las Estaciones
53 El Mundo
55 Los EEUU
56 Las Islas Británicas
57 Preposiciones
59 La Ciudad
61 Carreteras y Señales de Tráfico
63 Vehículos
64 El Coche
65 Bicicletas
66 El Ferrocarril
67 En el Aeropuerto
69 En el Puerto
71 Vacaciones
73 El Medio Ambiente
74 Hobbies
75 Instrumentos Musicales
76 Música y Teatro
77 Deportes
82 Manteniéndose en Forma
83 Verbos
87 Adjetivos Opuestos
89 Animales
91 Peces y Reptiles
92 Insectos y Otros Animales
93 Aves
94 Etiquetas para Inglés Británico y Americano
95 Símbolos Fonéticos
96 Indice Alfabético
124 Ejercicios
139 Soluciones a los Ejercicios

# Family Relationships 

| La Familia de John | John's Family |
|---|---|
| abuela | **1** grandmother |
| abuelo | **2** grandfather |
| tía | **3** aunt |
| tío | **4** uncle |
| madre | **5** mother |
| padre | **6** father |
| suegro | **7** father-in-law |
| suegra | **8** mother-in-law |
| primo, prima | **9** cousin |
| cuñado | **10** brother-in-law |
| hermana | **11** sister |
| esposa | **12** wife |
| cuñada | **13** sister-in-law |
| sobrina | **14** niece |
| sobrino | **15** nephew |
| hijo | **16** son |
| hija | **17** daughter |

| | |
|---|---|
| John es el **marido** de Ann. | **18** John is Ann's **husband**. |
| Tom y Lisa son los **hijos** de John y Ann. | **19** Tom and Lisa are John and Ann's **children**. |
| John y Ann son los **padres** de Tom y Lisa. | **20** John and Ann are Tom and Lisa's **parents**. |
| Mary y Bob Cox e Ian y Jane Hill son los **abuelos** de Tom y Lisa. | **21** Mary and Bob Cox and Ian and Jane Hill are Tom and Lisa's **grandparents**. |
| Tom es su **nieto**. | **22** Tom is their **grandson**. |
| Lisa es su **nieta**. | **23** Lisa is their **granddaughter**. |

# page 2 Family Relationships

1
Helen Jones
2
Andrew Jones
1
Joan Cox
2
Alan Cox
3
Sally Jones
4
David Jones
3
Jill Jones
5
Mary Cox
6
Bob Cox
7
Ian Hill
8
Jane Hill
9
Rita Jones
9
Sam Jones
10
Paul Day
11
Tina Day
John Cox
12
Ann Cox
13
Carol King
10
Joe King
14
Lucy Day
15
Nick Day
16
Tom Cox
17
Lisa Cox
15
Mark King
14
Sue King

# The Human Body 1

page 3

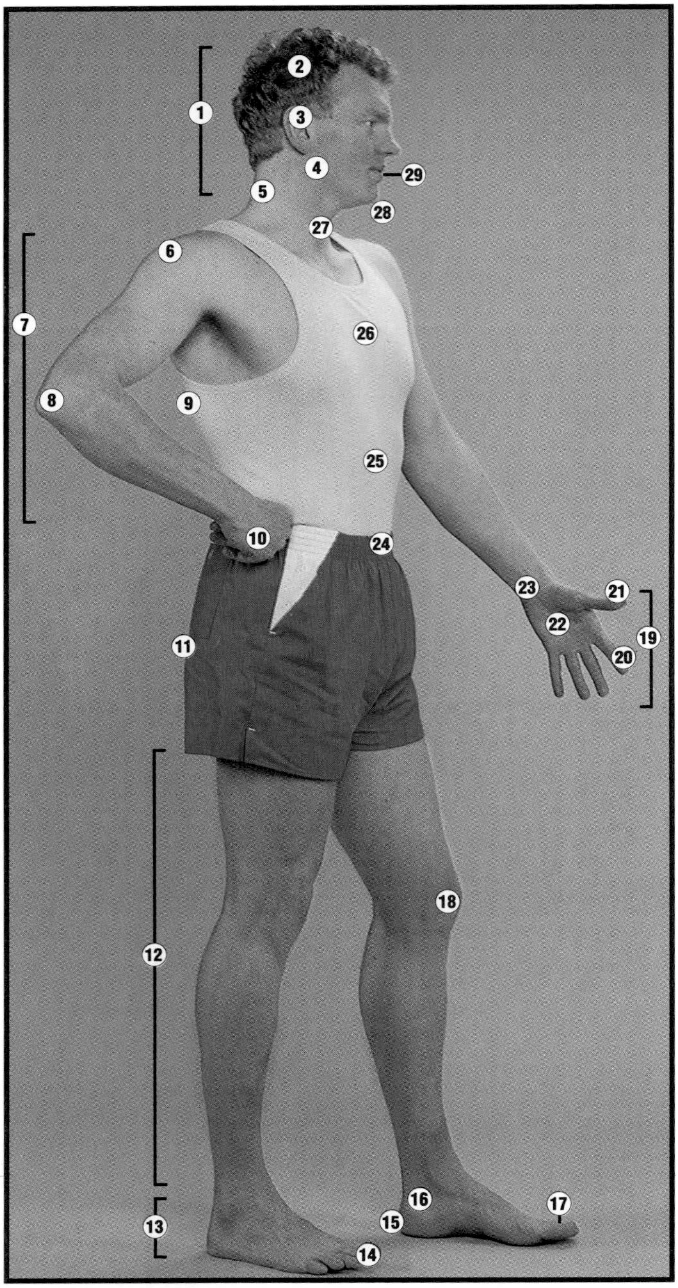


| | | |
|---|---|---|
| cabeza | **1** | head |
| pelo | **2** | hair |
| oreja | **3** | ear |
| mandídula | **4** | jaw |
| cuello | **5** | neck |
| hombro | **6** | shoulder |
| brazo | **7** | arm |
| codo | **8** | elbow |
| espalda | **9** | back |
| puño | **10** | fist |
| nalgas | **11** | buttocks/bottom |
| pierna | **12** | leg |
| pie | **13** | foot |
| dedo del pie | **14** | toe |
| talón | **15** | heel |
| tobillo | **16** | ankle |
| uña | **17** | nail |
| rodilla | **18** | knee |
| mano | **19** | hand |
| dedo | **20** | finger |
| pulgar | **21** | thumb |
| palma | **22** | palm |
| muñeca | **23** | wrist |
| cintura | **24** | waist |
| estómago | **25** | stomach |
| pecho | **26** | chest |
| garganta | **27** | throat |
| barbilla | **28** | chin |
| boca | **29** | mouth |

# The Human Body 2

page 4

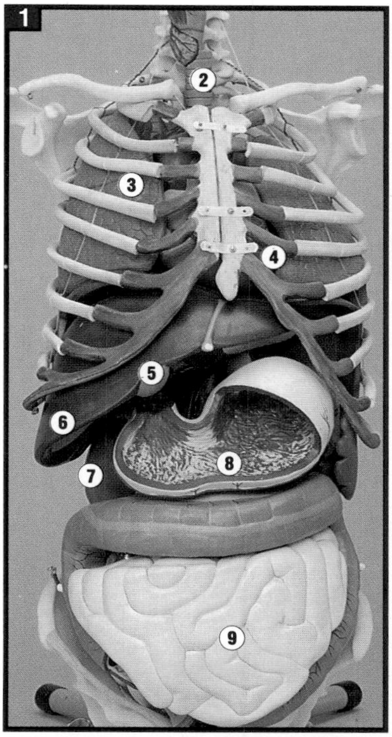


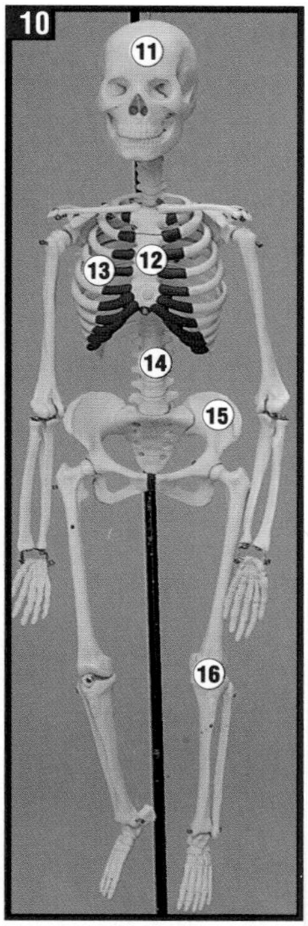


| | | |
|---|---|---|
| órganos internos | **1** | internal organs |
| tráquea | **2** | trachea/windpipe |
| pulmón | **3** | lung |
| corazón | **4** | heart |
| vesícula biliar | **5** | gall-bladder |
| hígado | **6** | liver |
| riñón | **7** | kidney |
| estómago | **8** | stomach |
| intestinos | **9** | intestines |
| esqueleto | **10** | skeleton |
| cráneo | **11** | skull |
| esternón | **12** | breastbone |
| costilla | **13** | rib |
| columna vertebral | **14** | spine/backbone |
| pelvis/hueso de la cadera | **15** | pelvis/hip-bone |
| rótula | **16** | kneecap |

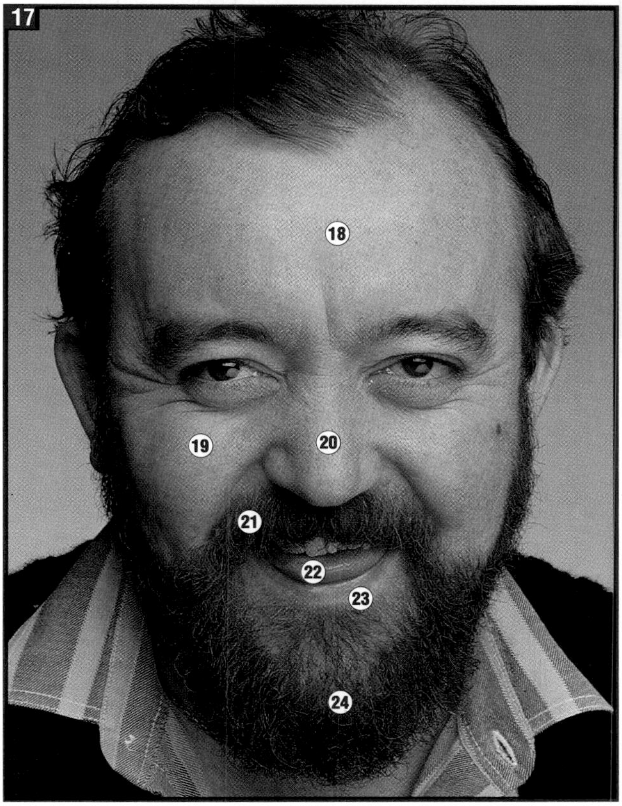


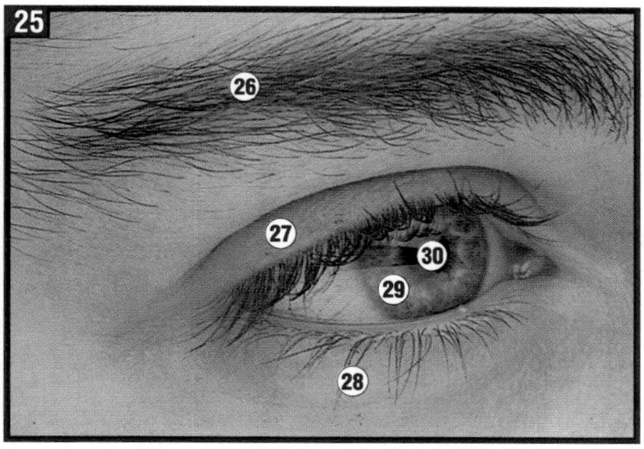


| | | |
|---|---|---|
| cara | **17** | face |
| frente | **18** | forehead |
| mejilla | **19** | cheek |
| nariz | **20** | nose |
| bigote | **21** | moustache |
| lengua | **22** | tongue |
| labio | **23** | lip |
| barba | **24** | beard |
| ojo | **25** | eye |
| ceja | **26** | eyebrow |
| párpado | **27** | eyelid |
| pestaña | **28** | eyelash |
| iris | **29** | iris |
| pupila | **30** | pupil |

# Physical Description

page 5

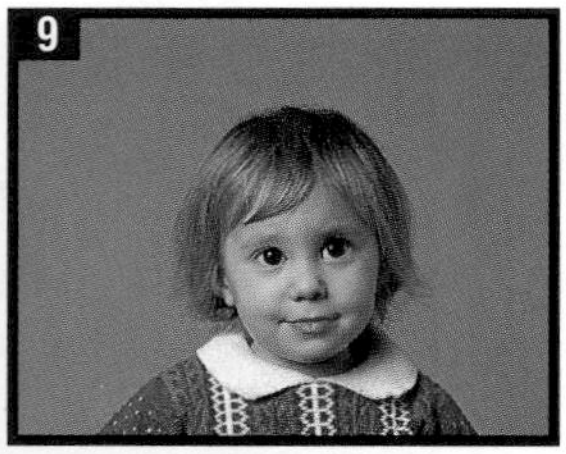


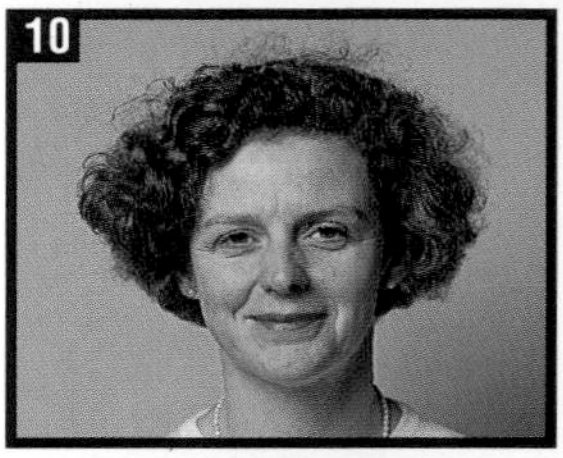

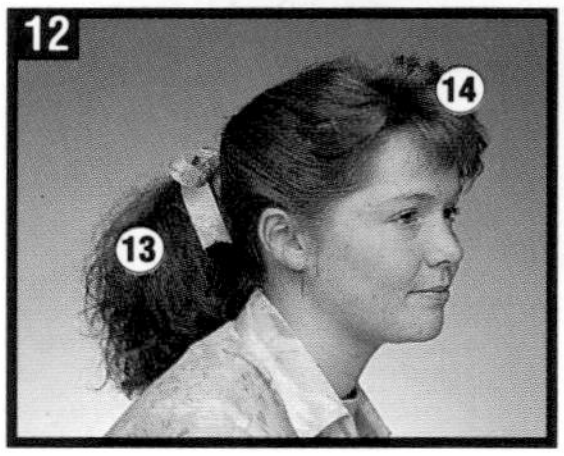


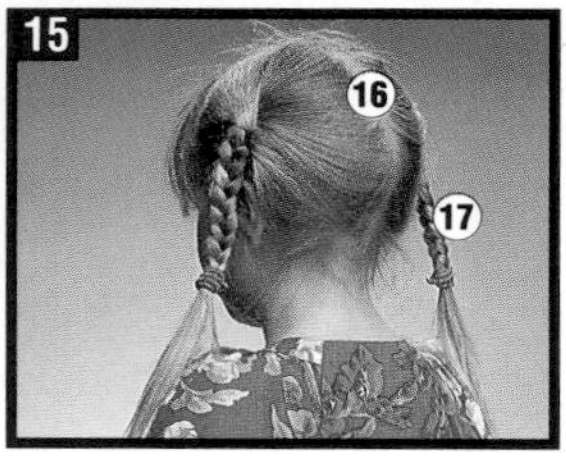


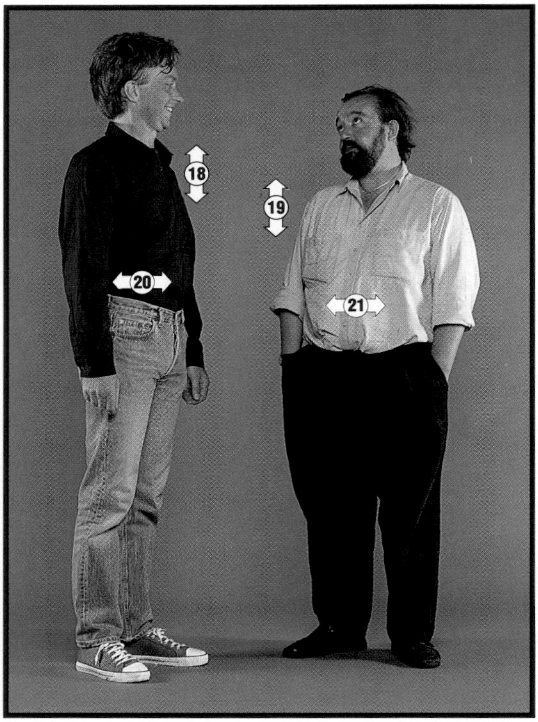


| | |
|---|---|
| **Edad** | **Age** |
| bebé | **1** baby |
| niño/chico | **2** child/(young) boy |
| adolescente/chica adolescente | **3** teenager/teenage girl |
| mujer adulta | **4** adult/woman |
| hombre adulto | **5** adult/man |
| hombre anciano (*o* viejo) | **6** elderly (*or* old) man |
| **Pelo** | **Hair** |
| calva | **7** bald head |
| corto liso moreno | **8** short straight dark |
| corto liso castaño | **9** short straight fair |
| corto rizado | **10** short curly |
| corto ondulado | **11** short wavy |
| largo rojo | **12** long red (*Brit also* ginger) |
| coleta | **13** pony tail |
| flequillo | **14** fringe (*US* bangs) |
| largo rubio | **15** long blonde |
| raya | **16** parting (*US* part) |
| trenza | **17** plait (*US* braid) |
| alto | **18** tall |
| bajo | **19** short |
| delgado | **20** thin |
| gordo | **21** fat |

# What's the matter?

page 6

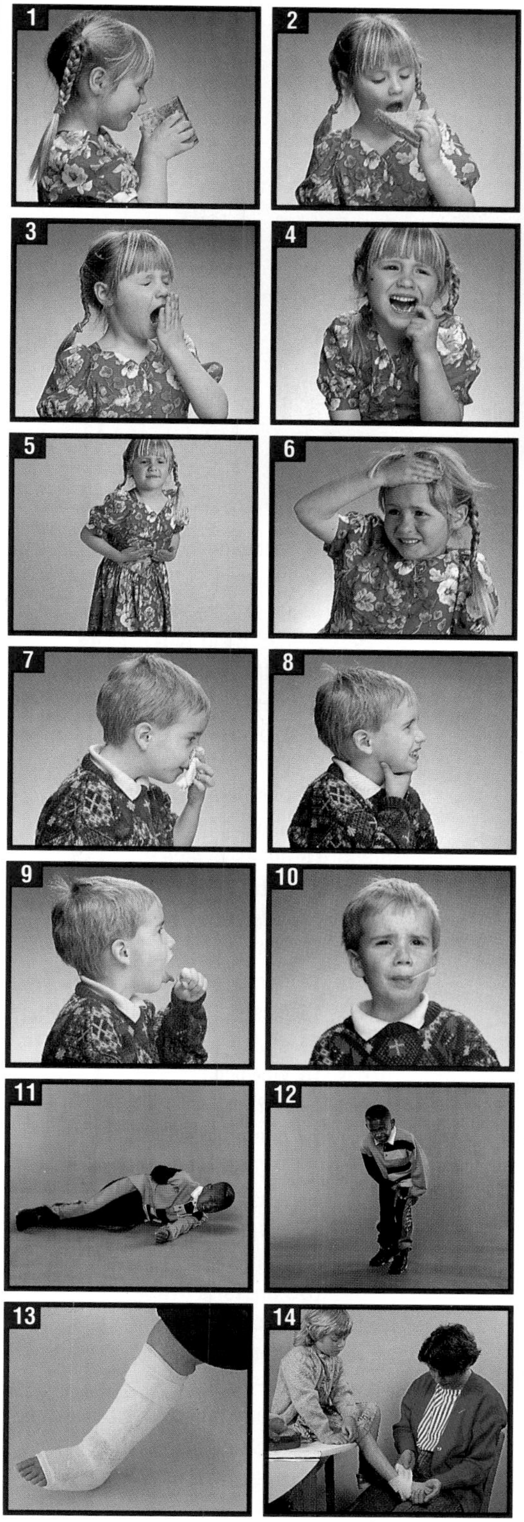

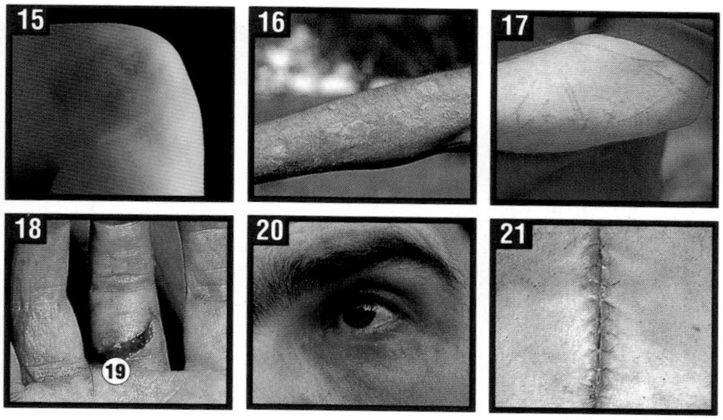

| | |
|---|---|
| Tiene sed. | **1** She's thirsty. |
| Tiene hambre. | **2** She's hungry. |
| Está cansada. | **3** She's tired. |
| Le duele una muela. | **4** She's got toothache. (*US* She has a toothache.) |
| Le duele el estómago. | **5** She's got stomach-ache. (*US* She has a stomachache.) |
| Le duele la cabeza. | **6** She's got a headache. (*US* She has a headache.) |
| Tiene un catarro. | **7** He's got a cold. (*US* He has a cold.) |
| Le duele la garganta. | **8** He's got a sore throat. (*US* He has a sore throat.) |
| Tiene tos. | **9** He's got a cough. (*US* He has a cough.) |
| Tiene fiebre. | **10** He's got a temperature. (*US* He has a temperature.) |
| **Accidentes** | **Accidents** |
| Se ha caído. | **11** He's fallen over. (*US* He fell over.) |
| Se ha hecho daño en la pierna. | **12** He's hurt his leg. (*US* He hurt his leg.) |
| Se ha roto la pierna. | **13** She's broken her leg. (*US* She broke her leg.) |
| Se ha torcido el tobillo. | **14** She's sprained her ankle. (*US* She sprained her ankle.) |
| cardenal | **15** bruise |
| quemaduras del sol | **16** sunburn |
| arañazo | **17** scratch |
| corte | **18** cut |
| sangre | **19** blood |
| ojo morado | **20** black eye |
| cicatriz | **21** scar |

# Health Care 1 page 7

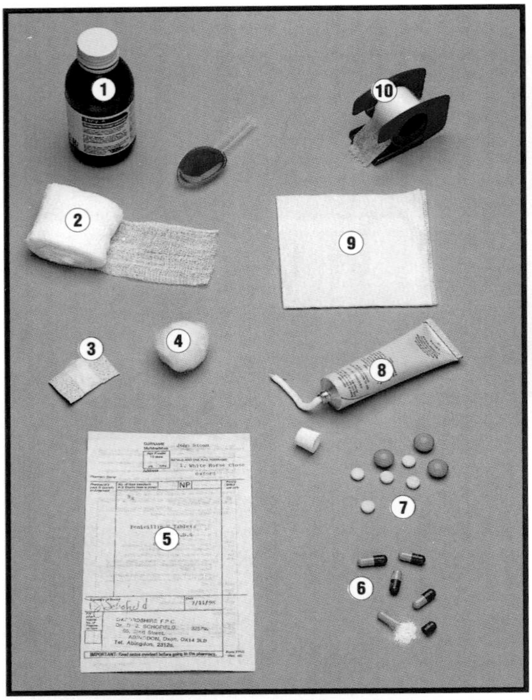


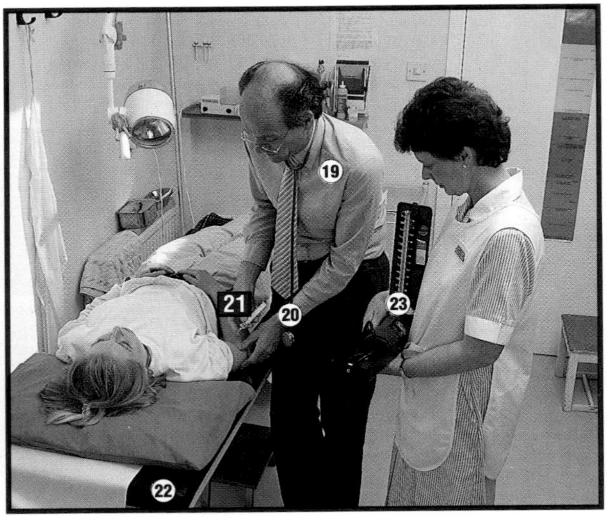


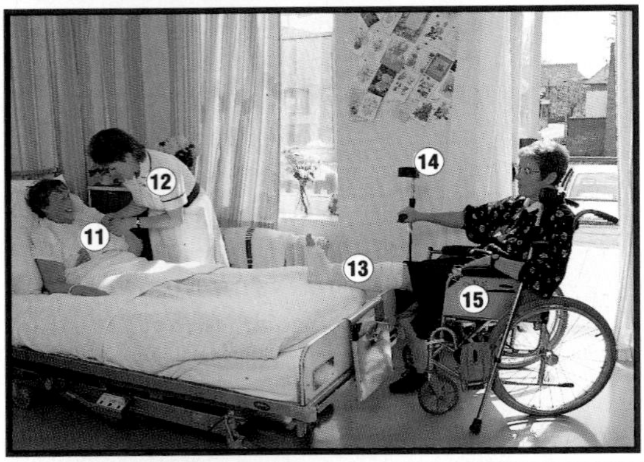


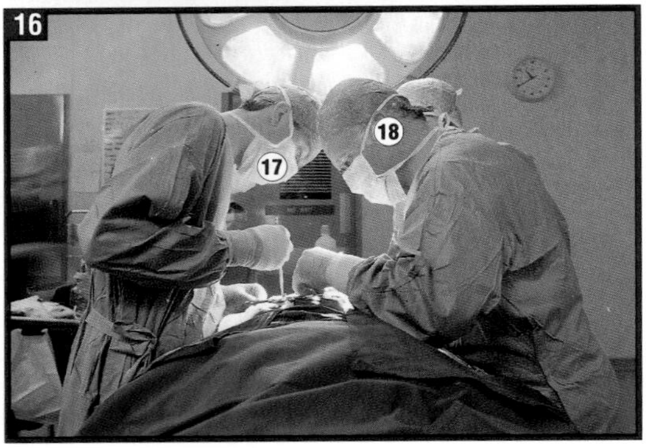


| | | |
|---|---|---|
| medicamento | **1** | medicine |
| venda | **2** | bandage |
| tirita | **3** | (sticking-)plaster (*US* Band-Aid) |
| algodón | **4** | cotton wool (*US* cotton ball) |
| receta | **5** | prescription |
| cápsula | **6** | capsule |
| pastilla/tableta | **7** | pill/tablet |
| pomada | **8** | ointment |
| gasa | **9** | gauze pad |
| esparadrapo | **10** | adhesive tape |
| **Habitación de Hospital** | | **Hospital Ward (*US also* Hospital Room)** |
| cabestrillo | **11** | sling |
| enfermera | **12** | nurse |
| escayola | **13** | plaster cast (*US* cast) |
| muleta | **14** | crutch |
| silla de ruedas | **15** | wheelchair |
| **Operación** | | **Operation** |
| quirófano | **16** | operating theatre (*US* operating room) |
| mascarilla | **17** | mask |
| cirujano | **18** | surgeon |
| **Consulta del Médico** | | **Doctor's Surgery (*US* Doctor's Office)** |
| médico | **19** | doctor |
| estetoscopio | **20** | stethoscope |
| inyección | **21** | injection |
| camilla | **22** | examination couch (*US* examining table/ examination table) |
| aparato de la tensión | **23** | blood pressure gauge |

# Health Care 2

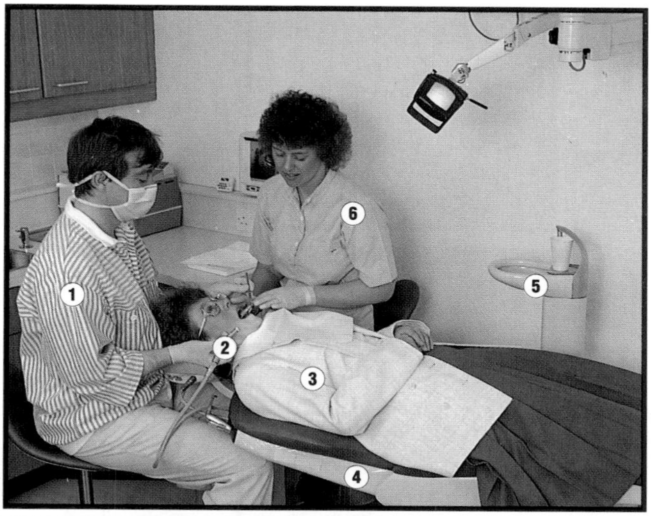


| En el Dentista | At the Dentist's |
|---|---|
| dentista | **1** dentist |
| fresa | **2** drill |
| paciente | **3** patient |
| sillón de dentista | **4** dentist's chair |
| lavabo | **5** basin |
| auxiliar del dentista | **6** dental nurse (*US* dental assistant) |
| encía | **7** gum |
| diente | **8** tooth |
| empaste | **9** filling |
| rayos X | **10** X-ray (*also* x-ray) |
| dientes | **11** front teeth |
| muelas | **12** back teeth |

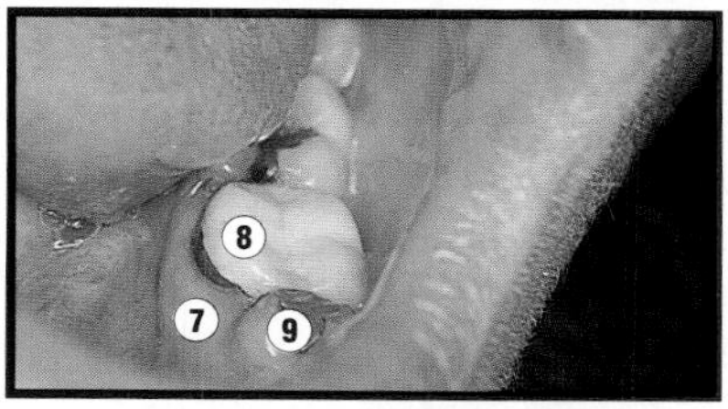


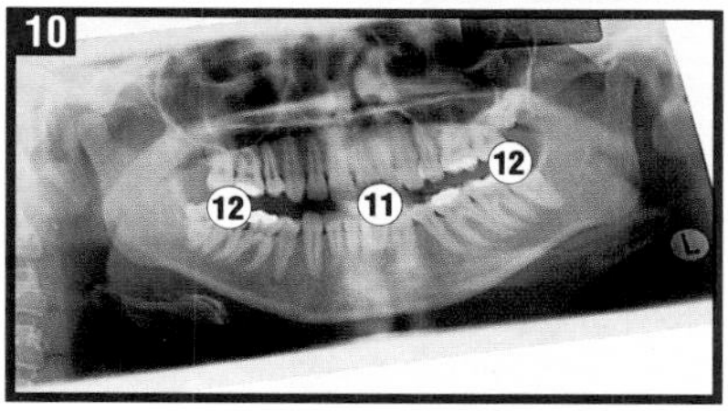


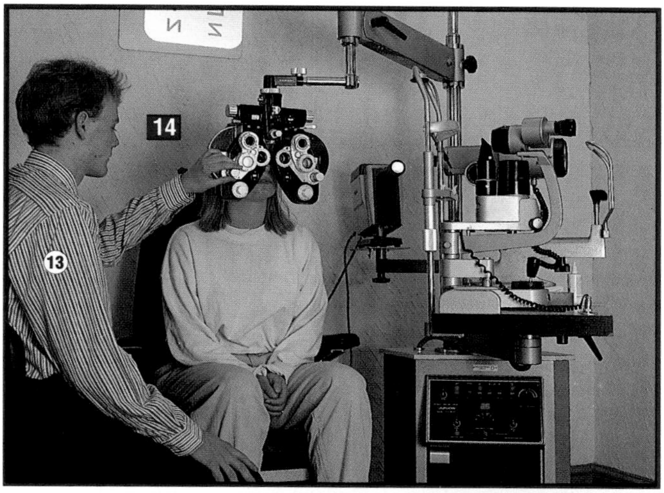


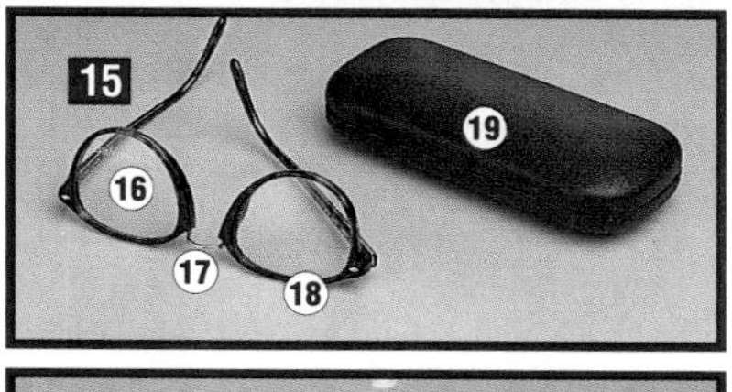


| En el Optico | At the Optician's |
|---|---|
| óptico | **13** optician |
| examen de la vista | **14** eye test |
| (par de) gafas | **15** (pair of) glasses |
| lente | **16** lens |
| puente | **17** bridge |
| montura | **18** frame |
| funda de gafas | **19** glasses case (*US also* eyeglass case) |
| lentes de contacto | **20** contact lens |
| colirio | **21** eye drops |
| limpiador de lentes de contacto | **22** contact lens cleaner |

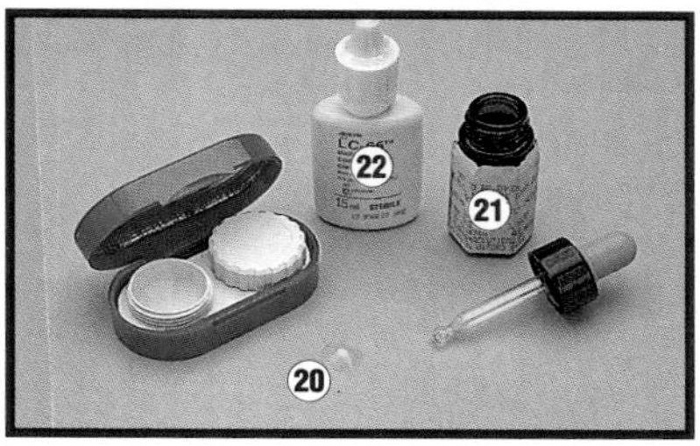

# Describing Clothes

page 9

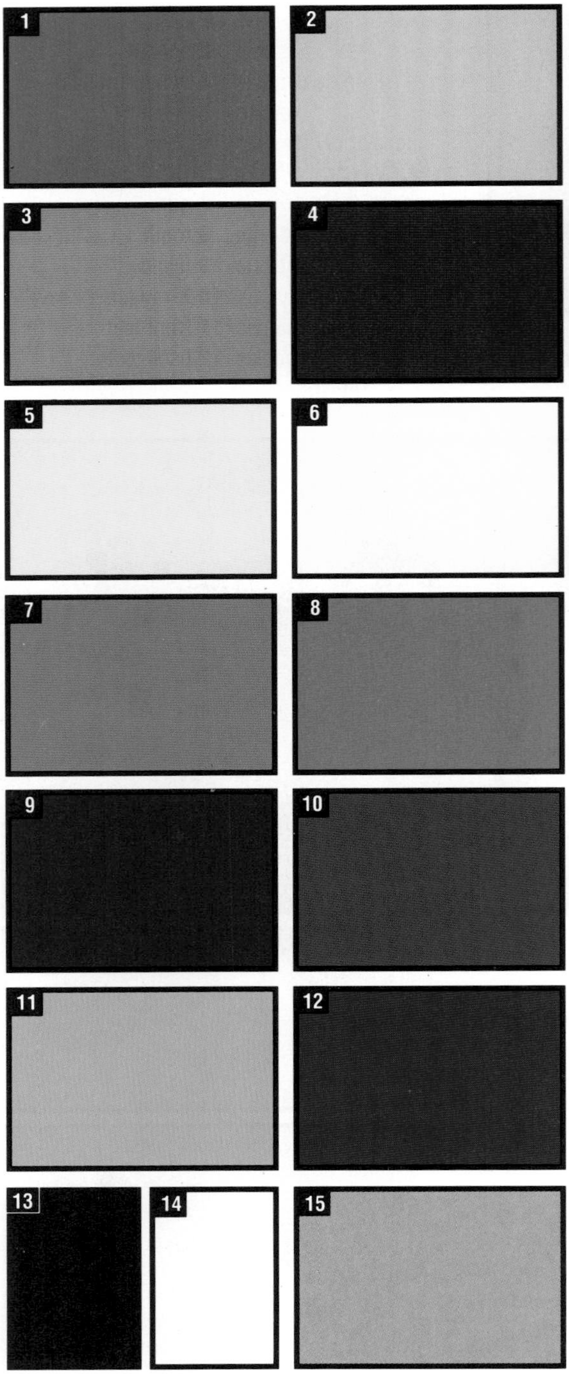

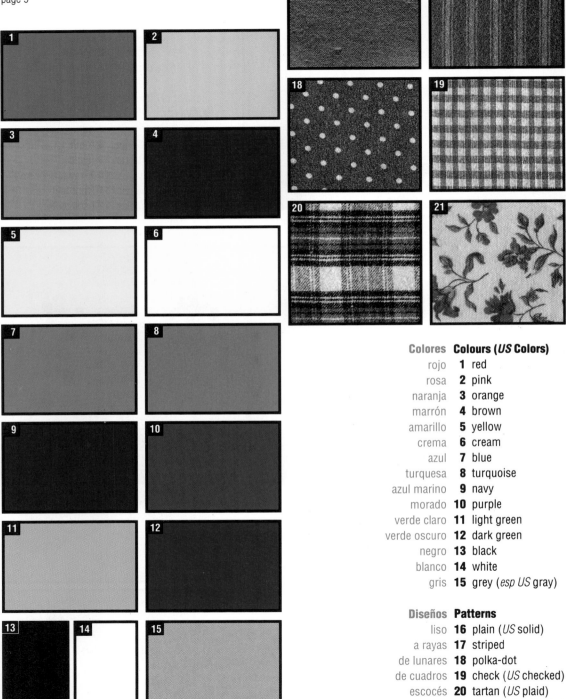

| **Colores** | **Colours (*US* Colors)** |
|---|---|
| rojo | **1** red |
| rosa | **2** pink |
| naranja | **3** orange |
| marrón | **4** brown |
| amarillo | **5** yellow |
| crema | **6** cream |
| azul | **7** blue |
| turquesa | **8** turquoise |
| azul marino | **9** navy |
| morado | **10** purple |
| verde claro | **11** light green |
| verde oscuro | **12** dark green |
| negro | **13** black |
| blanco | **14** white |
| gris | **15** grey (*esp US* gray) |

| **Diseños** | **Patterns** |
|---|---|
| liso | **16** plain (*US* solid) |
| a rayas | **17** striped |
| de lunares | **18** polka-dot |
| de cuadros | **19** check (*US* checked) |
| escocés | **20** tartan (*US* plaid) |
| estampado | **21** patterned (*US* print) |

page 10

# Clothes 1

| | | |
|---|---|---|
| uniforme escolar | **1** | school uniform |
| gorra | **2** | cap |
| americana | **3** | blazer |
| pantalones | **4** | trousers (*US* pants) |
| camiseta | **5** | T-shirt |
| jersey | **6** | sweater |
| vaqueros | **7** | jeans |
| chaquetón | **8** | jacket |
| blusa | **9** | blouse |
| bolso | **10** | handbag (*US also* purse) |
| falda | **11** | skirt |
| maletín | **12** | briefcase |
| bota | **13** | boot |
| bufanda | **14** | scarf |
| guante | **15** | glove |
| paraguas | **16** | umbrella |
| abrigo | **17** | coat |
| traje | **18** | suit |
| camisa | **19** | shirt |
| corbata | **20** | tie |
| pañuelo | **21** | handkerchief |
| gabardina | **22** | raincoat |
| zapato | **23** | shoe |

# Clothes 2 page 11

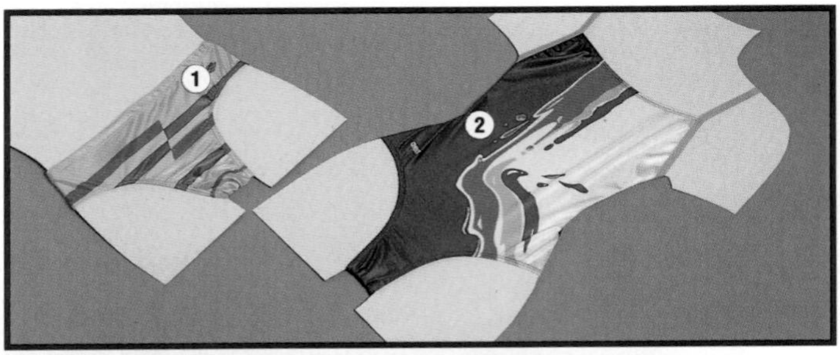


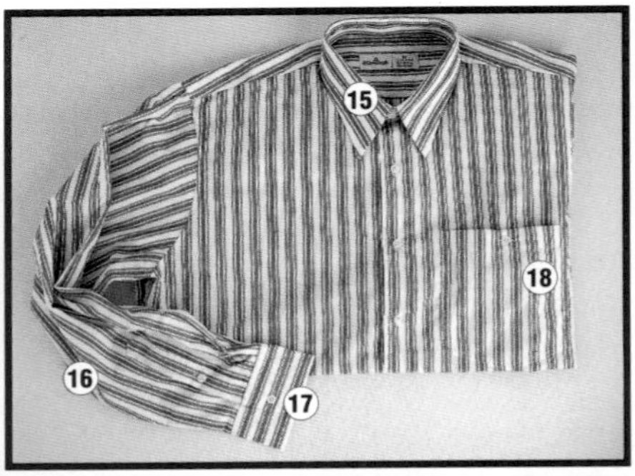

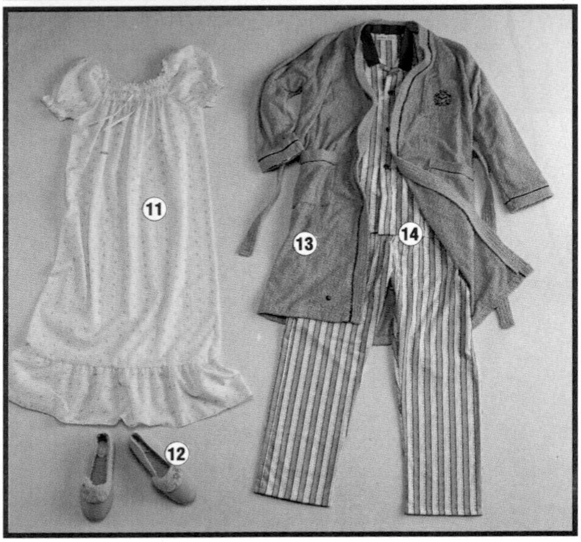


| | | |
|---|---|---|
| bañador | **1** | swimming-trunks (*US* bathing suit) |
| traje de baño | **2** | swimsuit (*US* bathing suit) |
| ropa interior | **3** | underwear |
| calcetines | **4** | socks |
| combinación | **5** | full slip |
| medias | **6** | stockings |
| pantis | **7** | tights (*US* pantyhose) |
| enagua | **8** | half slip |
| sujetador | **9** | bra |
| bragas/calzoncillos | **10** | pants (*US* underpants) |
| camisón | **11** | night-dress (*US* nightgown) |
| zapatilla | **12** | slipper |
| bata | **13** | dressing gown (*US* robe) |
| pijama | **14** | pyjamas (*US* pajamas) |
| cuello | **15** | collar |
| manga | **16** | sleeve |
| puño | **17** | cuff |
| bolsillo | **18** | pocket |
| hebilla | **19** | buckle |
| tacón | **20** | heel |
| cartera | **21** | wallet |
| monedero | **22** | purse (*US* wallet) |
| cordón de zapato | **23** | shoelace |

# Dressing up

| | |
|---|---|
| piloto de carreras | **1** racing driver (*US* race car driver) |
| casco | **2** helmet |
| chándal | **3** track suit (*US also* jogging suit) |
| zapatilla de deporte | **4** trainer (*US* sneaker) |
| gitana | **5** gypsy |
| pañuelo | **6** scarf |
| chaqueta | **7** cardigan |
| sandalia | **8** sandal |
| boxeador | **9** boxer |
| camiseta | **10** vest (*US* tank top) |
| cinturón | **11** belt |
| pantalones cortos | **12** shorts |
| monstruo | **13** monster |
| sudadera | **14** sweatshirt |
| reloj | **15** watch |
| bruja | **16** witch |
| sombrero | **17** hat |
| gafas de sol | **18** sun-glasses |
| vestido | **19** dress |
| maquillaje | **20** make-up |
| barra de labios | **21** lipstick |

| **Joyas** | **Jewellery (*esp US* Jewelry)** |
|---|---|
| broche | **22** brooch (*US* pin) |
| pulsera | **23** bracelet |
| anillo | **24** ring |
| cadena | **25** chain |
| collar | **26** necklace |
| pendiente | **27** earring |

# Buildings 1 page 13

| | |
|---|---|
| casa adosada | **1** terraced house (*US* town house) |
| tejado de pizarra | **2** slate roof |
| jardinera | **3** window-box |
| aldaba | **4** knocker |
| buzón | **5** letter-box (*US* mailbox) |
| escalón | **6** doorstep |
| pared de ladrillo | **7** brick wall |
| ventana de guillotina | **8** sash window |
| ventana del sótano | **9** basement window |
| bloque de pisos | **10** block of flats (*US* apartment house) |
| último piso | **11** top floor |
| balcón | **12** balcony |
| primer piso | **13** first floor (*US* second floor) |
| planta baja | **14** ground floor (*US also* first floor) |
| aparcamiento | **15** car-park (*US* parking lot) |
| **Materiales de Construcción** | **Building Materials** |
| ladrillo | **16** brick |
| piedra | **17** stone |
| hormigón | **18** concrete |
| teja | **19** tile |
| pizarra | **20** slate |
| paja | **21** thatch |
| madera | **22** wood |
| cristal | **23** glass |

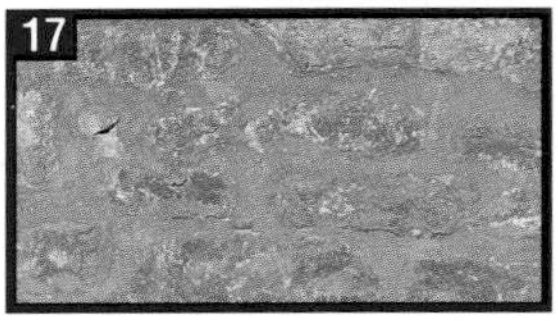

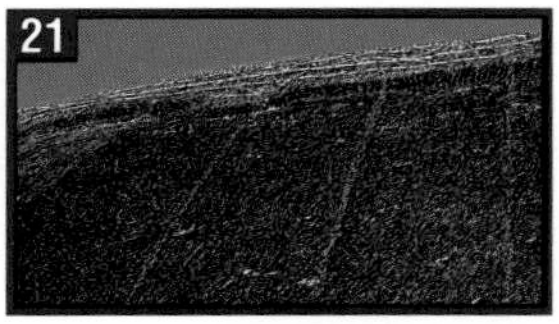

page 14

# Buildings 2

| | | |
|---|---|---|
| casa unifamiliar | **1** | detached house (*US* one-family house) |
| garaje | **2** | garage |
| puerta principal | **3** | front door |
| pilar | **4** | pillar |
| contraventana | **5** | shutter |
| casa adosada | **6** | semi-detached house (*US* two-family house) |
| chimenea | **7** | chimney |
| ventana | **8** | window |
| alféizar | **9** | window-sill/window-ledge |
| arco | **10** | arch |
| ventana en saledizo | **11** | bay window |
| muro de hormigón | **12** | concrete wall |
| casa de campo | **13** | cottage |
| tejado de paja | **14** | thatched roof |
| buhardilla | **15** | dormer |
| porche | **16** | porch |
| puerta de madera | **17** | wooden gate |
| muro de piedra | **18** | stone wall |
| chalé | **19** | bungalow (*US* ranch house) |
| antena | **20** | TV aerial (*US* antenna) |
| tubería | **21** | drainpipe |
| canal | **22** | gutter |
| tejado de tejas | **23** | tiled roof |

# The Dining-room

page 15

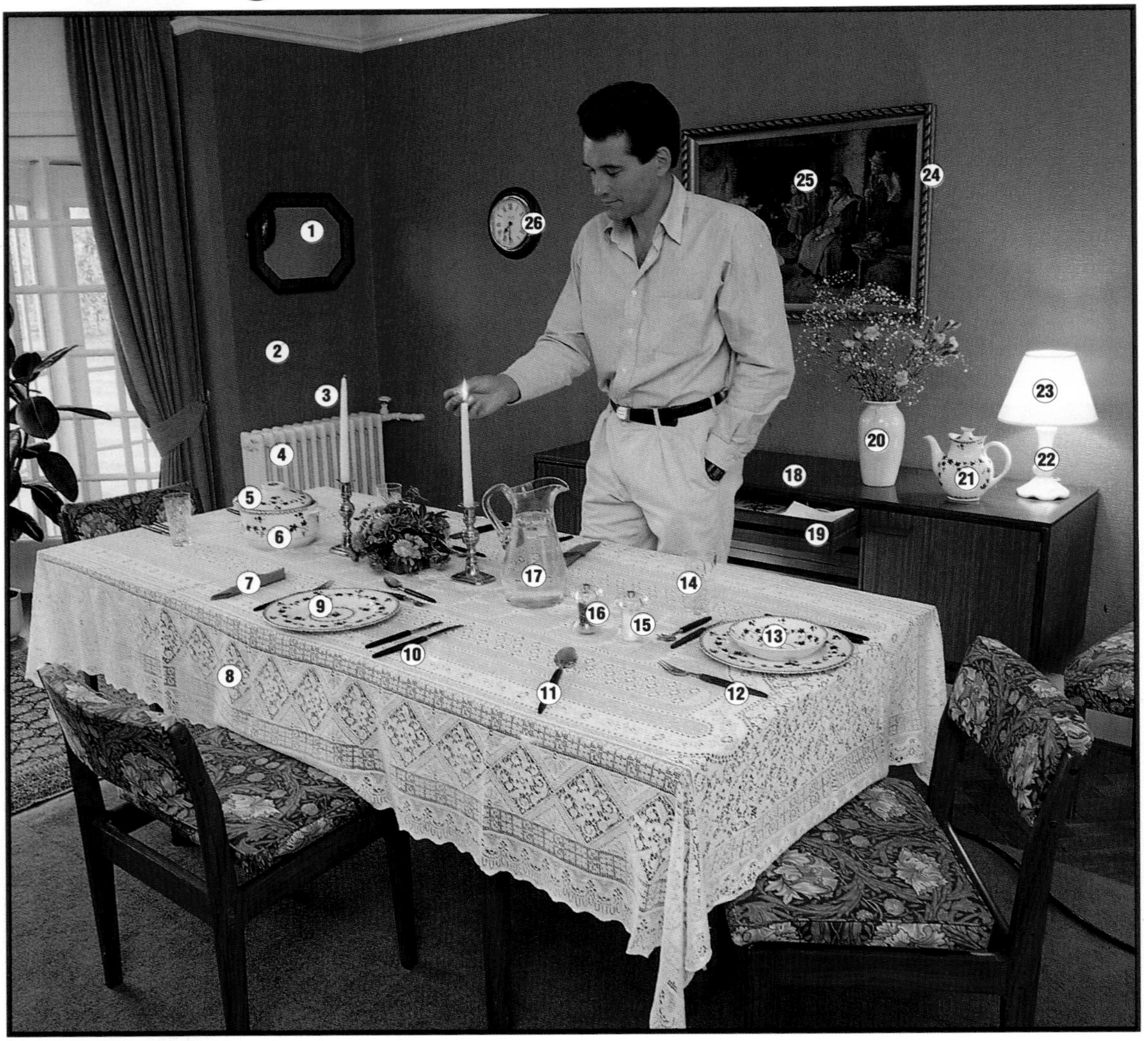


| | |
|---|---|
| espejo | **1** mirror |
| pared | **2** wall |
| vela | **3** candle |
| radiador | **4** radiator |
| tapa | **5** lid |
| sopera | **6** dish |
| servilleta | **7** napkin |
| mantel | **8** table-cloth |
| plato | **9** plate |
| cuchillo | **10** knife |
| cuchara | **11** spoon |
| tenedor | **12** fork |
| bol | **13** bowl |
| vaso | **14** glass |
| sal | **15** salt |
| pimienta | **16** pepper |
| jarra | **17** jug (*US* pitcher) |
| aparador | **18** sideboard (*US* buffet) |
| cajón | **19** drawer |
| jarrón | **20** vase |
| cafetera | **21** coffee-pot |
| lámpara | **22** lamp |
| pantalla | **23** lampshade |
| marco | **24** frame |
| cuadro | **25** painting |
| reloj | **26** clock |

# The Living-room

| | | |
|---|---|---|
| techo | **1** | ceiling |
| repisa de la chimenea | **2** | mantelpiece (*US* mantel) |
| chimenea | **3** | fireplace |
| fuego | **4** | fire |
| leño | **5** | log |
| alfombra | **6** | rug |
| moqueta | **7** | carpet |
| mesa de café | **8** | coffee-table |
| mando a distancia | **9** | remote control |
| lata de galletas | **10** | biscuit tin (*US* cookie tin) |
| tetera | **11** | teapot |
| bandeja | **12** | tray |
| platito | **13** | saucer |
| taza | **14** | cup |
| cucharilla | **15** | teaspoon |
| papelera | **16** | waste-paper basket |
| sofá | **17** | sofa (*esp US* couch) |
| cojín | **18** | cushion |
| planta | **19** | plant |
| cortinas | **20** | curtains (*US* drapes) |
| estantería | **21** | wall unit |
| sillón | **22** | armchair |
| televisión | **23** | television/TV |
| vídeo | **24** | video cassette recorder/VCR |

# The Bathroom page 17

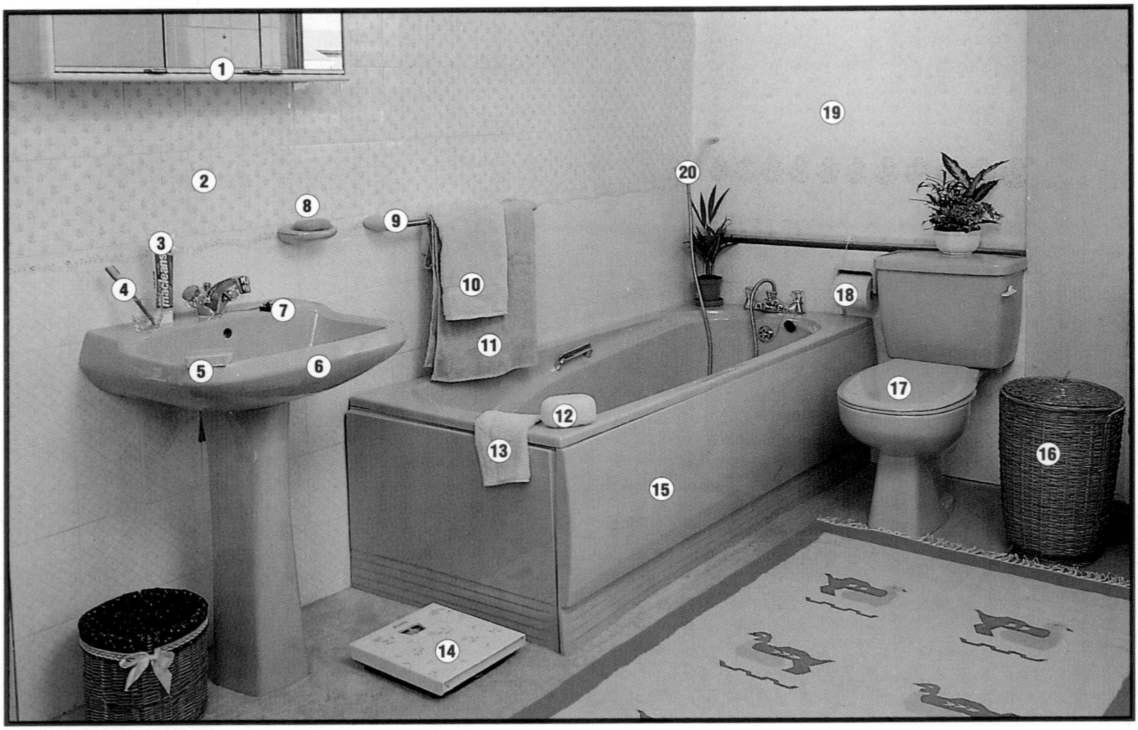


| | | |
|---|---|---|
| armario de baño | **1** | bathroom cabinet (*US* medicine chest/cabinet) |
| baldosa | **2** | tile |
| tubo de pasta de dientes | **3** | tube of toothpaste |
| cepillo de dientes | **4** | toothbrush |
| cepillo de uñas | **5** | nail-brush |
| lavabo | **6** | wash-basin (*US* sink) |
| tapón | **7** | plug (*US* stopper) |
| pastilla de jabón | **8** | bar of soap |
| toallero | **9** | towel-rail (*US* towel rack) |
| toalla de manos | **10** | hand-towel |
| toalla de baño | **11** | bath-towel |
| esponja | **12** | sponge |
| toalla de cara | **13** | flannel (*US* washcloth) |
| báscula | **14** | (bathroom) scales (*US* scale) |
| bañera | **15** | bath (*US* bathtub) |
| cesta de ropa | **16** | laundry basket (*US* hamper) |
| retrete | **17** | toilet |
| papel higiénico | **18** | toilet paper |
| persiana | **19** | blind (*US* shade) |
| ducha | **20** | shower |

| | | |
|---|---|---|
| aftershave | **21** | aftershave (*US* after-shave lotion) |
| maquinilla eléctrica | **22** | electric razor |
| maquinilla de afeitar | **23** | razor |
| cuchilla de afeitar | **24** | razor-blade |
| espuma de afeitar | **25** | shaving-foam (*US* shaving cream) |
| champú | **26** | shampoo |
| peine | **27** | comb |
| polvos de talco | **28** | talcum powder (*also* talc) |

page 18

# The Bedroom

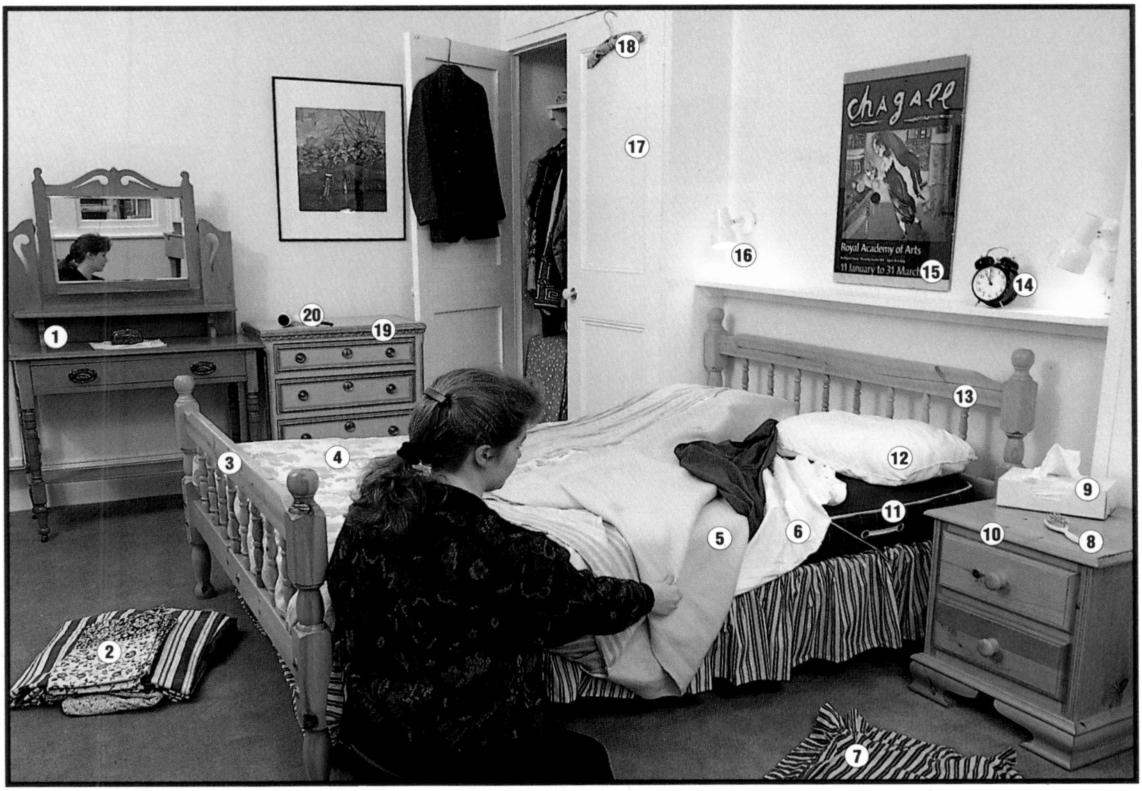


tocador **1** dressing table (*US* dresser)
ropa de cama **2** bed-linen
cama **3** bed
colcha **4** bedspread
manta **5** blanket
sábana **6** sheet
almohadón **7** pillowcase
cepillo del pelo **8** hairbrush
caja de pañuelos de papel **9** box of tissues
mesilla **10** bedside cabinet (*US* night table)
colchón **11** mattress
almohada **12** pillow
cabecera **13** headboard
despertador **14** alarm clock
póster **15** poster
luz **16** light
armario **17** wardrobe (*US* closet)
percha **18** coat-hanger (*esp US* hanger)
cómoda **19** chest of drawers (*US also* bureau)
secador **20** hair-drier (*or* hair-dryer)

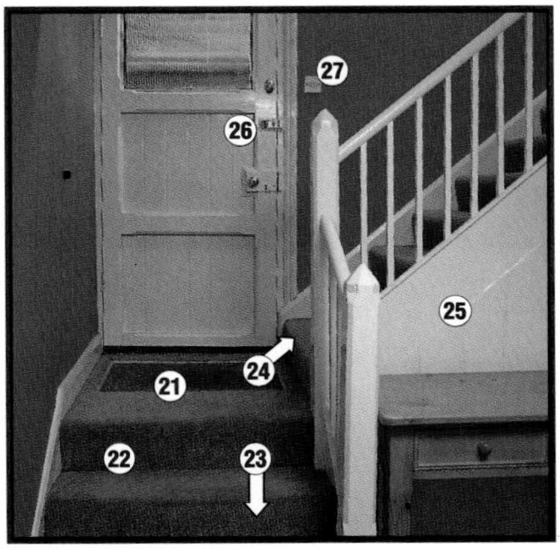


felpudo **21** doormat
escalón **22** stair (*esp US* step)
abajo **23** downstairs
arriba **24** upstairs
escalera **25** staircase
cerradura **26** lock
interruptor **27** light switch

# The Utility Room (*US also* Laundry Room)

page 19

| | | |
|---|---|---|
| detergente | **1** | detergent |
| fregadero | **2** | sink |
| lavadora | **3** | washing-machine |
| recogedor | **4** | dustpan |
| cepillo | **5** | brush |
| cubo | **6** | bucket (*esp US* pail) |
| aspiradora | **7** | vacuum cleaner (*Brit also* Hoover) |
| fregona | **8** | mop |
| tabla de planchar | **9** | ironing-board |
| pinza | **10** | clothes-peg (*US* clothespin) |
| cable | **11** | flex (*esp US* cord) |
| enchufe | **12** | plug |
| plancha | **13** | iron |
| trapo del polvo | **14** | duster (*US* dust cloth) |
| bombilla | **15** | light-bulb |
| colgador | **16** | hook |
| linterna | **17** | torch (*US* flashlight) |
| cepillo | **18** | scrubbing-brush (*US* scrub brush) |
| grifo de agua fría | **19** | cold(-water) tap (*US* cold water faucet) |
| grifo de agua caliente | **20** | hot(-water) tap (*US* hot water faucet) |
| enchufe | **21** | socket (*US also* outlet) |
| tendedero | **22** | clothes-line |

# The Kitchen

| | | |
|---|---|---|
| cazuela | **1** | casserole |
| tamiz | **2** | sieve (*esp US* strainer) |
| bol | **3** | mixing bowl |
| libro de cocina | **4** | cookery book (*US* cookbook) |
| lavavajillas | **5** | washing-up liquid (*US* dishwashing liquid) |
| estropajo | **6** | scourer (*US* scouring pad) |
| paño de cocina | **7** | tea towel (*US* dish towel) |
| batidora | **8** | mixer |
| colador | **9** | colander |
| abrelatas | **10** | tin-opener (*US* can opener) |
| cazo | **11** | ladle |
| rodillo | **12** | rolling-pin |
| encimera | **13** | work surface (*US* counter) |
| nevera | **14** | fridge (*esp US* refrigerator) |
| congelador | **15** | freezer |
| taza | **16** | mug |
| tostador | **17** | toaster |
| tabla de cortar | **18** | breadboard (*US* cutting board) |
| hervidora | **19** | kettle (*US* electric teakettle) |
| armario | **20** | cupboard (*esp US* cabinet) |
| guante del horno | **21** | oven glove (*US* pot holder) |
| horno | **22** | oven |
| estante | **23** | shelf |
| sartén | **24** | frying-pan |
| robot de cocina | **25** | food processor |
| cazo | **26** | saucepan/pot |
| cocina | **27** | burner |

# Tools page 21

| | | |
|---|---|---|
| caja de herramientas | **1** | tool-box |
| mazo | **2** | mallet |
| papel de lija | **3** | sandpaper |
| navaja | **4** | penknife (*esp US* pocketknife) |
| banco de carpintero | **5** | workbench |
| alicates | **6** | pliers |
| nivel | **7** | spirit-level (*US* level) |
| cepillo | **8** | plane |
| sierra eléctrica | **9** | power saw |
| taladro eléctrico | **10** | electric drill |
| torno | **11** | vice (*US* vise) |
| serrucho | **12** | handsaw (*esp US* saw) |
| lima | **13** | file |
| formón | **14** | chisel |
| berbiquí | **15** | brace |
| martillo | **16** | hammer |
| hacha | **17** | hatchet |
| taladro | **18** | hand drill |
| llave inglesa | **19** | wrench |
| sierra de pelo | **20** | coping saw |

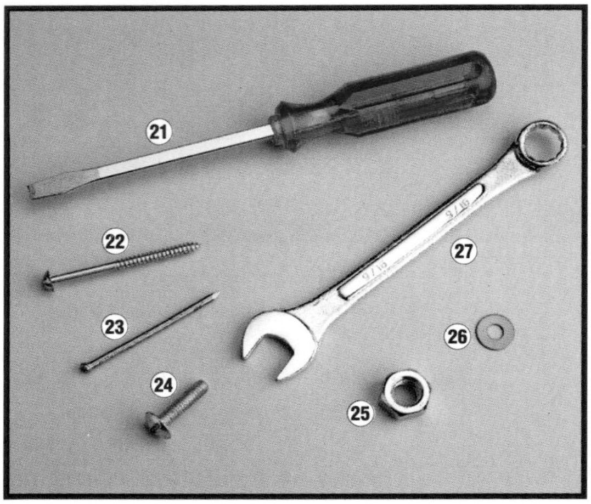


| | | |
|---|---|---|
| destornillador | **21** | screwdriver |
| tornillo | **22** | screw |
| clavo | **23** | nail |
| perno | **24** | bolt |
| tuerca | **25** | nut |
| arandela | **26** | washer |
| llave fija | **27** | spanner (*US* wrench) |

# page 22 The Garden

| | | |
|---|---|---|
| jardín trasero | **1** | back garden (*US* backyard) |
| columpio | **2** | swing |
| hierba/césped | **3** | grass/lawn |
| árbol | **4** | tree |
| cortacésped | **5** | lawnmower |
| regadera | **6** | watering-can |
| rastrillo | **7** | rake |
| tijeras de jardín | **8** | shears |
| arbusto | **9** | bush |
| maceta | **10** | flowerpot |
| empedrado | **11** | patio |
| transplantador | **12** | trowel |
| escoba | **13** | broom |
| banco | **14** | bench |
| valla | **15** | fence |
| barbacoa | **16** | barbecue |
| carretilla | **17** | wheelbarrow |
| horquilla | **18** | fork |
| pala | **19** | spade |
| cubo de la basura | **20** | dustbin (*US* garbage can) |

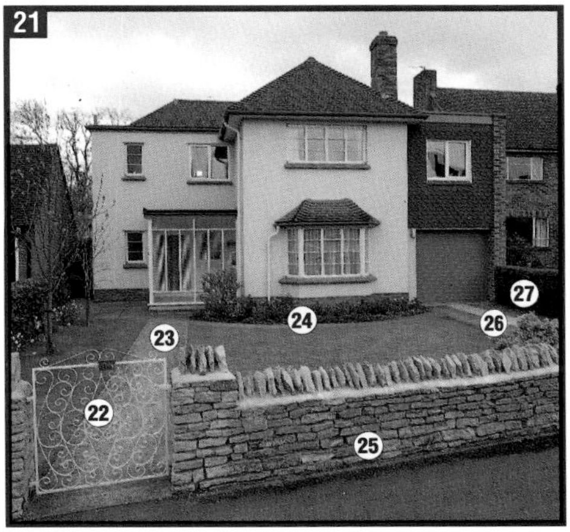

| | | |
|---|---|---|
| jardín delantero | **21** | front garden (*US* front yard) |
| puerta | **22** | gate |
| camino | **23** | path (*US* front walk) |
| macizo de flores | **24** | flower-bed |
| muro | **25** | wall |
| camino | **26** | drive (*US* driveway) |
| seto | **27** | hedge |

# In the Market 1 page 23

| Verduras | Vegetables |
|---|---|
| puesto | **1** market stall (*US* stand) |
| ajo | **2** garlic |
| pimiento verde | **3** green pepper |
| coliflor | **4** cauliflower |
| espárrago | **5** asparagus |
| rábano | **6** radish |
| lechuga | **7** lettuce |
| remolacha | **8** beetroot (*US* beet) |
| patata | **9** potato |
| pepino | **10** cucumber |
| cebolla | **11** onion |

| | |
|---|---|
| calabacín | **12** courgette (*US* zucchini) |
| berro | **13** watercress |
| zanahoria | **14** carrot |
| col de Bruselas | **15** Brussels sprout (*US* brussels sprout) |
| apio | **16** celery |
| brócoli | **17** broccoli |
| nabo | **18** turnip |
| tomate | **19** tomato |
| berenjena | **20** aubergine (*US* eggplant) |
| col | **21** cabbage |
| bolsa de papel | **22** paper bag |

page 24

# In the Market 2

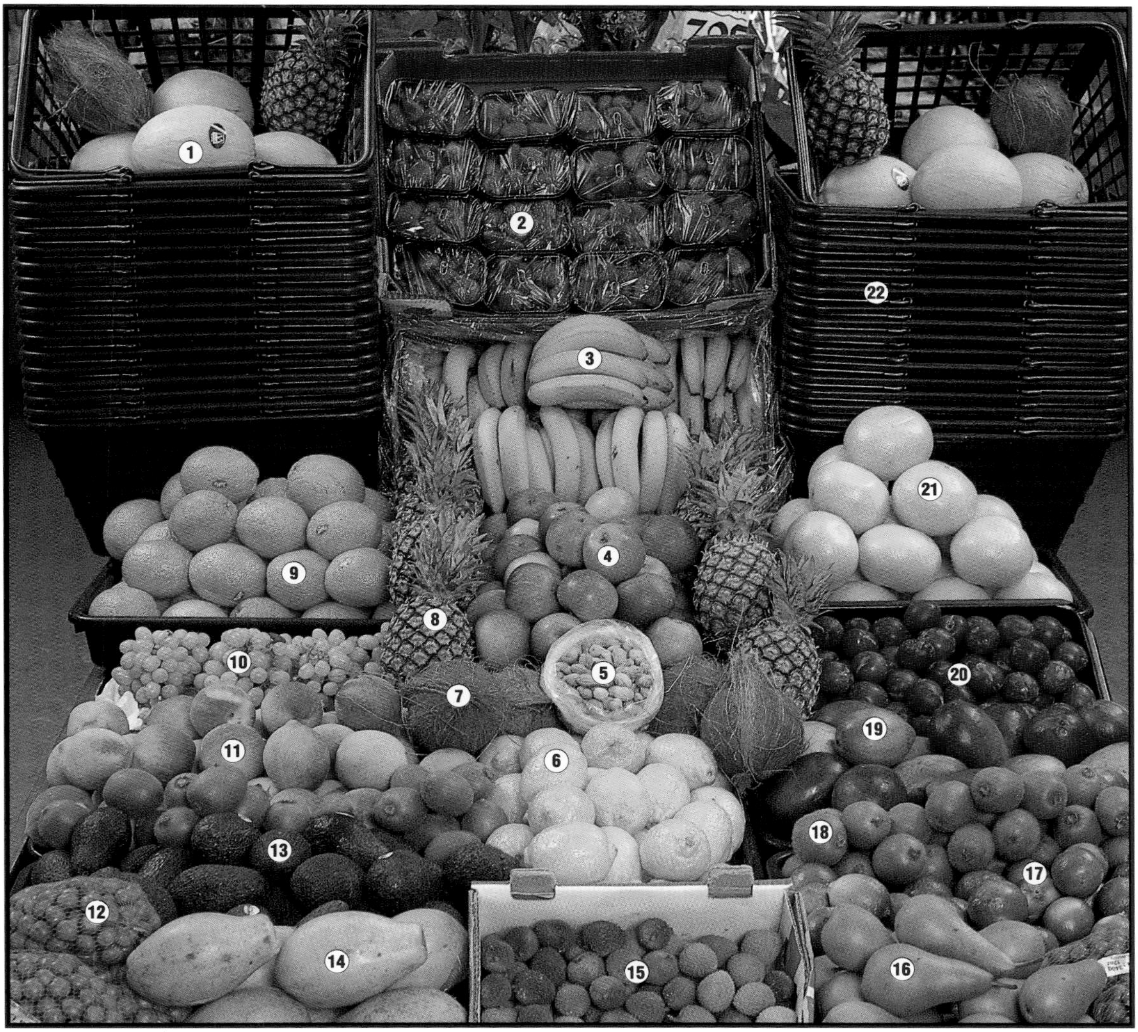


| | |
|---|---|
| **Fruta** | **Fruit** |
| melón | **1** melon |
| caja de fresas | **2** punnet of strawberries (*US* basket of strawberries) |
| racimo de plátanos | **3** bunch of bananas |
| manzana | **4** apple |
| cacahuete | **5** peanut |
| limón | **6** lemon |
| coco | **7** coconut |
| piña | **8** pineapple |
| naranja | **9** orange |
| racimo de uvas | **10** bunch of grapes |
| melocotón | **11** peach |
| bolsa de frutos secos | **12** bag of nuts |
| aguacate | **13** avocado |
| papaya | **14** pawpaw (*esp US* papaya) |
| lichi | **15** lychee (*also* litchi) |
| pera | **16** pear |
| lima | **17** lime |
| kiwi | **18** kiwi fruit |
| mango | **19** mango |
| ciruela | **20** plum |
| pomelo | **21** grapefruit |
| pila de cestas | **22** stack of baskets |

# At the Florist's page 25

| | | |
|---|---|---|
| abeto | **1** | pine tree (*also* Christmas tree) |
| tronco | **2** | trunk |
| raíces | **3** | roots |
| pétalo | **4** | petal |
| helecho | **5** | fern |
| cesta | **6** | basket |
| rama | **7** | branch |
| corteza | **8** | bark |
| ramo de flores secas | **9** | bunch of dried flowers |
| centro de flores secas | **10** | dried flower arrangement |
| hoja | **11** | leaf |
| bonsai | **12** | bonsai |
| bulbo | **13** | bulb |
| narciso | **14** | daffodil |
| crisantemo | **15** | chrysanthemum |
| palmera | **16** | palm |
| rosa | **17** | rose |
| orquídea | **18** | orchid |
| tallo | **19** | stem |
| fresia | **20** | freesia |
| cactus | **21** | cactus |
| piña | **22** | pine cone |
| margarita | **23** | daisy |
| clavel | **24** | carnation |
| tulipán | **25** | tulip |
| azucena | **26** | lily |
| capullo | **27** | bud |
| lirio | **28** | iris |

# At the Newsagent's (*US* Newsstand)

| Papelería | Stationery |
|---|---|
| rollo de celo | **1** reel of Sellotape (*US* roll of Scotch tape) |
| rollo de cuerda | **2** ball of string |
| paquete de sobres | **3** packet of envelopes (*US* pack of envelopes) |
| papel de carta | **4** writing-paper |
| caja de rotuladores | **5** set of coloured pens (*US* set of colored pens) |
| rollo de papel de regalo | **6** roll of wrapping paper |
| hilera de revistas | **7** row of magazines |
| pila de periódicos | **8** pile of newspapers |

| Golosinas | Confectionery (*US* Candy) |
|---|---|
| caja de bombones | **9** box of chocolates (*US* box of chocolate) |
| bolsa de dulces | **10** bag of sweets (*US* bag of candy) |
| tableta de chocolate | **11** bar of chocolate |
| paquete doble | **12** twin-pack |
| paquete triple | **13** triple-pack |
| paquete de dulces | **14** packet of sweets (*US* pack of candy) |
| paquete de dulces | **15** packet of sweets (*US* roll of candy) |
| paquete de patatas fritas | **16** packet of crisps (*US* bag of potato chips) |
| chocolate | **17** chocolate |
| dulces | **18** sweets (*US* candy) |
| patatas fritas | **19** crisps (*US* potato chips) |

# At the Delicatessen page 27

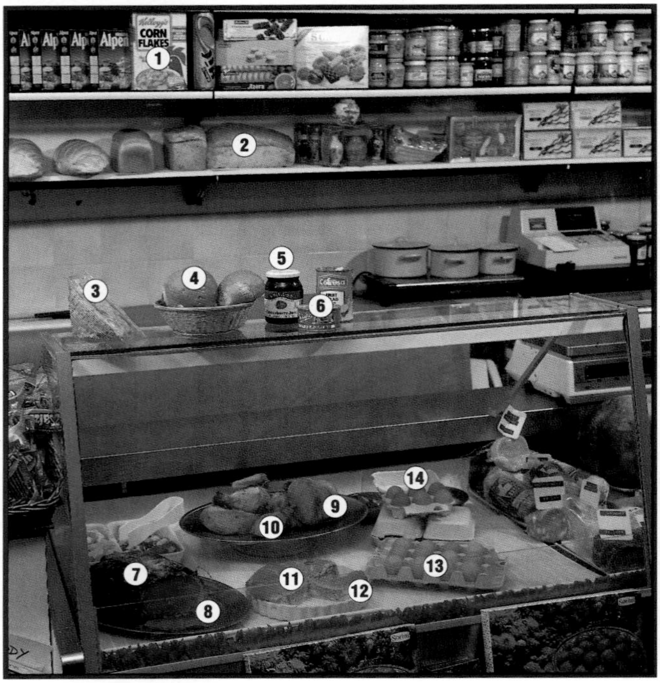

| | | |
|---|---|---|
| caja de cereales | **1** | box of cereal |
| pan de molde | **2** | loaf of bread |
| sandwiches | **3** | sandwiches |
| bollo | **4** | roll |
| tarro de mermelada | **5** | jar of jam/pot of jam |
| lata de atún | **6** | tin of tuna (*US* can of tuna) |
| pieza de carne cocida | **7** | joint of cooked meat (*US* roast) |
| loncha de carne | **8** | slice of meat |
| pollo asado | **9** | roast chicken |
| trozo de pollo | **10** | chicken portion (*US* piece of chicken) |
| pastel | **11** | pie |
| trozo de pastel | **12** | piece of pie |
| docena de huevos | **13** | dozen eggs |
| media docena de huevos | **14** | half a dozen eggs |
| galleta | **15** | biscuit (*US* cookie) |
| paquete de galletas | **16** | packet of biscuits (*US* package of cookies) |
| mermelada | **17** | jam |
| atún | **18** | tuna |
| vaso de yogur | **19** | pot of yoghurt (*US* container of yogurt) |
| tarrina de margarina | **20** | tub of margarine |
| caja de zumo de naranja | **21** | carton of orange juice |
| queso | **22** | cheese |
| aceitunas rellenas | **23** | stuffed olives |
| pinta de leche | **24** | pint of milk |
| botella de agua mineral | **25** | bottle of mineral water |
| lata de refresco | **26** | can of fizzy drink (*US* can of soda) |
| yogur | **27** | yoghurt (*esp US* yogurt) |
| margarina | **28** | margarine |
| mantequilla | **29** | butter |

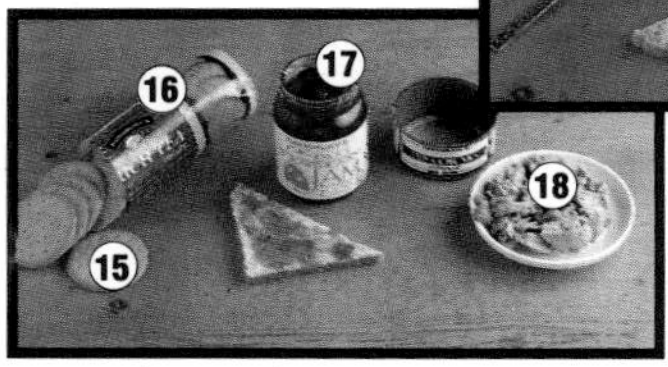

# At the Restaurant

page 28

| | | |
|---|---|---|
| **Primeros Platos** | | **Starters (*US* Appetizers)** |
| guinda | **1** | cherry |
| melón | **2** | melon |
| salmón ahumado | **3** | smoked salmon |
| paté con tostadas | **4** | pâté with toast |
| sopa de tomate | **5** | tomato soup |
| **Postres** | | **Desserts** |
| carrito de los postres | **6** | dessert trolley (*US* dessert cart) |
| fruta | **7** | fruit |
| tarta de manzana | **8** | apple pie |
| pastel de queso | **9** | cheesecake |
| helado de frambuesa | **10** | raspberry ice-cream |
| macedonia de frutas | **11** | fruit cocktail |
| nata | **12** | cream |
| tarta de chocolate | **13** | chocolate gateau (*US* chocolate cake) |
| camarero | **14** | waiter |
| menú | **15** | menu |
| **Segundos Platos** | | **Main Courses** |
| ternera asada | **16** | roast beef |
| trucha con almendras | **17** | trout with almonds |
| filete | **18** | steak |
| chuletas de cordero | **19** | lamb chops |
| **Verduras** | | **Vegetables** |
| maíz | **20** | sweet corn (*US* corn) |
| champiñones | **21** | mushrooms |
| ensalada | **22** | salad |
| judías verdes | **23** | runner beans (*US* string beans) |
| guisantes | **24** | peas |
| patata asada | **25** | jacket potato (*esp US* baked potato) |
| patatas cocidas | **26** | boiled potatoes |
| patatas fritas | **27** | chips (*US* French fries) |

# At the Camera Shop (*US* Camera Store) page 29

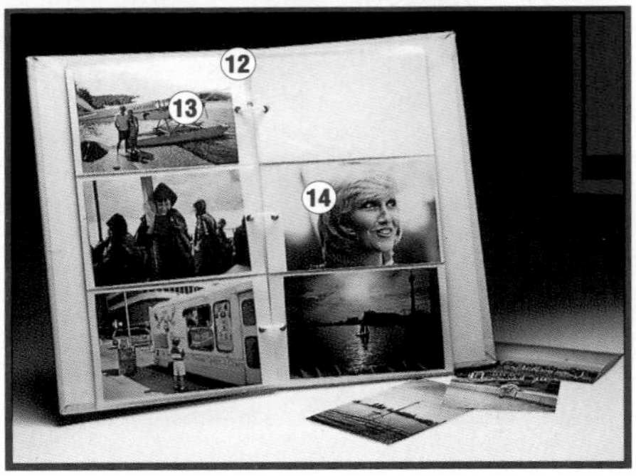

cliente **1** customer
recibo **2** receipt
caja registradora **3** cash register
trípode **4** tripod
telescopio **5** telescope
dependiente **6** shop assistant (*US* salesperson)
prismáticos **7** binoculars
proyector de diapositivas **8** slide projector
diapositiva **9** slide
negativo **10** negative
carrete de fotos **11** reel of film (*US* roll of film)
álbum de fotos **12** photo album
foto en color **13** colour print (*US* color print)
foto en blanco y negro **14** black and white print

teleobjetivo **15** zoom lens
cámara réflex **16** single lens reflex/SLR camera
lente **17** lens
flash **18** flash (gun)
cámara compacta de 35 mm **19** 35 mm* compact camera
flash incorporado **20** built-in flash
funda de cámara **21** camera case
correa **22** strap
cámara polaroid **23** polaroid camera

*milímetro* **mm = millimetre (US millimeter)*

# At the Hi-fi Shop (*US* Electronics Store)

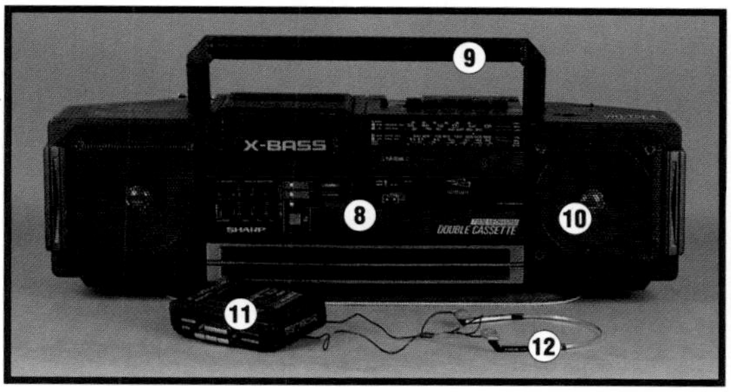

cámara de vídeo **1** camcorder
micrófono **2** microphone
visor **3** viewfinder
cinta de vídeo **4** (video)tape
disco **5** record
casete **6** cassette
disco compacto **7** compact disc/CD
radiocasete **8** radio cassette recorder (*US also* AM/FM cassette recorder)
asa **9** handle
altavoz **10** speaker
Walkman **11** Walkman (*Brit also* personal stereo)
auriculares **12** headphones

cadena de sonido **13** stereo/stereo system (*US also* sound system) (*Brit also* hi-fi)
plato **14** turntable
radio **15** radio
amplificador **16** amplifier
ecualizador gráfico **17** graphic equalizer
pletina **18** cassette deck/tape deck
reproductor de disco compacto **19** compact disc player/CD player

# Postal Services 1 page 31

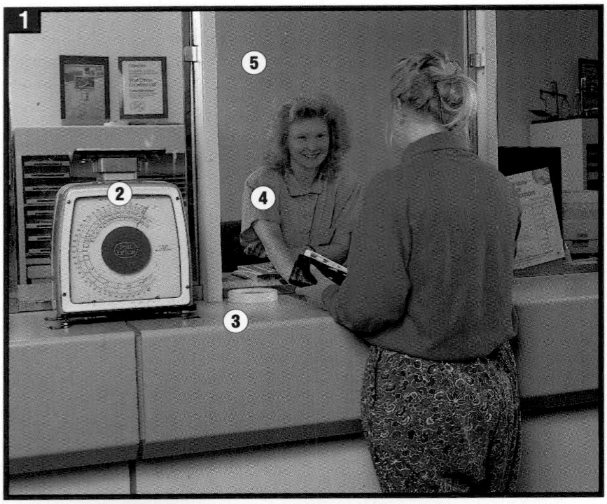

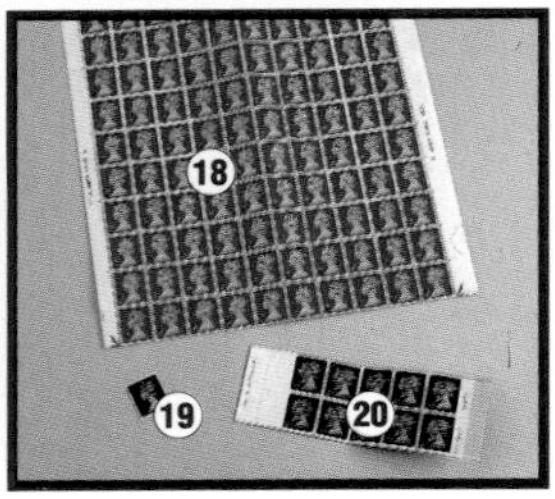

| | | |
|---|---|---|
| oficina de correos | **1** | post office |
| balanza | **2** | scales (*US* scale) |
| mostrador | **3** | counter |
| empleada | **4** | counter assistant (*US* postal clerk) |
| ventanilla | **5** | window |
| recogida | **6** | collection |
| furgoneta de correos | **7** | post office van (*US* mail truck) |
| cartero | **8** | postman (*US* mailman) |
| saca de correos | **9** | mailbag |
| correo | **10** | post (*US* mail) |
| buzón | **11** | letter-box/postbox (*US* mailbox) |
| reparto | **12** | delivery |
| saco postal | **13** | postbag (*esp US* mailbag) |
| buzón | **14** | letter-box (*US* mailbox) |
| reparto por mensajero | **15** | delivery by courier (*US* delivery by messenger) |
| mensajero | **16** | despatch-rider (*US* messenger) |
| máquina de sellos | **17** | stamp machine |
| pliego de sellos | **18** | sheet of stamps |
| sello | **19** | stamp |
| librillo de sellos | **20** | book of stamps |

page 32

# Postal Services 2

Británico **British** Americano **American**

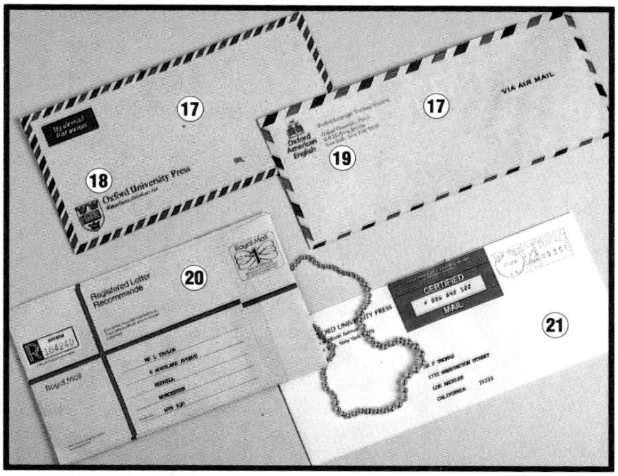

| | |
|---|---|
| paquete | **1** parcel (*esp US* package) |
| cinta | **2** tape |
| rótulo | **3** label |
| tarjeta de felicitación | **4** greetings card (*US* greeting card) |
| carta | **5** letter |
| sobre | **6** envelope |
| solapa | **7** flap |
| tarjeta postal | **8** postcard |
| texto | **9** message |
| dirección | **10** address |
| correo de primera clase | **11** first-class post (*Brit*) |
| matasellos | **12** postmark |
| código postal | **13** postcode (*also* postal code) (*Brit*) |
| correo de primera clase | **14** first class mail (*US*) |
| correo de segunda clase | **15** second-class post (*Brit*) |
| código postal | **16** zip code (*US*) |
| correo aéreo | **17** airmail |
| dirección del remitente | **18** address of sender (*Brit*) |
| dirección del remitente | **19** return address (*US*) |
| correo certificado | **20** registered post (*Brit*) |
| correo certificado | **21** certified mail (*US*) |
| giro postal | **22** postal order (*Brit*) |
| giro postal | **23** money order (*US*) |
| entrega urgente | **24** Special Delivery (*Brit*) |
| entrega urgente | **25** Express Mail (*US*) |

# Numbers/The Date page 33

| | | | | | |
|---|---|---|---|---|---|
| **JULY 1998** | | | | | |
| **Sunday** | | **5** | **12** | **19** | **26** |
| **Monday** | | **6** | **13** | **20** | **27** |
| **Tuesday** | | **7** | **14** | **21** | **28** |
| **Wednesday** | **1** | **8** | **15** | **22** | **29** |
| **Thursday** | **2** | **9** | **16** | **23** | **30** |
| **Friday** | **3** | **10** | **17** | **24** | **31** |
| **Saturday** | **4** | **11** | **18** | **25** | |

| | | |
|---|---|---|
| uno | **1** | one |
| dos | **2** | two |
| tres | **3** | three |
| cuatro | **4** | four |
| cinco | **5** | five |
| seis | **6** | six |
| siete | **7** | seven |
| ocho | **8** | eight |
| nueve | **9** | nine |
| diez | **10** | ten |
| once | **11** | eleven |
| doce | **12** | twelve |
| trece | **13** | thirteen |
| catorce | **14** | fourteen |
| quince | **15** | fifteen |
| dieciséis | **16** | sixteen |
| diecisiete | **17** | seventeen |
| dieciocho | **18** | eighteen |
| diecinueve | **19** | nineteen |
| veinte | **20** | twenty |
| veintiuno | **21** | twenty-one |
| treinta | **30** | thirty |
| cuarenta | **40** | forty |
| cincuenta | **50** | fifty |
| sesenta | **60** | sixty |
| setenta | **70** | seventy |
| ochenta | **80** | eighty |
| noventa | **90** | ninety |
| cien | **100** | one hundred |
| ciento uno | **101** | one hundred and one |
| mil | **1000** | one thousand |
| dos mil doscientos diez | **2210** | two thousand, two hundred and ten |
| un millón | **1000000** | one million |

| | | |
|---|---|---|
| primero | **1st** | first |
| segundo | **2nd** | second |
| tercero | **3rd** | third |
| cuarto | **4th** | fourth |
| quinto | **5th** | fifth |
| sexto | **6th** | sixth |
| séptimo | **7th** | seventh |
| octavo | **8th** | eighth |
| noveno | **9th** | ninth |
| décimo | **10th** | tenth |
| undécimo | **11th** | eleventh |
| décimo segundo | **12th** | twelfth |
| décimo tercero | **13th** | thirteenth |
| vigésimo | **20th** | twentieth |
| vigésimo primero | **21st** | twenty-first |
| vigésimo segundo | **22nd** | twenty-second |
| vigésimo tercero | **23rd** | twenty-third |
| trigésimo | **30th** | thirtieth |
| trigésimo primero | **31st** | thirty-first |

***Británico*** ***British***

3.5.98 3rd May 1998
3/5/98 3 May 1998

Tres de mayo de mil novecientos noventa y ocho. The third of May nineteen ninety-eight/ May the third, nineteen ninety-eight.

***Americano*** ***American***

5/3/98 May 3, 1998

Tres de mayo de mil novecientos noventa y ocho. May third, nineteen ninety-eight.

# At the Bank

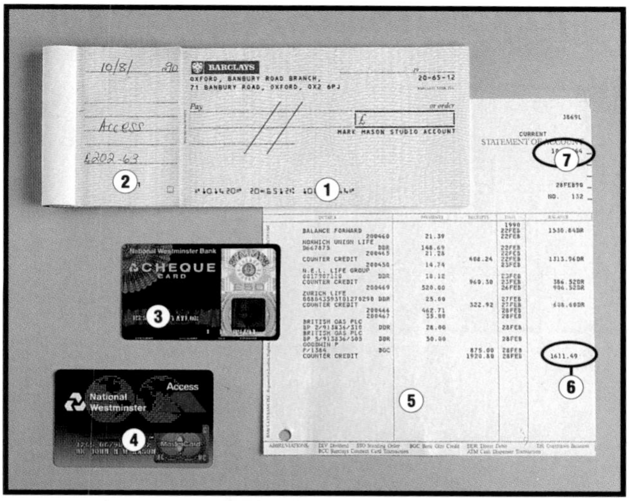

| | | |
|---|---|---|
| talonario de cheques | **1** | cheque book (*US* checkbook) |
| matriz | **2** | counterfoil/cheque stub (*US* check stub) |
| tarjeta de garantía de cheques | **3** | cheque (guarantee) card (*Brit only*) |
| tarjeta de crédito | **4** | credit card |
| estado de cuenta | **5** | bank statement (*esp US* monthly statement) |
| saldo de cuenta | **6** | (bank) balance |
| número de cuenta | **7** | (bank) account number |
| tipos de cambio | **8** | exchange rates |
| cajero | **9** | cashier (*US* teller) |
| cambiar un cheque de viajero | **10** | changing a traveller's cheque (*US* cashing a traveler's check) |
| cheque de viajero | **11** | traveller's cheque (*US* traveler's check) |
| cambiar dinero | **12** | changing money |
| moneda extranjera | **13** | foreign currency |
| cobrar un cheque | **14** | cashing a cheque (*US* cashing a check) |
| sacar dinero | **15** | withdrawing cash |
| cajero automático | **16** | cash dispenser/cashpoint (*US* cash machine/ automatic teller) |
| ingresar dinero | **17** | paying in (*US* making a deposit) |
| recibo de depósito | **18** | paying-in slip (*US* deposit slip) |
| recibo de reintegro | **19** | withdrawal slip |

# American Money

page 35

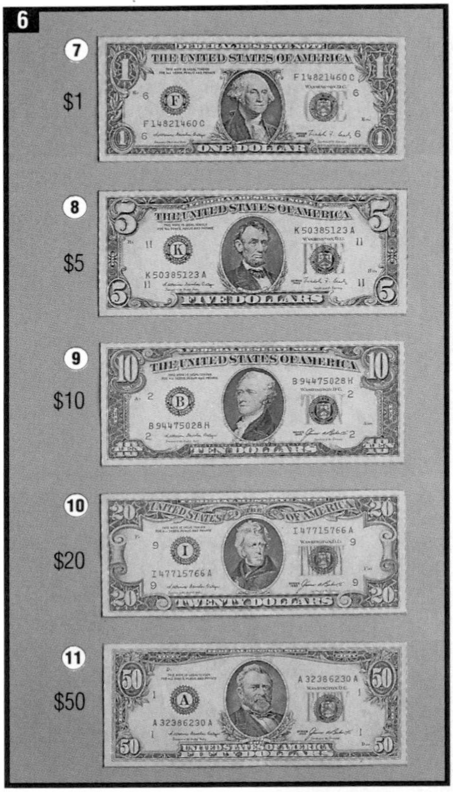


| | | |
|---|---|---|
| **monedas** | **1** | **coins** |
| una moneda de un centavo | **2** | a penny |
| una moneda de cinco centavos | **3** | a nickel |
| una moneda de diez centavos | **4** | a dime |
| una moneda de veinticinco centavos | **5** | a quarter |
| **billetes** | **6** | **bills** |
| un billete de dólar | **7** | a dollar bill |
| un billete de cinco dólares | **8** | a five dollar bill |
| un billete de diez dólares | **9** | a ten dollar bill |
| un billete de veinte dólares | **10** | a twenty dollar bill |
| un billete de cincuenta dólares | **11** | a fifty dollar bill |

| | | |
|---|---|---|
| **Pagando en metálico** | | **Paying (in) cash** |
| veinte dólares | **12** | twenty dollars |
| siete dólares y noventa y cinco centavos/ siete noventa y cinco | **13** | seven dollars and ninety-five cents/ seven ninety-five |
| recibo | **14** | receipt |
| total | **15** | total |
| cambio | **16** | change |

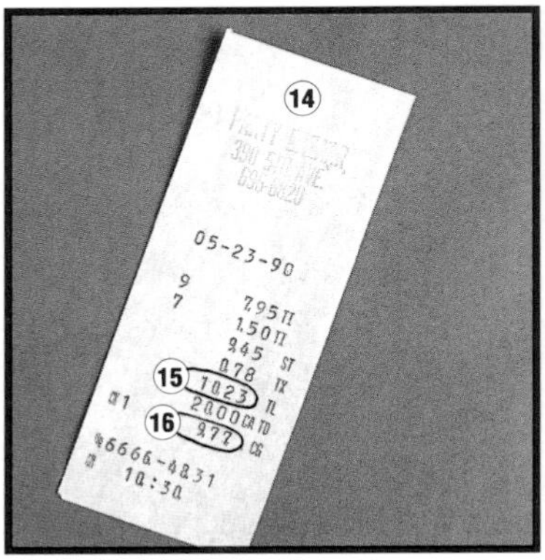

# British Money

**monedas** **1 coins**
una moneda de un penique **2** a one pence piece/a penny
una moneda de dos peniques **3** a two pence piece
una moneda de cinco peniques **4** a five pence piece
una moneda de diez peniques **5** a ten pence piece
una moneda de veinte peniques **6** a twenty pence piece
una moneda de cincuenta peniques **7** a fifty pence piece
una moneda de una libra **8** a pound coin
una moneda de dos libras **9** a two pound coin

**billetes** **10 notes**
un billete de cinco libras **11** a five pound note
un billete de diez libras **12** a ten pound note
un billete de veinte libras **13** a twenty pound note
un billete de cincuenta libras **14** a fifty pound note

**¿Cuánto cuesta?** **How much is it?**
veinte peniques **15** twenty pence (*also* 20p)
diez peniques **16** ten pence (*also* 10p)
cincuenta peniques **17** fifty pence (*also* 50p)
tres libras ochenta y dos peniques/tres libras ochenta y dos **18** three pounds eighty-two pence/three pounds eighty-two
dos libras **19** two pounds

# Time page 37

**24 hours = 1 day**
**7 days = 1 week (wk)**
**365 days = 1 year (yr)**
**100 years = 1 century (c)**

| | |
|---|---|
| las tres en punto | **1** three o'clock |
| esfera del reloj | **2** clock-face |
| minutero | **3** minute-hand |
| horario | **4** hour-hand |
| segundero | **5** second-hand |
| las nueve y cinco | **6** five past nine (*US also* five after nine)/ nine o five |
| las nueve y diez | **7** ten past nine (*US also* ten after nine)/ nine ten |
| las nueve y cuarto | **8** a quarter past nine (*US also* a quarter after nine)/ nine fifteen |
| las nueve y media | **9** half past nine/nine thirty |
| las diez menos veinte | **10** twenty to ten/nine forty |
| las diez menos cuarto | **11** a quarter to ten/ nine forty-five |
| las diez menos diez | **12** ten to ten/nine fifty |
| las doce en punto/mediodía *también* medianoche | **13** twelve o'clock/midday (*esp US* noon*) also* midnight |
| las doce y siete minutos | **14** seven minutes past twelve (*US also* seven minutes after twelve)/twelve o seven |
| las siete de la mañana | **15** seven am (*US* A.M.)/ seven o'clock in the morning |
| las cinco de la tarde | **16** five pm (*US* P.M.)/ five o'clock in the afternoon |
| las ocho de la tarde | **17** eight pm (*US* P.M.)/ eight o'clock in the evening |
| las once y media de la noche | **18** eleven thirty pm (*US* P.M.) half past eleven at night |

page 38

# Emergency Services

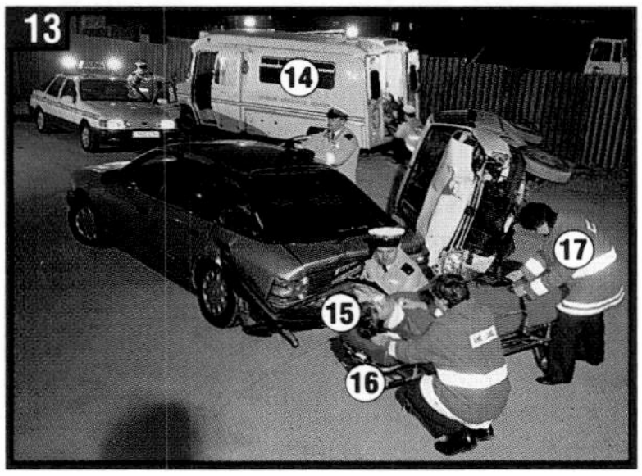


| | |
|---|---|
| **Policía** | **Police** |
| comisaría | **1** police station |
| coche de policía | **2** police car |
| (oficial de) policía | **3** police officer |
| **Bomberos** | **Fire Brigade** (***US*** **Fire Department)** |
| coche de bomberos | **4** fire-engine |
| escalera | **5** ladder |
| agua | **6** water |
| humo | **7** smoke |
| fuego | **8** fire |
| extintor de incendios | **9** fire extinguisher |
| bombero | **10** fireman (*esp US* fire fighter) |
| hidrante | **11** hydrant |
| manguera | **12** hose |
| **Servicio de Ambulancias** | **Ambulance Service** |
| accidente de coche | **13** car accident |
| ambulancia | **14** ambulance |
| hombre herido | **15** injured man |
| camilla | **16** stretcher |
| paramédico | **17** paramedic |
| prefijo internacional | **18** international code |
| prefijo del país | **19** country code |
| prefijo nacional | **20** area code |
| prefijo local | **21** (tele)phone number |
| cabina de teléfonos | **22** (tele)phone box (*esp US* telephone booth) |
| auricular | **23** receiver |
| tarjeta de teléfono | **24** phonecard (*Brit only*) |
| ranura | **25** slot |
| teclado | **26** dial |

(18) 00 (19) 44 1865 556767

01865 (20) 556767 (21)

*In Britain the telephone number for the police, fire and ambulance services is 999. In the US the emergency number is 911.*

*En Gran Bretaña el número de teléfono de la policía, los bomberos y la ambulancia es 999. En EEUU el número de emergencia es 911.*

# Jobs 1 page 39

artista **1** artist
jardinero, jardinera **2** gardener
disc jockey **3** disc jockey (*US* disk jockey)
locutora, locutor **4** newsreader (*esp US* newscaster)

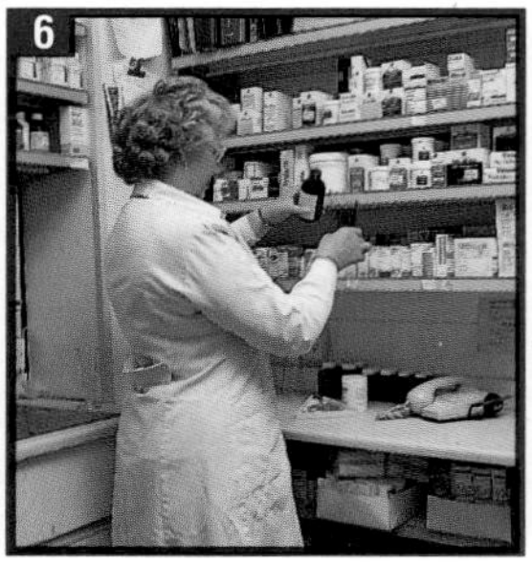

peluquera, peluquero **5** hairdresser
farmacéutica, farmacéutico **6** pharmacist
panadero, panadera **7** baker
carnicero, carnicera **8** butcher

agricultor, agricultora **9** farmer
pescador **10** fisherman
marinero **11** sailor
soldado **12** soldier

page 40

# Jobs 2

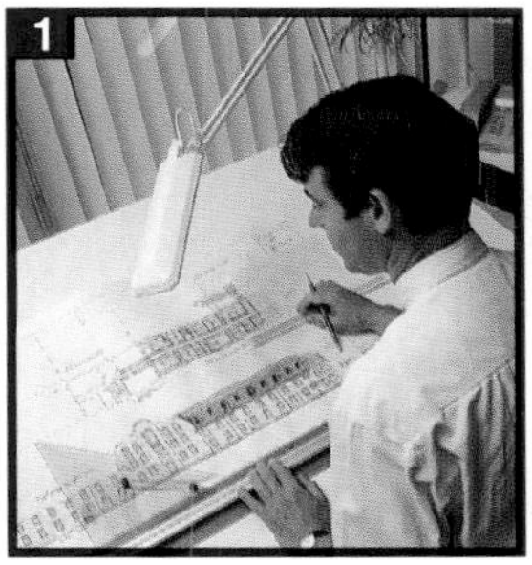

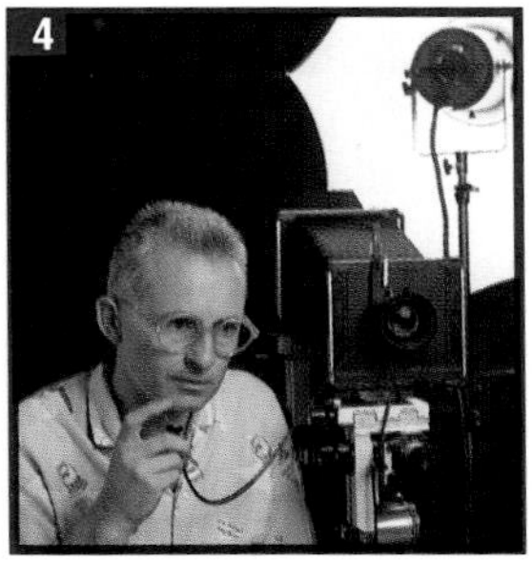


arquitecto, arquitecta **1** architect
camionero, camionera **2** lorry driver (*US* truck driver)
agente de viajes **3** travel agent
fotógrafo, fotógrafa **4** photographer

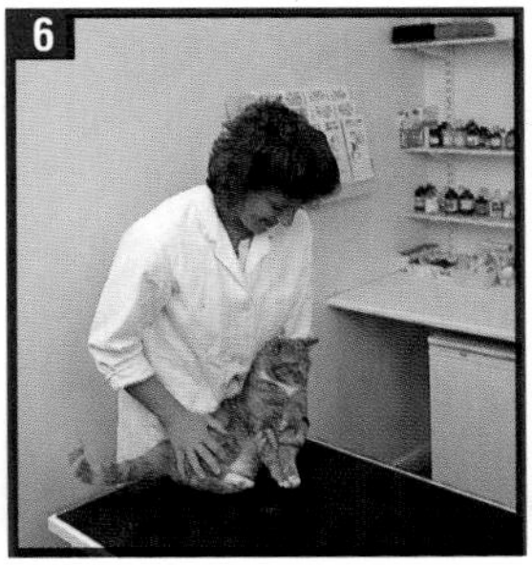

programador de ordenadores, programadora de ordenadores **5** computer programmer
veterinaria, veterinario **6** vet
electricista **7** electrician
carpintero, carpintera **8** carpenter

soldador, soldadora **9** welder
fontanero, fontanera **10** plumber
mecánico, mecánica **11** mechanic
albañil **12** bricklayer

# Daily Routine page 41

Se despierta. **1** He wakes up.
Se levanta. **2** He gets up/He gets out of bed.
Baja. **3** He goes downstairs.
Va a correr. **4** He goes jogging.

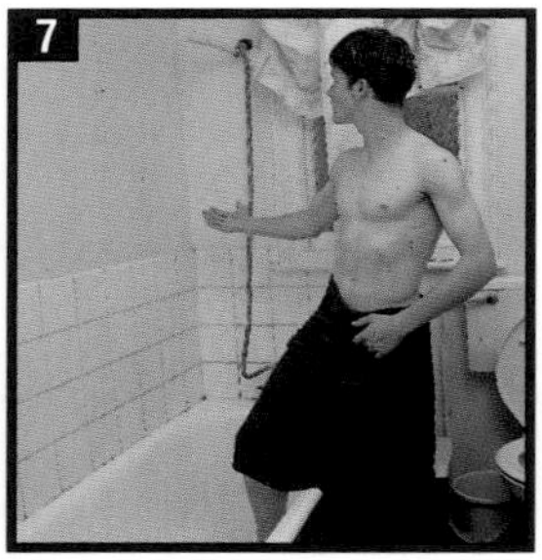

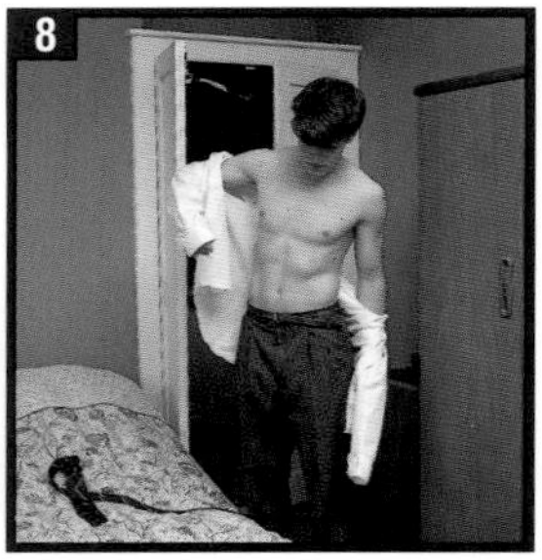


Vuelve. **5** He comes back.
Coge el correo. **6** He picks up the post (*US* mail).
Se ducha. **7** He has a shower.
(*esp US* He takes a shower.)
Se viste. **8** He gets dressed.

Desayuna. **9** He has breakfast/He eats breakfast.
Se va de casa. **10** He leaves home.
Compra un periódico. **11** He buys a newspaper.
Escucha música. **12** He listens to music.

page 42

# Daily Routine 2

Coge el tren. **13** He catches the train.
Lee el periódico. **14** He reads the newspaper.
Empieza a trabajar. **15** He starts work.
Se toma una taza de café. **16** He has a cup of coffee.
He drinks some coffee.

Come. **17** He has lunch/He eats lunch.
Termina de trabajar. **18** He finishes work.
Va en coche al club deportivo. **19** He drives to the sports centre (*US* health club).
Se encuentra con sus amigos. **20** He meets his friends.

Juega al squash. **21** He plays squash.
Cena. **22** He has dinner/He eats dinner.
Ve la televisión. **23** He watches television/TV.
Se va a la cama. **24** He goes to bed.

# Office Verbs page 43

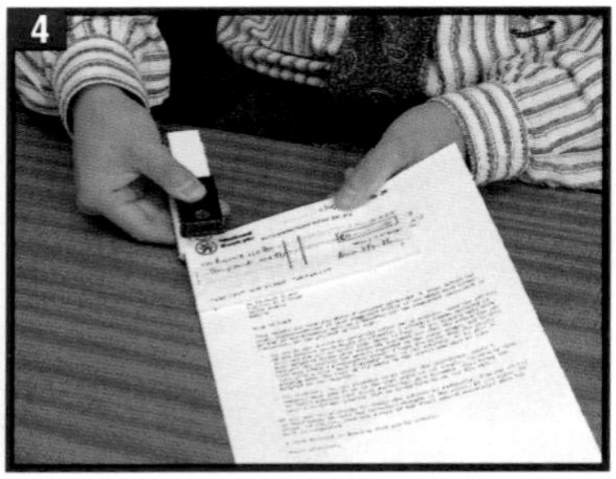


| | |
|---|---|
| Está dictando una carta. | **1** She is dictating a letter. |
| dictáfono | **2** Dictaphone/dictating machine |
| Está mecanografiando una carta. | **3** He is typing a letter. |
| Está mecanografiando. | He is typing. |
| Está grapando un cheque a una carta. | **4** He is stapling a cheque to a letter. (*US* check) |

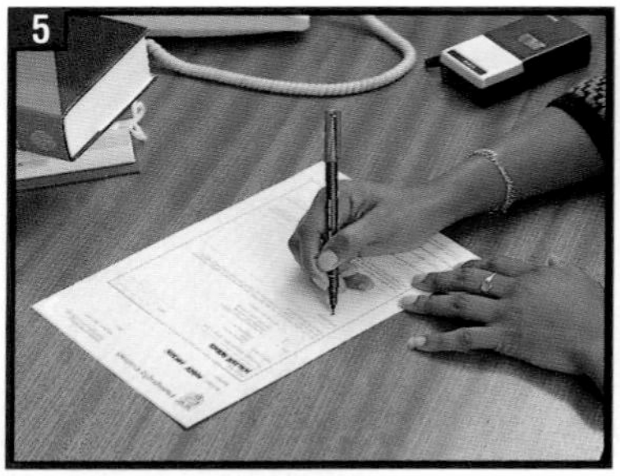

| | |
|---|---|
| Está rellenando un impreso. | **5** She is filling in a form. (*US* She is filling out a form.) |
| Está firmando una carta. | **6** She is signing a letter. |
| firma | **7** signature |
| Está tomando nota de una cita. | **8** She is making a note of an appointment. |

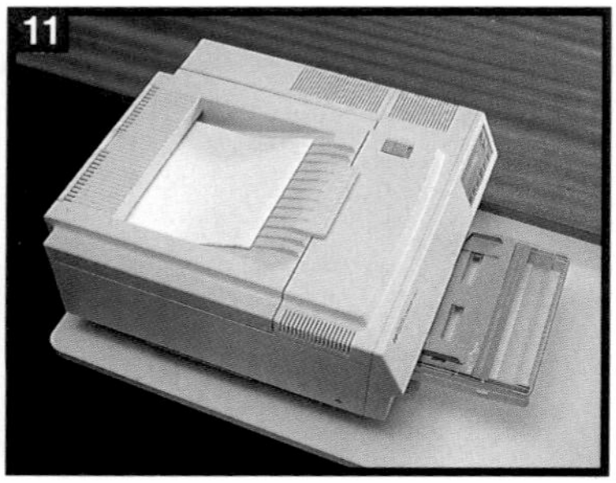


| | |
|---|---|
| Está archivando. | **9** He is filing. |
| Está mandando un fax. | **10** He is sending a fax. |
| Está mandando una carta por fax. | He is faxing a letter. |
| Está imprimiendo. | **11** It is printing. |
| Está imprimiendo una copia. | It is printing a copy. |

page 44

# The Office

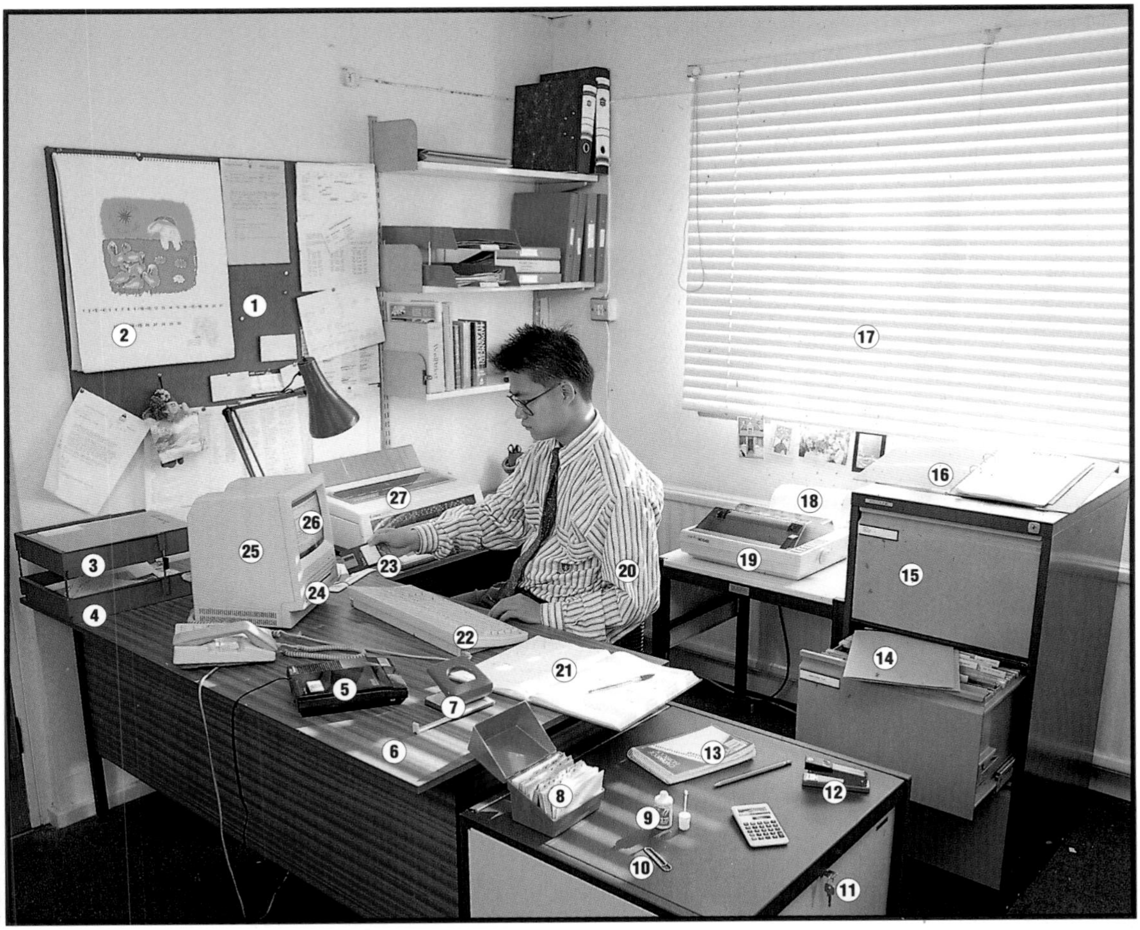

| | | |
|---|---|---|
| tablón de anuncios | **1** | notice-board (*US* bulletin board) |
| calendario | **2** | calendar |
| bandeja de entrada | **3** | in-tray (*US* in box) |
| bandeja de salida | **4** | out-tray (*US* out box) |
| contestador automático | **5** | answering machine (*Brit also* answerphone) |
| mesa | **6** | desk |
| perforador | **7** | hole-punch |
| fichero | **8** | card index (*US* card file) |
| Tipp-Ex líquido corrector | **9** | Tipp-Ex (*esp US* correction fluid) |
| clip | **10** | paper-clip |
| llave | **11** | key |
| grapadora | **12** | stapler |
| libreta | **13** | notebook |
| archivador | **14** | file |
| archivo | **15** | filing cabinet (*US* file cabinet) |
| bloc de anillas | **16** | ring binder |
| persiana | **17** | venetian blind |
| impresión | **18** | printout |
| impresora | **19** | printer |
| administrativo/secretaria | **20** | secretary |
| agenda | **21** | diary (*US* appointment book) |
| teclado | **22** | keyboard |
| disco flexible | **23** | floppy disk |
| unidad de disco | **24** | disk drive |
| ordenador personal | **25** | personal computer/PC |
| pantalla | **26** | screen |
| máquina de escribir | **27** | typewriter |

# A Science Laboratory 1 page 45

gafas protectoras **1** goggles
tubo de ensayo **2** test-tube
llama **3** flame
tubo de goma **4** rubber tubing
quemador de Bunsen **5** Bunsen burner
soporte **6** rack
mano de mortero **7** pestle
mortero **8** mortar
matraz de fondo plano **9** flat bottom flask
embudo **10** funnel
filtro de papel **11** filter paper
prisma **12** prism
pinzas **13** tongs
lupa **14** magnifying glass
émbolo **15** plunger

jeringa **16** syringe
matraz cónico **17** conical flask
tubo en U **18** U-tube
taburete **19** stool
soporte con abrazadera **20** clamp stand (*US* ring stand)
termómetro **21** thermometer
matraz de fondo redondo **22** round bottom flask
condensador **23** condenser
vaso de precipitación **24** measuring beaker (*US* graduated beaker)
tela metálica **25** gauze (*US* wire mesh screen)
trípode **26** tripod

# A Science Laboratory 2

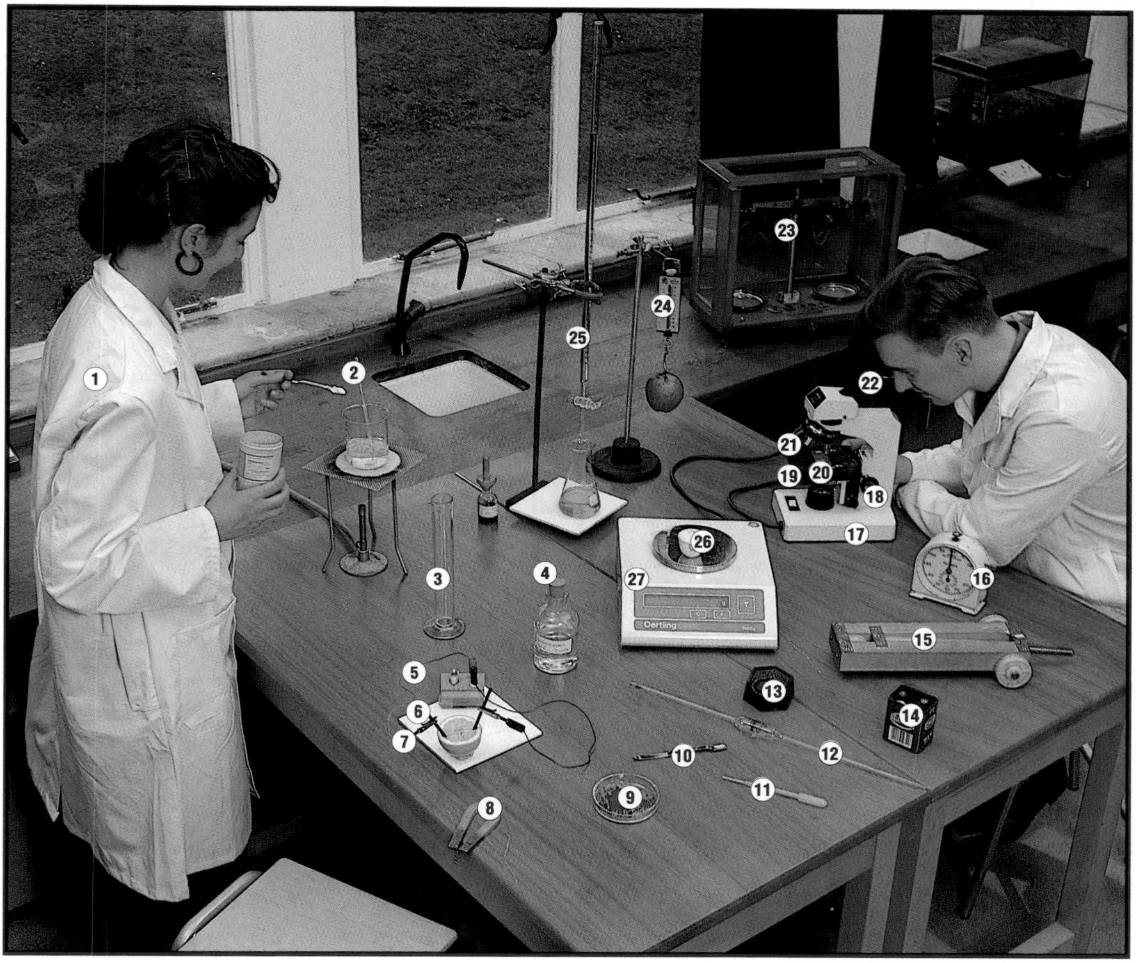


| | | |
|---|---|---|
| bata | **1** | lab coat |
| varilla de vidrio | **2** | glass rod |
| probeta | **3** | measuring cylinder (*US* graduated cylinder) |
| tapón | **4** | stopper |
| cable | **5** | wire |
| electrodo | **6** | electrode |
| pinza | **7** | crocodile clip (*US* alligator clip) |
| imán | **8** | magnet |
| cápsula de Petri | **9** | Petri dish (*US* petri dish) |
| espátula | **10** | spatula |
| cuentagotas | **11** | dropper |
| pipeta | **12** | pipette |
| pesa | **13** | weight |
| batería | **14** | battery |
| carrito | **15** | trolley (*US* cart) |
| cronómetro | **16** | stop clock (*US* timer) |
| microscopio | **17** | microscope |
| control de enfoque | **18** | focusing control (*US also* focusing knob) |
| portaobjeto | **19** | stage |
| preparación | **20** | slide |
| lente | **21** | objective lens |
| visor | **22** | eyepiece |
| balanza | **23** | balance/scales (*US* scale) |
| balanza de tensión | **24** | spring balance |
| bureta | **25** | burette |
| crisol | **26** | crucible |
| balanza electrónica | **27** | microbalance |

# Shapes and Lines page 47

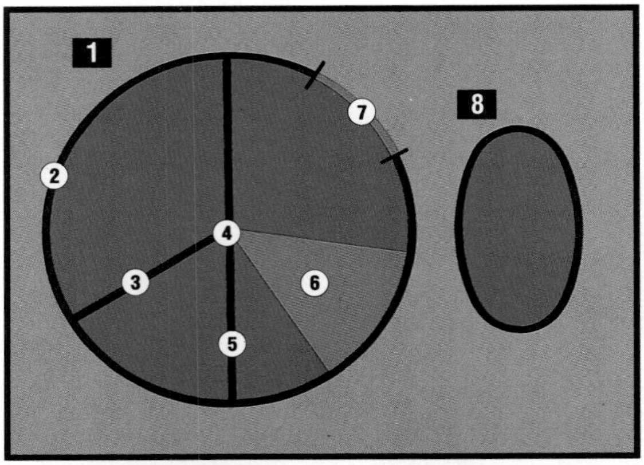


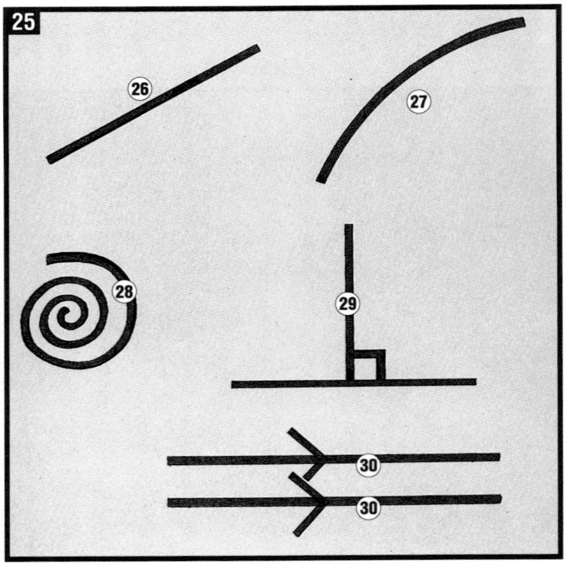


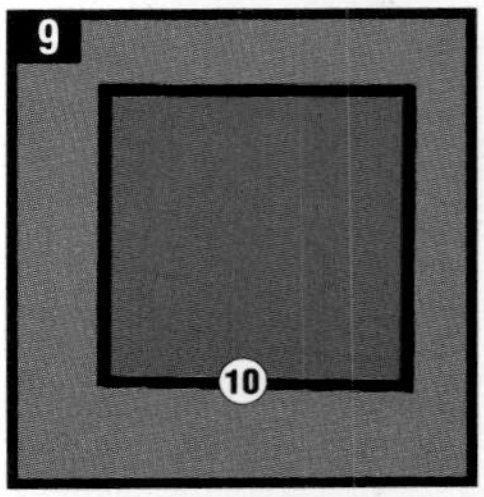


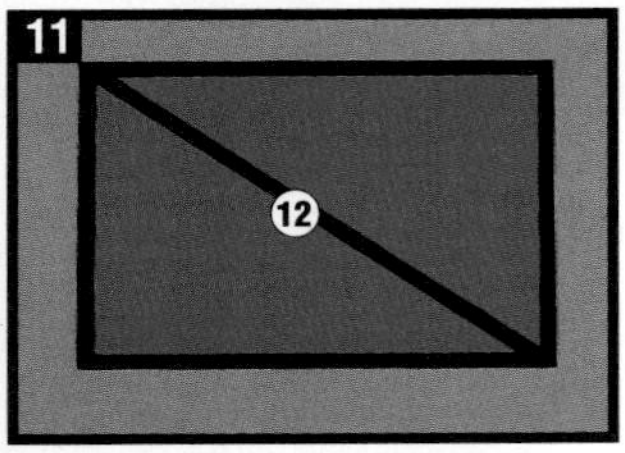


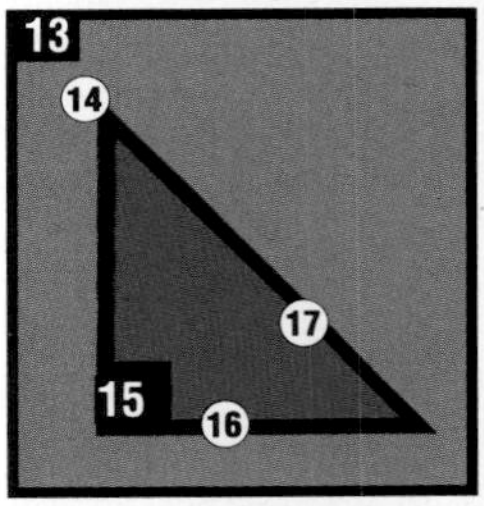


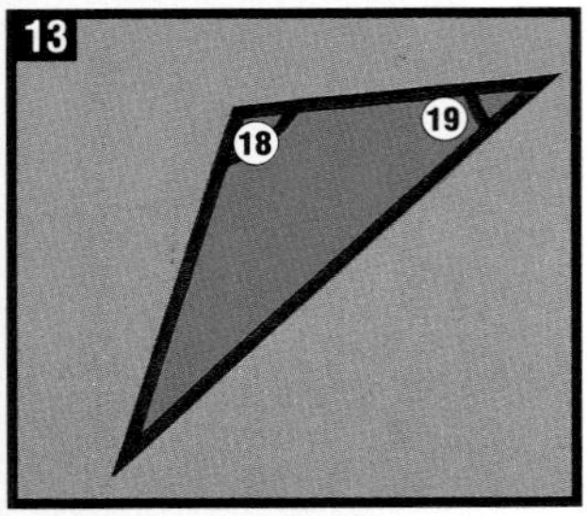


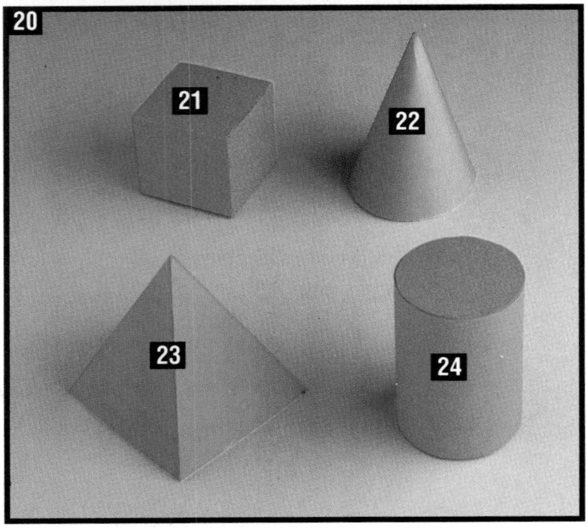


| | | |
|---|---|---|
| círculo | **1** | circle |
| circunferencia | **2** | circumference |
| radio | **3** | radius |
| centro | **4** | centre (*US* center) |
| diámetro | **5** | diameter |
| sector | **6** | sector |
| arco | **7** | arc |
| óvalo | **8** | oval |
| cuadrado | **9** | square |
| lado | **10** | side |
| rectángulo | **11** | rectangle |
| diagonal | **12** | diagonal |
| triángulo | **13** | triangle |
| vértice | **14** | apex |
| ángulo recto | **15** | right angle |
| base | **16** | base |
| hipotenusa | **17** | hypotenuse |
| ángulo obtuso | **18** | obtuse angle |
| ángulo agudo | **19** | acute angle |
| cuerpos sólidos | **20** | solid figures |
| cubo | **21** | cube |
| cono | **22** | cone |
| pirámide | **23** | pyramid |
| cilindro | **24** | cylinder |
| líneas | **25** | lines |
| línea recta | **26** | straight line |
| curva | **27** | curve |
| espiral | **28** | spiral |
| línea perpendicular | **29** | perpendicular line |
| líneas paralelas | **30** | parallel lines |

$$7 \overset{\text{⑪}}{+} 11 = 18$$

$$80 \overset{\text{⑫}}{-} 13 = 67$$

$$40 \overset{\text{⑬}}{\times} 4 = 160$$

$$32 \div 8 \overset{\text{⑭}}{=} 4 \text{ ⑮}$$

$$\overset{\text{⑯}}{2.5} \qquad \overset{\text{⑰}}{50\%}$$

| Spanish | | English |
|---|---|---|
| profundidad | **1** | depth |
| altura | **2** | height |
| anchura | **3** | width |
| borde | **4** | edge |
| ángulo | **5** | corner |
| longitud | **6** | length |
| frente | **7** | front |
| fondo | **8** | bottom |
| lado | **9** | side |
| parte trasera | **10** | back |
| más | **11** | plus |
| menos | **12** | minus |
| por | **13** | multiplied by/times |
| entre | **14** | divided by |
| igual a | **15** | equals |
| dos coma cinco | **16** | two point five |
| cincuenta por ciento | **17** | fifty per cent |
| fracciones | **18** | fractions |
| un cuarto | **19** | a quarter/ ¼ |
| un tercio | **20** | a third/ ⅓ |
| un medio | **21** | a half/ ½ |
| tres cuartos | **22** | three quarters/ ¾ |
| peso | **23** | weight |
| 10 gramos | **24** | 10 grams* |
| kilogramo | **25** | kilogram* |
| capacidad | **26** | capacity |
| mililitro | **27** | millilitre (*US* milliliter)* |
| litro | **28** | litre (*US* liter)* |
| milímetro | **29** | millimetre (*US* millimeter)* |
| centímetro | **30** | centimetre (*US* centimeter)* |

*Estas medidas no se usan normalmente en el inglés americano.*

*\*These measurements are not usually used in US English.*

1000 grams (g) = 1 kilogram (kg)

1000 millilitres (ml) = 1 litre (l)

10 millimetres (mm) = 1 centimetre (cm)
100 centimetres = 1 metre (m)
1000 metres = 1 kilometre (km)

cm 1 2 3 4

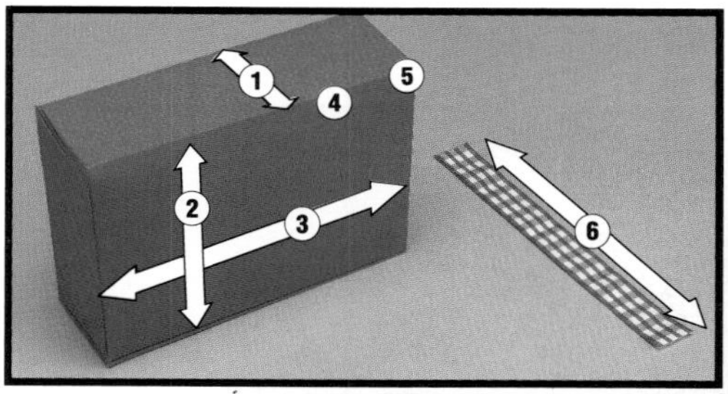

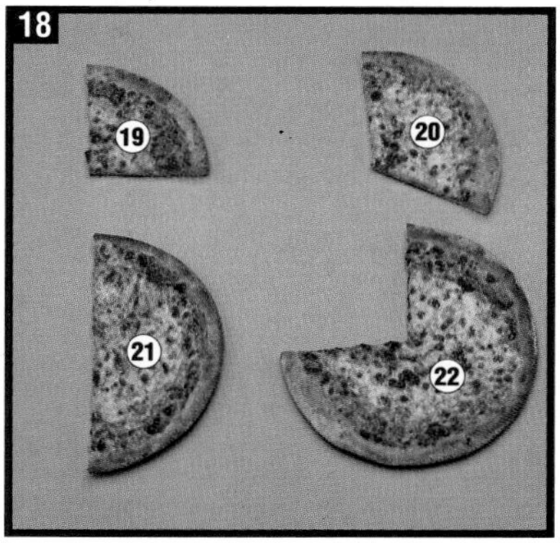

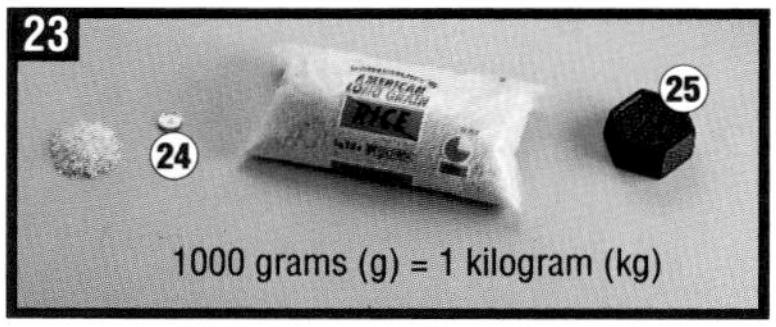

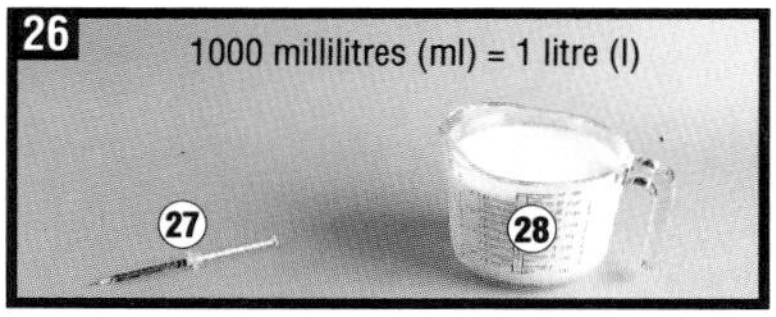

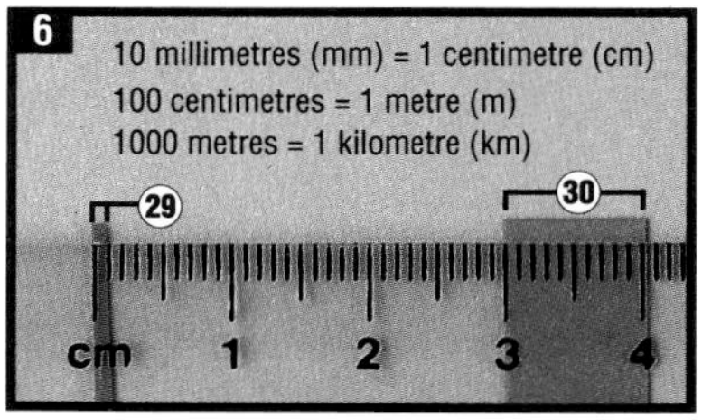

# The Classroom page 49

| | | |
|---|---|---|
| pizarra | **1** | blackboard (*US also* chalkboard) |
| alumna | **2** | pupil (*esp US* student) |
| libro de texto | **3** | textbook |
| cuaderno | **4** | exercise book (*US* notebook) |
| calculadora | **5** | calculator |
| escuadra | **6** | set square (*US* triangle) |
| transportador | **7** | protractor |
| mochila | **8** | school bag |
| suelo de baldosas | **9** | (tiled) floor |
| silla | **10** | chair |
| globo terráqueo | **11** | globe |
| tijeras | **12** | scissors |
| caballete | **13** | easel |
| pincel | **14** | paintbrush |
| caja de pinturas | **15** | paintbox |
| profesora | **16** | teacher |
| mural | **17** | picture |
| mapa | **18** | map |

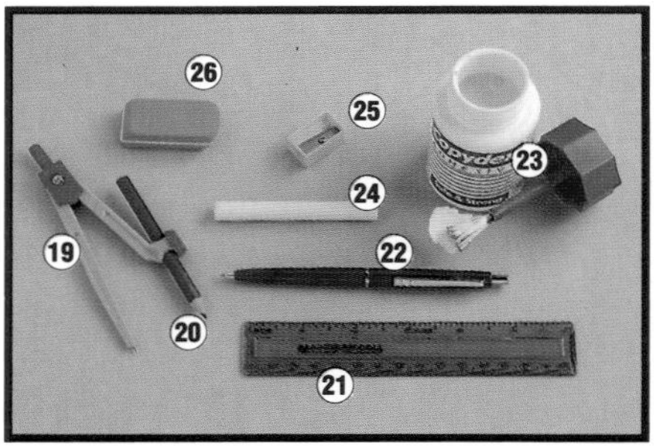


| | | |
|---|---|---|
| compás | **19** | (pair of) compasses (*also* compass) |
| lápiz | **20** | pencil |
| regla | **21** | ruler |
| bolígrafo | **22** | pen |
| pegamento | **23** | glue |
| (trozo de) tiza | **24** | (piece of) chalk |
| sacapuntas | **25** | pencil-sharpener |
| goma | **26** | rubber (*US* eraser) |

page 50

# Space

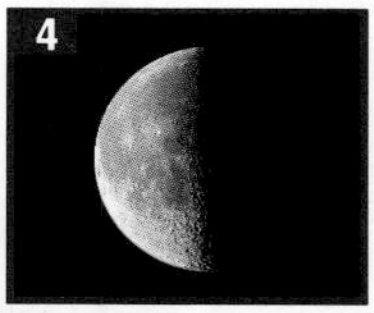

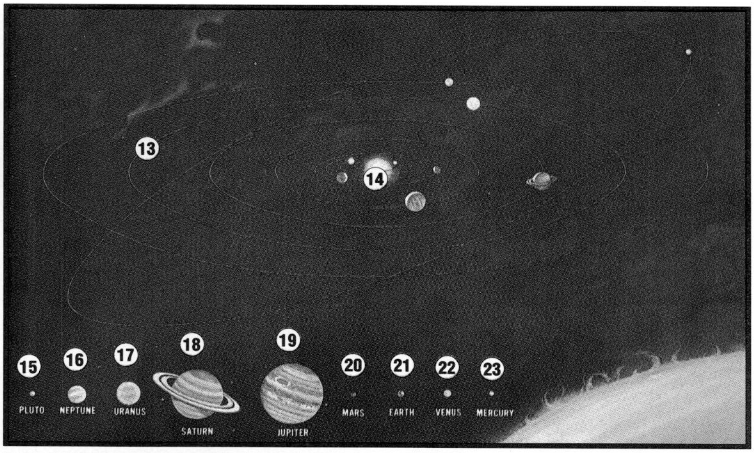

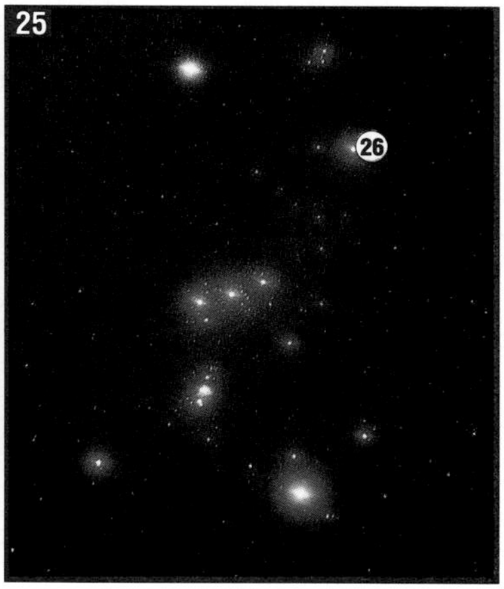

| | |
|---|---|
| cuarto creciente | **1** new moon (*esp US* crescent moon) |
| media luna | **2** half moon (*US also* first quarter) |
| luna llena | **3** full moon |
| cuarto menguante | **4** old moon (*US* half moon/last quarter) |
| módulo lunar | **5** lunar module |
| astronauta | **6** astronaut |
| traje espacial | **7** spacesuit |
| vehículo lunar | **8** lunar vehicle |
| satélite | **9** satellite |
| cohete | **10** rocket |
| transbordador espacial | **11** space shuttle |
| plataforma de lanzamiento | **12** launch pad |

| | |
|---|---|
| **El Sistema Solar** | **The Solar System** |
| órbita | **13** orbit |
| Sol | **14** Sun |
| **Los Planetas** | **The Planets** |
| Plutón | **15** Pluto |
| Neptuno | **16** Neptune |
| Urano | **17** Uranus |
| Saturno | **18** Saturn |
| Júpiter | **19** Jupiter |
| Marte | **20** Mars |
| Tierra | **21** Earth |
| Venus | **22** Venus |
| Mercurio | **23** Mercury |
| **Espacio Exterior** | **Outer Space** |
| galaxia | **24** galaxy |
| constelación | **25** constellation |
| estrella | **26** star |

# The Weather page 51

Hace sol. **1** It's sunny.
Está lloviendo. **2** It's raining. (*US also* It's rainy.)
Está nevando. **3** It's snowing. (*US also* It's snowy.)
nieve **4** snow
Hace viento. **5** It's windy.

Hay niebla. **6** It's misty.
Hay mucha niebla. **7** It's foggy.
Está nublado. **8** It's cloudy.
Hay tormenta. **9** It's stormy.

tormenta **10** thunderstorm
rayo **11** lightning
arco iris **12** rainbow
Está despejado. **13** It's bright.
Está oscuro. **14** It's dull. (*US* It's dark.)

# The Temperature
# The Seasons

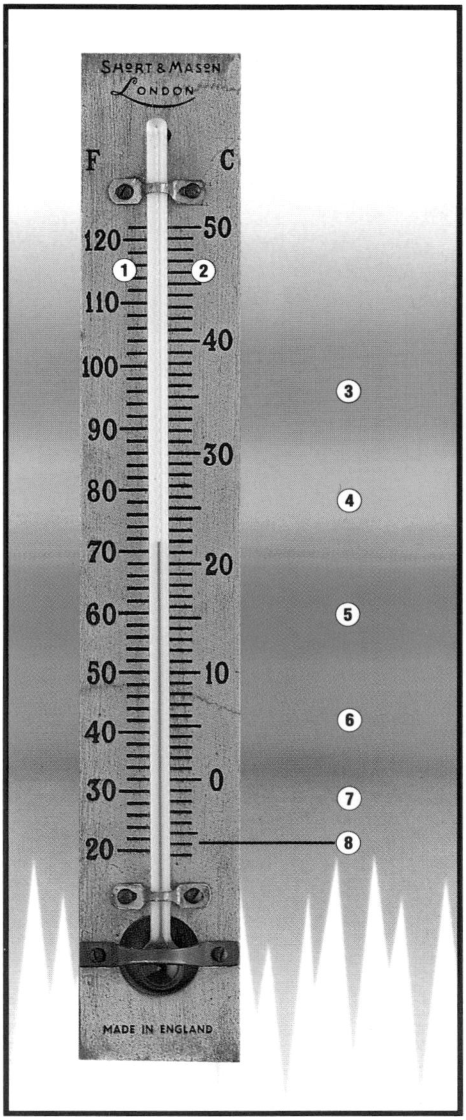

| La Temperatura | The Temperature |
|---|---|
| grados Fahrenheit | **1** degrees Fahrenheit |
| grados Celsius (*o* centígrados) | **2** degrees Celsius (*or* centigrade) |
| Hace mucho calor. | **3** It's hot. |
| Hace calor. | **4** It's warm. |
| Hace fresco. | **5** It's cool. |
| Hace frío. | **6** It's cold. |
| Hace un frío helador. | **7** It's freezing. |
| Hay seis grados bajo cero. | **8** It's minus six (degrees). (*US* It's six (degrees) below zero.) |

| Las Estaciones | The Seasons |
|---|---|
| en primavera | **9** in (the) spring |
| en verano | **10** in (the) summer |
| en otoño | **11** in (the) autumn (*US* in the fall) |
| en invierno | **12** in (the) winter |

| Los Meses | The Months |
|---|---|
| enero | January |
| febrero | February |
| marzo | March |
| abril | April |
| mayo | May |
| junio | June |
| julio | July |
| agosto | August |
| septiembre | September |
| octubre | October |
| noviembre | November |
| diciembre | December |

# The World page 53

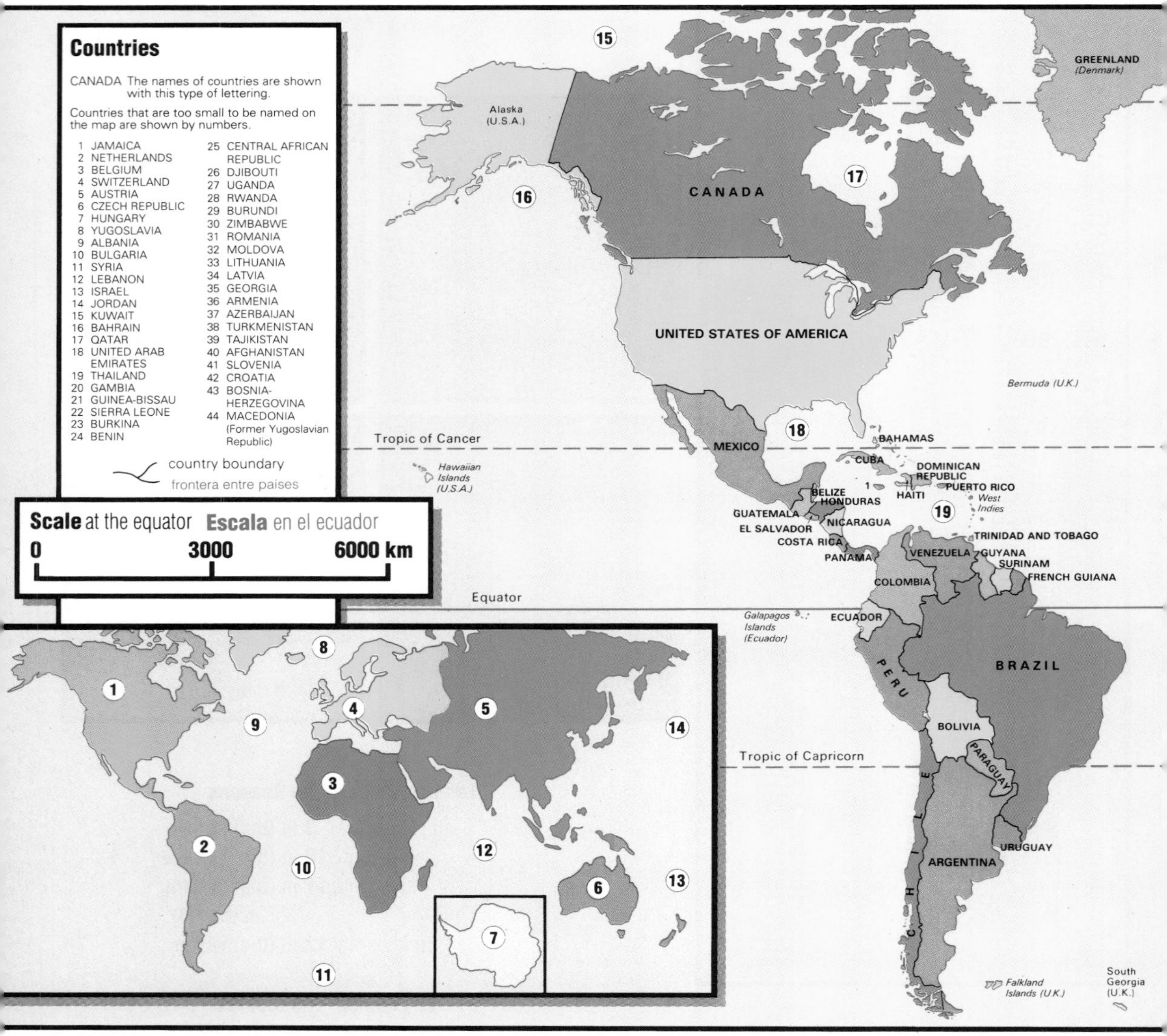


| Continentes | Continents |
|---|---|
| América del Norte | **1** North America |
| América del Sur | **2** South America |
| Africa | **3** Africa |
| Europa | **4** Europe |
| Asia | **5** Asia |
| Australia | **6** Australia |
| Antártica | **7** Antarctica |
| **Océanos** | **Oceans** |
| Artico | **8** Arctic |
| Atlántico Norte | **9** North Atlantic |
| Atlántico Sur | **10** South Atlantic |
| Antártico | **11** Antarctic |
| Indico | **12** Indian |
| Pacífico Sur | **13** South Pacific |
| Pacífico Norte | **14** North Pacific |
| **Mares, Golfos, y Bahías** | **Seas, Gulfs, and Bays** |
| Mar de Beaufort | **15** Beaufort Sea |
| Golfo de Alaska | **16** Gulf of Alaska |
| Bahía de Hudson | **17** Hudson Bay |
| Golfo de Méjico | **18** Gulf of Mexico |
| Mar Caribe | **19** Caribbean Sea |

page 54

# The World

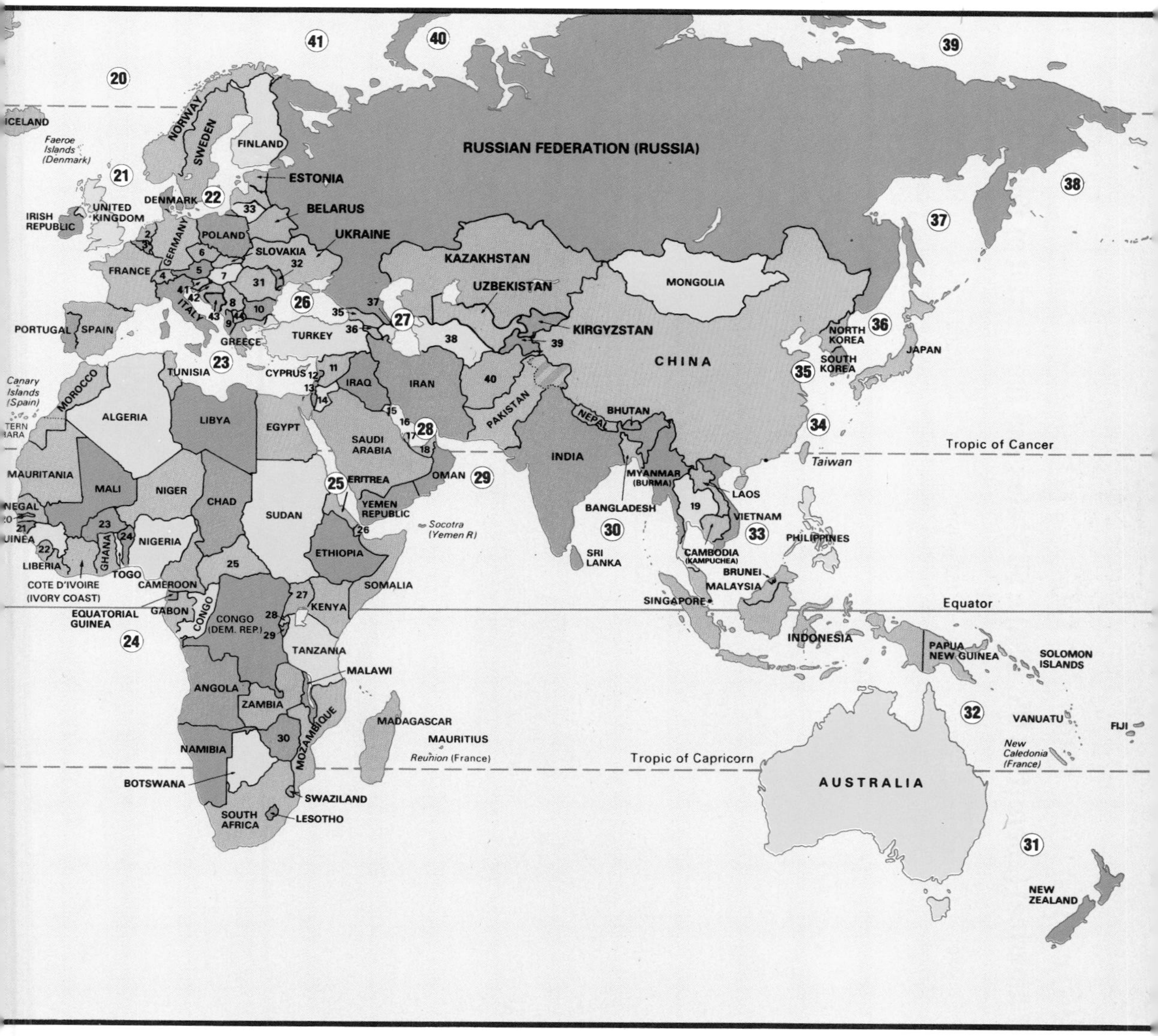


Mar de Noruega **20** Norwegian Sea
Mar del Norte **21** North Sea
Mar Báltico **22** Baltic Sea
Mar Mediterráneo **23** Mediterranean Sea
Golfo de Guinea **24** Gulf of Guinea
Mar Rojo **25** Red Sea
Mar Negro **26** Black Sea
Mar Caspio **27** Caspian Sea
Golfo Pérsico **28** The Gulf
Mar de Arabia **29** Arabian Sea
Bahía de Bengala **30** Bay of Bengal

Mar de Tasmania **31** Tasman Sea
Mar del Coral **32** Coral Sea
Mar de la China Sur **33** South China Sea
Mar de la China Este **34** East China Sea
Mar Amarillo **35** Yellow Sea
Mar de Japón **36** Sea of Japan
Mar de Okhotsk **37** Sea of Okhotsk
Mar de Bering **38** Bering Sea
Mar de Laptev **39** Laptev Sea
Mar de Kara **40** Kara Sea
Mar de Barents **41** Barents Sea

# The USA

page 55

**los Estados Unidos (de América) (*abrv.* EEUU) = 50 Estados y el Distrito de Columbia**

**the United States (of America) (*abbrs* (the) US, USA) = 50 States and the District of Columbia**

- state line — línea de estado
- lake — lago
- mountain — montaña
- main river — río principal
- island — isla
- city *or* town — ciudad

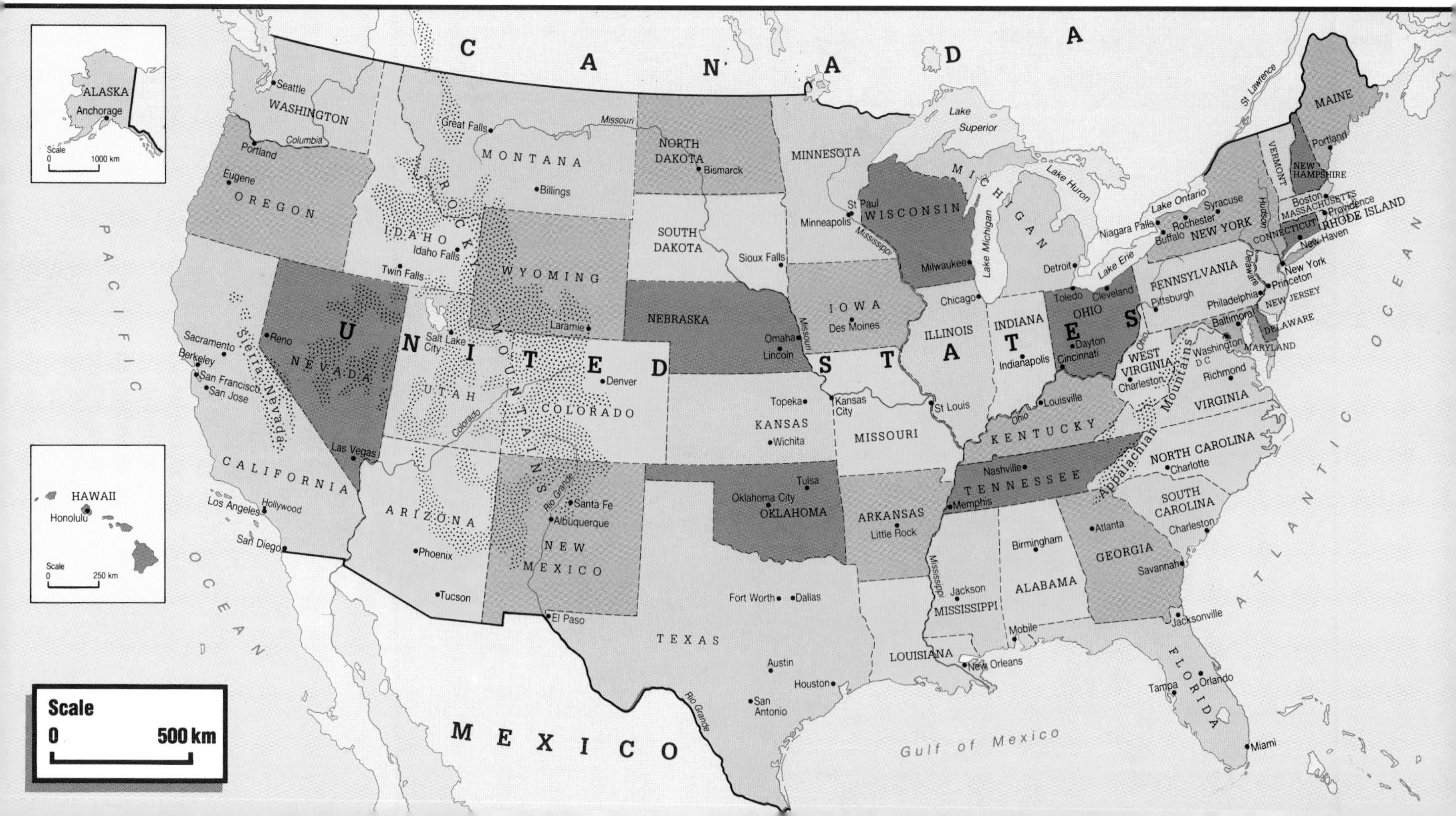

# The British Isles



- international boundary
- national boundary
- boundaries of districts in Northern Ireland, counties in the Republic of Ireland, and counties and unitary authorities in England, Scotland, and Wales
- ■ capital city
- • city *or* town

**Scale**
0 75 150 km

**N** north
**W** west
**S** south
**E** east
**NW** north-west

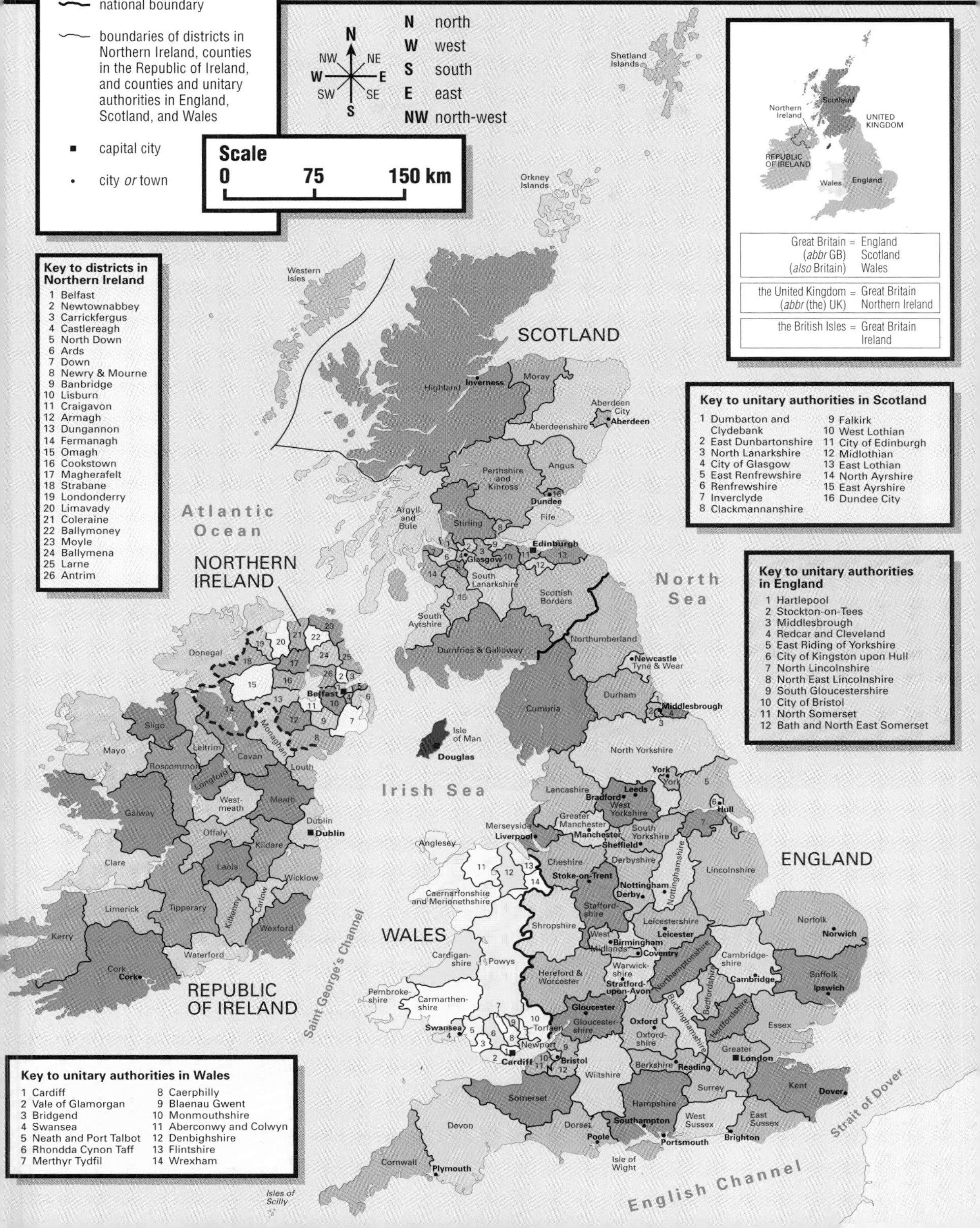


Great Britain (*abbr* GB) (*also* Britain) = England, Scotland, Wales

the United Kingdom (*abbr* (the) UK) = Great Britain, Northern Ireland

the British Isles = Great Britain, Ireland

**Key to districts in Northern Ireland**

1 Belfast
2 Newtownabbey
3 Carrickfergus
4 Castlereagh
5 North Down
6 Ards
7 Down
8 Newry & Mourne
9 Banbridge
10 Lisburn
11 Craigavon
12 Armagh
13 Dungannon
14 Fermanagh
15 Omagh
16 Cookstown
17 Magherafelt
18 Strabane
19 Londonderry
20 Limavady
21 Coleraine
22 Ballymoney
23 Moyle
24 Ballymena
25 Larne
26 Antrim

**Key to unitary authorities in Scotland**

1 Dumbarton and Clydebank
2 East Dunbartonshire
3 North Lanarkshire
4 City of Glasgow
5 East Renfrewshire
6 Renfrewshire
7 Inverclyde
8 Clackmannanshire
9 Falkirk
10 West Lothian
11 City of Edinburgh
12 Midlothian
13 East Lothian
14 North Ayrshire
15 East Ayrshire
16 Dundee City

**Key to unitary authorities in England**

1 Hartlepool
2 Stockton-on-Tees
3 Middlesbrough
4 Redcar and Cleveland
5 East Riding of Yorkshire
6 City of Kingston upon Hull
7 North Lincolnshire
8 North East Lincolnshire
9 South Gloucestershire
10 City of Bristol
11 North Somerset
12 Bath and North East Somerset

**Key to unitary authorities in Wales**

1 Cardiff
2 Vale of Glamorgan
3 Bridgend
4 Swansea
5 Neath and Port Talbot
6 Rhondda Cynon Taff
7 Merthyr Tydfil
8 Caerphilly
9 Blaenau Gwent
10 Monmouthshire
11 Aberconwy and Colwyn
12 Denbighshire
13 Flintshire
14 Wrexham

# Prepositions 1 page 57

| | |
|---|---|
| Está mirando por la ventana. | **1** She is looking **out of** the window. |
| Está cruzando el patio. | **2** She is walking **across** the courtyard. |
| El árbol crece a través del asiento. | **3** The tree is growing **through** the seat. |
| Tira un papel a la papelera. | **4** He is throwing some paper **into** the bin (*US* trash can). |
| Tira papel al suelo. | **5** He is throwing some paper **onto** the ground. |
| Va a la biblioteca. | **6** She is going **to** the library. |
| Viene de la biblioteca. | **7** He is coming **from** the library. |
| El papel se está cayendo de la mesa. | **8** The paper is falling **off** the table. |
| Se aleja del tablón. | **9** She is walking **away from** the notice (*US* sign). |
| Camina hacia el tablón. | **10** She is walking **towards** (*esp US* **toward**) the notice (*US* sign). |
| Sube las escaleras. | **11** She is walking **up** the steps. |
| Las flores crecen a lo largo de la pared. | **12** The flowers are growing **along** the wall. |
| Baja las escaleras. | **13** He is walking **down** the steps. |
| Está mirando desde la terraza. | **14** He is looking **over** the balcony. |

page 58

# Prepositions 2

| | | |
|---|---|---|
| El arbusto está fuera de la ventana. | **1** | The bush is **outside** the window. |
| La cinta está alrededor de la cesta. | **2** | The ribbon is **round** the basket (*esp US* **around** the basket). |
| Los casetes están en el cajón. | **3** | The cassettes are **in/inside** the drawer. |
| El libro está contra la mesa. | **4** | The book is **against** the table. |
| La taza está debajo de la mesa. | **5** | The mug is **under/underneath** the table. |
| La mesa está junto a la chimenea. | **6** | The table is **by/near** the fireplace. |
| Las flores secas están en la chimenea. | **7** | The dried flowers are **in** the fireplace. |
| El reloj está entre las velas. | **8** | The clock is **between** the candles. |
| La vela está en la repisa de la chimenea. | **9** | The candle is **on** the mantelpiece (*US* mantel). |
| El cuadro está sobre la chimenea. | **10** | The picture is **over** the mantelpiece (*US* mantel). |
| La planta está encima de la estantería. | **11** | The plant is **on top of** the bookcase. |
| La figura está en la parte alta de la estantería. | **12** | The ornament is **at the top of** the bookcase. |
| El plato está en el centro de la estantería. | **13** | The plate is **in the middle of** the bookcase. |
| Los libros están en la parte inferior de la estantería. | **14** | The books are **at the bottom of** the bookcase. |
| Los platos están encima de los libros. | **15** | The plates are **above** the books. |
| Las tazas están debajo de la tetera. | **16** | The cups are **below** the teapot. |
| La tetera está junto al plato. | **17** | The teapot is **beside/next to** the plate. |
| La televisión está delante de las revistas. | **18** | The television is **in front of** the magazines. |
| Las revistas están detrás de la televisión. | **19** | The magazines are **behind** the television. |

señal **1** road sign
señal de aparcamiento **2** parking notice (*US* parking sign)
buzón **3** letter-box/pillar-box (*US* mailbox)
cafetería **4** café (*also* cafe)
policía **5** police officer
acera **6** pavement (*US* sidewalk)
tapa de registro **7** manhole cover
arroyo **8** gutter
bordillo **9** kerb (*US* curb)
calle **10** street
esquina **11** street corner
tienda **12** shop (*esp US* store)
tráfico **13** traffic
papelera **14** litter-bin (*US* trash can/garbage can)
kiosco **15** news-stand
periódico **16** newspaper
vendedor de periódicos **17** news-vendor (*Brit only*)
grandes almacenes **18** department store
bandera **19** flag

anuncio **20** advertisement
parada de autobús **21** bus shelter
parada de autobús **22** bus stop
fábrica **23** factory
paso de peatones **24** pedestrian crossing (*US* crosswalk)

page 60

# The City 2

| | | |
|---|---|---|
| edificio | **1** | building |
| parque | **2** | park |
| cochecito (de niño) | **3** | pram (*US* baby carriage) |
| sillita (de niño) | **4** | pushchair (*US* stroller) |
| calle lateral | **5** | side street |
| taxi | **6** | taxi/cab |
| farola | **7** | lamppost |
| peatón | **8** | pedestrian |
| verja | **9** | railings |
| placa de la calle | **10** | street sign |
| barco | **11** | boat |
| rascacielos | **12** | tower block (*esp US* skyscraper) |
| cielo | **13** | sky |
| perfil urbano | **14** | skyline |
| puente | **15** | bridge |
| embarcadero | **16** | pier |
| río | **17** | river |
| orilla | **18** | bank |
| **En las afueras** | | **In the suburbs** |
| semáforo | **19** | traffic-lights (*US* traffic light) |
| ciclista | **20** | cyclist (*US* bicyclist) |
| cruce | **21** | crossroads (*US* intersection) |
| doble línea amarilla | **22** | double yellow lines (*Brit only*) |
| indicador | **23** | signpost |
| coche | **24** | car |
| autobús de dos pisos | **25** | double-decker bus |
| rotonda | **26** | roundabout (*US* traffic circle/rotary) |

# Roads and Road Signs 1 page 61

| | | |
|---|---|---|
| ceda el paso | **1** | give way (*US* yield) |
| stop | **2** | stop |
| dirección prohibida | **3** | no entry (*US* do not enter) |
| tráfico de doble sentido | **4** | two-way traffic |
| prohibido girar en U | **5** | no U-turn |
| límite de velocidad | **6** | speed limit |
| prohibido girar a la izquierda | **7** | no left turn |
| curva peligrosa a la derecha | **8** | bend to right (*US* curve to right) |
| calle para peatones y bicicletas | **9** | cycle and pedestrian route (*US* bike and pedestrian path) |
| calle de sentido único | **10** | one-way street |
| área de servicio | **11** | service station (*US* service area) |
| giro obligatorio a la derecha | **12** | turn right |
| carretera en obras | **13** | roadworks (*US* road work) |
| volquete | **14** | dumper (truck) (*esp US* dump truck) |
| trabajador de la construcción | **15** | construction worker |
| taladro neumático | **16** | pneumatic drill (*US also* jackhammer) |
| cono | **17** | cone |
| excavadora | **18** | JCB (*US* backhoe) |
| tierra | **19** | soil |

page 62

# Roads and Road Signs 2

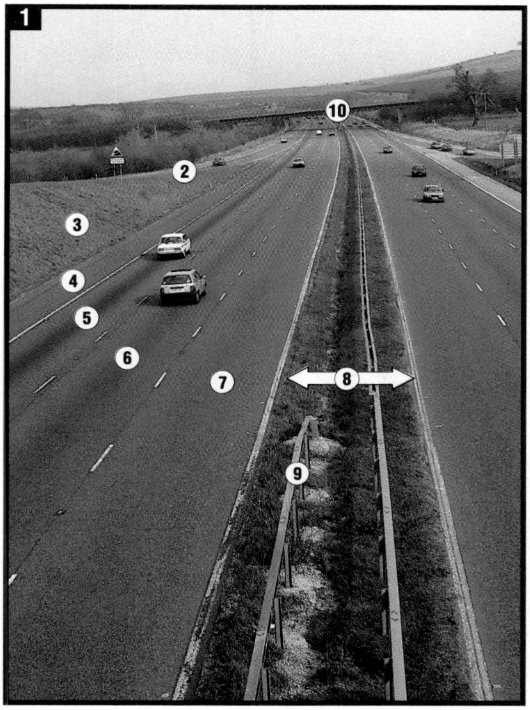

| | | |
|---|---|---|
| autopista | **1** | motorway (*Brit*) |
| rampa de acceso | **2** | slip-road (*Brit*) |
| terraplén | **3** | embankment (*Brit*) |
| arcén | **4** | hard shoulder (*Brit*) |
| carril de la izquierda | **5** | inside lane/slow lane (*Brit*) |
| carril central | **6** | middle lane/centre lane (*Brit*) |
| carril de la derecha | **7** | outside lane/fast lane (*Brit*) |
| mediana | **8** | central reservation (*Brit*) |
| valla de seguridad | **9** | crash barrier (*Brit*) |
| paso elevado | **10** | flyover (*Brit*) |
| autopista | **11** | freeway/ interstate highway (*US*) |
| rampa de acceso | **12** | exit ramp (*US*) |
| terraplén | **13** | bank (*US*) |
| arcén | **14** | shoulder (*US*) |
| carril de la derecha | **15** | right lane/slow lane (*US*) |
| carril central | **16** | center lane/middle lane (*US*) |
| carril de la izquierda | **17** | left lane/fast lane/ passing lane (*US*) |
| mediana | **18** | median strip (*US*) |
| valla de seguridad | **19** | guardrail (*US*) |
| paso elevado | **20** | overpass (*US*) |

| | | |
|---|---|---|
| paso inferior | **21** | underpass |
| pasarela peatonal | **22** | footbridge |
| cuneta | **23** | grass verge (*US* shoulder) |
| carretera | **24** | road (*US* highway) |
| intersección | **25** | junction (*esp US* intersection) |

# Vehicles page 63

| | | |
|---|---|---|
| transporte | **1** | transporter |
| autobús | **2** | coach (*US* bus) |
| camión cisterna | **3** | tanker (*US* fuel truck) |
| camión | **4** | lorry (*US* truck) |
| furgoneta | **5** | van |
| hormigonera | **6** | cement-mixer (*US* cement truck) |
| camioneta | **7** | pick-up truck |
| carretilla elevadora | **8** | fork-lift truck |
| caravana | **9** | caravan (*US* trailer) |
| jeep | **10** | jeep |
| deportivo | **11** | sports car |
| berlina | **12** | saloon (*US* sedan) |
| descapotable | **13** | convertible |
| familiar | **14** | estate (*US* station wagon) |
| tres puertas/cinco puertas | **15** | hatchback |

# The Car

| | | |
|---|---|---|
| gasolinera | **1** | filling-station (*US also* gas station) |
| espejo retrovisor | **2** | wing mirror (*US* side mirror) |
| intermitente | **3** | indicator (*US* turn signal) |
| faro | **4** | headlight |
| matrícula | **5** | number-plate (*US* license plate) |
| tubo de escape | **6** | exhaust-pipe |
| parachoques | **7** | bumper |
| piloto trasero | **8** | rear-light (*US* taillight) |
| maletero | **9** | boot (*US* trunk) |
| limpiaparabrisas trasero | **10** | rear windscreen wiper (*US* rear windshield wiper) |
| surtidor de gasolina | **11** | petrol pump (*US* gas pump) |
| manguera | **12** | hose |
| boquilla | **13** | nozzle |
| capó | **14** | bonnet (*US* hood) |
| motor | **15** | engine |
| filtro del aire | **16** | air filter |
| culata del cilindro | **17** | cylinder head |
| parrilla del radiador | **18** | radiator grille |

| | | |
|---|---|---|
| parabrisas | **19** | windscreen (*US* windshield) |
| salpicadero | **20** | dashboard |
| palanca de cambio | **21** | gear lever (*US* gearshift) |
| volante | **22** | steering-wheel |
| indicador de combustible | **23** | fuel gauge (*US also* gas gauge) |
| velocímetro | **24** | speedometer |
| encendido | **25** | ignition |
| embrague | **26** | clutch |
| freno de pie | **27** | footbrake |
| acelerador | **28** | accelerator (*US also* gas pedal) |

# Bikes page 65

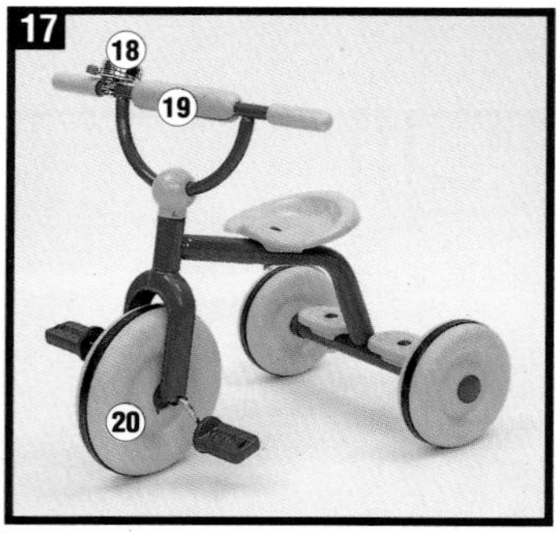

| | | |
|---|---|---|
| bicicleta/bici | **1** | bicycle/bike |
| sillín | **2** | saddle (*esp US* seat) |
| bomba | **3** | pump |
| cuadro | **4** | frame |
| biela | **5** | crank |
| candado | **6** | lock |
| radios | **7** | spokes |
| cadena | **8** | chain |
| pedal | **9** | pedal |
| plato | **10** | chain-wheel |
| válvula | **11** | valve |
| cubo | **12** | hub |
| palanca de cambio | **13** | gear lever (*US* gear changer) |
| reflector | **14** | reflector |
| cable | **15** | cable |
| palanca de freno | **16** | brake lever |

| | | |
|---|---|---|
| triciclo | **17** | tricycle |
| timbre | **18** | bell |
| manillar | **19** | handlebar |
| rueda | **20** | wheel |
| motocicleta | **21** | scooter |
| guardabarros | **22** | mudguard (*US* fender) |
| sillín | **23** | seat |
| portaequipajes | **24** | top box (*US* top case) |
| motocicleta | **25** | motor cycle (*Brit also* motor bike) |
| acelerador | **26** | accelerator/throttle |
| neumático | **27** | tyre (*US* tire) |
| motor | **28** | engine |
| amortiguadores | **29** | shock absorbers |

page 66

# The Railway (*US* Railroad)

garita de señales **1** signal-box (*US* signal tower)
paso a nivel **2** level crossing (*US* grade crossing)
locomotora **3** engine
vagón **4** coach (*US* passenger car)

**El Metro** **The Underground (*US* The Subway)**

señal de salida **5** exit sign
andén **6** platform
vías **7** line(s) (*esp US* track)
tren **8** train
túnel **9** tunnel

**En la Estación** **At the Station**

despacho de billetes **10** ticket office (*US* ticket counter)
ventanilla **11** window
cola **12** queue (*US* line)
bolsa **13** bag
maleta **14** suitcase
horario **15** timetable
mochila **16** rucksack (*esp US* backpack)
pantalla de salidas **17** departures board (*US* departure board)
numero de vía **18** platform number (*US* track number)
picador de billetes **19** ticket-collector (*US* ticket taker)
pasajero **20** passenger
entrada (a la vía 10) **21** entrance (to platform 10)
barrera **22** barrier (*esp US* gate)

# At the Airport 1 page 67

| En la terminal | In the terminal |
|---|---|
| facturación | **1** check-in |
| billete de avión | **2** airline ticket |
| tarjeta de embarque | **3** boarding pass |
| mostrador de facturación | **4** check-in desk (*US* check-in counter) |
| control de pasaportes | **5** passport control |
| pasaporte | **6** passport |
| seguridad | **7** security |
| detector de metales | **8** metal detector |
| rayos X | **9** X-ray scanner |
| tienda libre de impuestos | **10** duty-free shop |
| perfume | **11** perfume |
| sala de embarque | **12** departures lounge (*US* departure lounge/ waiting area) |
| asiento | **13** seat |
| azafata | **14** steward (*US* flight attendant) |
| puerta | **15** gate |
| recogida de equipajes | **16** luggage reclaim (*US* baggage reclaim) |
| equipaje | **17** luggage |
| carro | **18** trolley (*US* cart) |
| aduana | **19** customs |
| oficial de aduanas | **20** customs officer |

page 68

# At the Airport 2

embarque **1** boarding
pasajero **2** passenger
carro **3** trailer (*US* cart)
torre de control **4** control tower
controlador aéreo **5** air traffic controller
despegue **6** take-off
pista **7** runway
aterrizaje **8** landing
helicóptero **9** helicopter
hélice **10** rotor
piloto **11** pilot
avión **12** plane
morro **13** nose
cabina de la tripulación **14** cockpit
hélice **15** propeller
ala **16** wing
fuselaje **17** fuselage
cola **18** tail
motor a reacción **19** jet engine

# In Port 1 page 69

barco de vela **1** sailing-ship
mástil **2** mast
vela **3** sail
cubierta **4** deck
cabina **5** cabin
cable **6** cable (*US* line)
barca de remos **7** rowing-boat (*US* rowboat)
remo **8** oar
barcaza **9** barge

puerto deportivo **10** marina
lancha motora **11** motor boat
velero **12** yacht (*US also* sailboat)
yate **13** cabin cruiser
barco de pesca **14** fishing boat
amarre **15** mooring
proa **16** bow
popa **17** stern
bote salvavidas **18** lifeboat
canoa **19** canoe (*US* kayak)
remo **20** paddle

page 70

# In Port 2

| | | |
|---|---|---|
| muelle | **1** | dock |
| grúa | **2** | crane |
| almacén | **3** | warehouse |
| carga | **4** | cargo |
| barco | **5** | ship |
| petrolero | **6** | (oil-)tanker |
| hidroala | **7** | hydrofoil |
| aerodeslizador | **8** | hovercraft |
| ferry | **9** | ferry |
| chimenea | **10** | funnel (*US* smokestack) |
| transatlántico | **11** | liner (*esp US* ocean liner) |
| faro | **12** | lighthouse |
| rocas | **13** | rocks |
| lancha inflable | **14** | inflatable dinghy (*US* rubber raft) |
| motor fueraborda | **15** | outboard motor |
| ancla | **16** | anchor |

# Holidays 1 (*US* Vacations) page 71

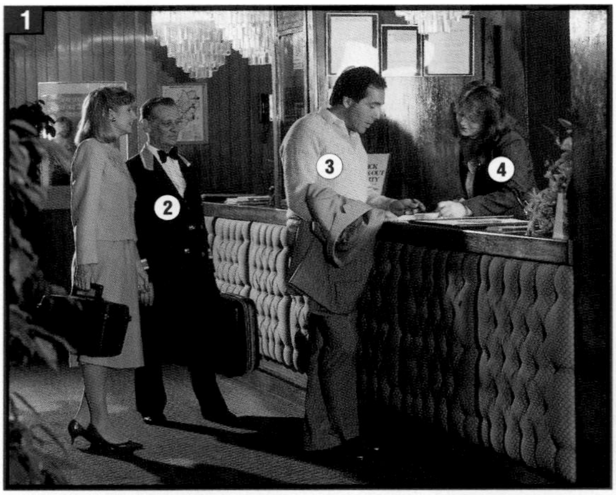

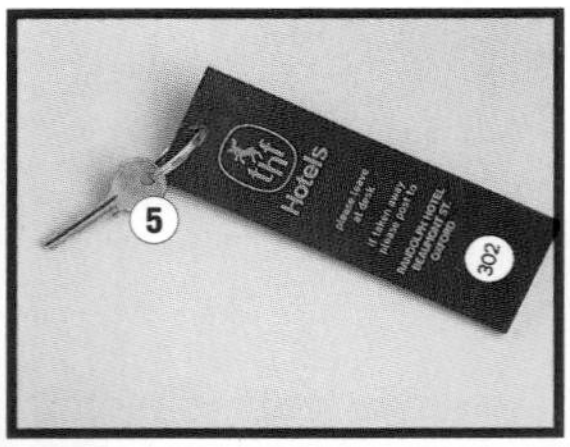

| | | |
|---|---|---|
| recepción del hotel | **1** | hotel reception (*US* front desk) |
| botones | **2** | porter (*US also* bellhop) |
| huésped | **3** | guest |
| recepcionista | **4** | receptionist |
| llave de la habitación | **5** | room key |
| habitación individual | **6** | single room |
| habitación doble | **7** | double room |
| habitación de dos camas | **8** | twin room (*US* room with twin beds) |
| visita a monumentos | **9** | sightseeing |
| guía | **10** | tour guide |
| grupo de turistas | **11** | party of tourists |
| turista | **12** | tourist |
| castillo | **13** | castle |
| mansión | **14** | country house |
| pueblo | **15** | village |
| el campo | **16** | the countryside |
| merienda | **17** | picnic |
| acampada | **18** | camping |
| tienda | **19** | tent |
| tela impermeable | **20** | groundsheet |
| saco de dormir | **21** | sleeping-bag |
| hornillo | **22** | camping stove (*US* camp stove) |
| excursionismo | **23** | hiking |
| excursionista | **24** | hiker |
| mochila | **25** | rucksack (*esp US* backpack) |
| camping para caravanas | **26** | caravan site (*US* trailer camp) |
| caravana | **27** | caravan (*US* trailer) |

page 72

# Holidays 2 (*US* Vacations)

| | |
|---|---|
| la costa | **1** the seaside (*esp US* the beach) |
| centro turístico | **2** holiday resort |
| playa | **3** beach |
| dique | **4** sea wall |
| paseo | **5** promenade (*esp US* seafront) |
| crucero | **6** cruise |
| tumbona | **7** sunbed |
| veraneante | **8** sunbather |
| sombrilla | **9** sunshade |
| vela | **10** sailing |
| vacaciones en barco | **11** boating holiday (*US* boating vacation) |
| canal | **12** canal |
| pesca | **13** fishing |
| pescador | **14** angler |
| caña de pescar | **15** fishing-rod |
| equitación | **16** pony-trekking (*US* horseback riding) |
| safari | **17** safari |
| paracaidismo | **18** parachuting |
| paracaidas | **19** parachute |
| ascensionismo | **20** ballooning |
| globo | **21** hot-air balloon |
| vuelo delta | **22** hang-gliding |
| ala delta | **23** hang-glider |
| alpinismo | **24** climbing |
| alpinista | **25** climber |
| guarniciones | **26** harness |

# The Environment page 73

| | | |
|---|---|---|
| montaña | **1** | mountain |
| pico | **2** | peak |
| valle | **3** | valley |
| lago | **4** | lake |
| bosque | **5** | forest |
| cascada | **6** | waterfall |
| corriente | **7** | stream |
| mar | **8** | sea |
| rocas | **9** | rocks |
| playa | **10** | beach |
| acantilado | **11** | cliff |
| colina | **12** | hill |
| pantano | **13** | reservoir |
| presa | **14** | dam |
| desierto | **15** | desert |
| arena | **16** | sand |
| duna de arena | **17** | sand-dune |
| meseta | **18** | plateau |
| bosque | **19** | wood (*esp US* woods) |
| granja | **20** | farm |
| casa de la granja | **21** | farmhouse |
| granero | **22** | barn |
| estanque | **23** | pond |
| campo | **24** | field |
| cosechadora | **25** | combine harvester (*US* combine) |
| campo de cereal | **26** | cornfield |
| grano | **27** | grain |
| tractor | **28** | tractor |
| arado | **29** | plough (*esp US* plow) |
| surco | **30** | furrow |

page 74

# Hobbies

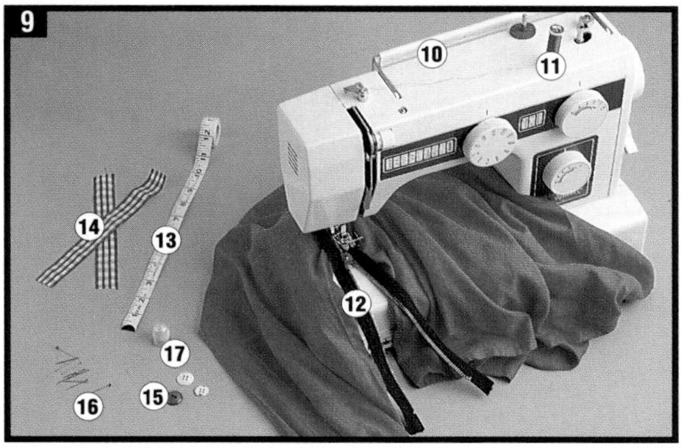


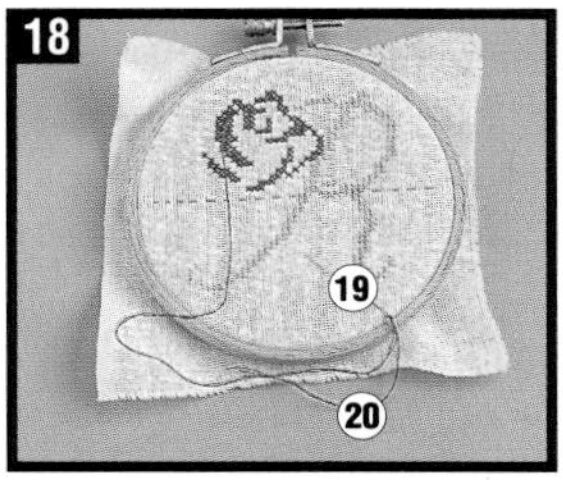


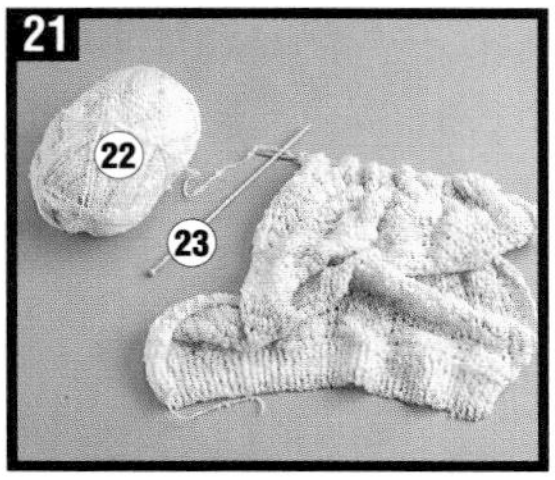


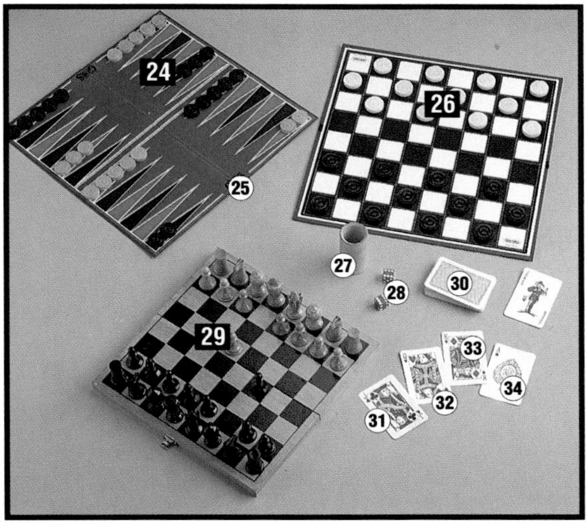


| | | |
|---|---|---|
| pintura | **1** | painting |
| dibujo | **2** | drawing |
| alfarería | **3** | pottery |
| filatelia | **4** | stamp collecting |
| álbum de sellos | **5** | stamp album |
| modelismo | **6** | making models |
| juego de modelismo | **7** | kit |
| maqueta | **8** | model |
| costura | **9** | sewing |
| máquina de coser | **10** | sewing-machine |
| bobina de hilo | **11** | reel of cotton (*US* spool of thread) |
| cremallera | **12** | zip (*esp US* zipper) |
| metro | **13** | tape-measure |
| cinta | **14** | ribbon |
| botón | **15** | button |
| alfiler | **16** | pin |
| dedal | **17** | thimble |
| bordado | **18** | embroidery |
| aguja | **19** | needle |
| hilo | **20** | thread |
| punto | **21** | knitting |
| lana | **22** | wool |
| aguja de punto | **23** | knitting-needle |
| backgammon | **24** | backgammon |
| tablero | **25** | board |
| damas | **26** | draughts (*US* checkers) |
| cubilete | **27** | shaker |
| dados | **28** | dice |
| ajedrez | **29** | chess |
| baraja | **30** | pack of playing-cards |
| J de tréboles | **31** | jack/knave of clubs |
| reina de corazones | **32** | queen of hearts |
| rey de diamantes | **33** | king of diamonds |
| as de espadas | **34** | ace of spades |

# Musical Instruments

page 75

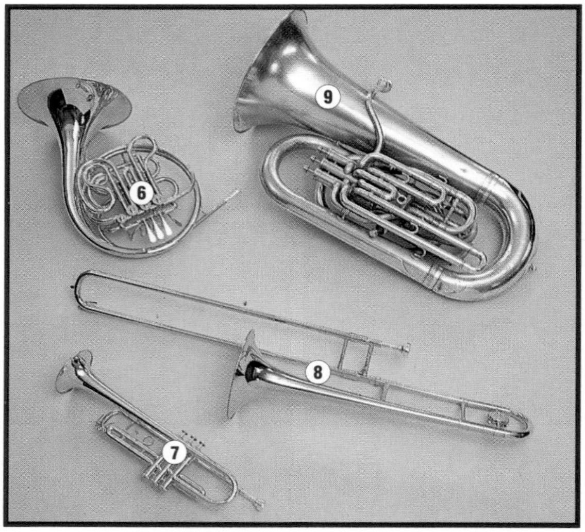


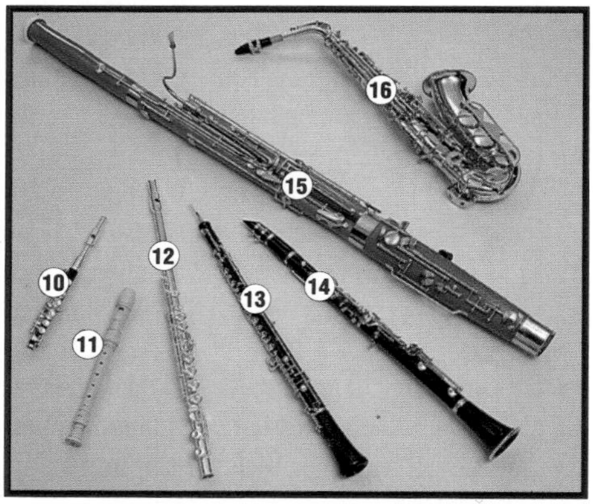

| | |
|---|---|
| **Cuerda** | **Strings** |
| viola | **1** viola |
| arco | **2** bow |
| violoncelo | **3** cello |
| violín | **4** violin |
| bajo | **5** (double-)bass |
| **Viento-Metal** | **Brass** |
| corno francés | **6** French horn |
| trompeta | **7** trumpet |
| trombón | **8** trombone |
| tuba | **9** tuba |
| **Viento-Madera** | **Woodwind** |
| flautín | **10** piccolo |
| flauta de pico | **11** recorder |
| flauta | **12** flute |
| oboe | **13** oboe |
| clarinete | **14** clarinet |
| fagot | **15** bassoon |
| saxofón | **16** saxophone |
| **Percusión** | **Percussion** |
| timbal | **17** kettledrum |
| pandereta | **18** tambourine |
| baquetas | **19** drumsticks |
| bongos | **20** bongos |
| platillos | **21** cymbals |
| conga | **22** conga |
| **Otros instrumentos** | **Other instruments** |
| acordeón | **23** accordion |
| teclas | **24** keys |
| armónica | **25** harmonica |

page 76 **Music and Theatre (*US* Theater)**

# Music and Theatre (*US* Theater)

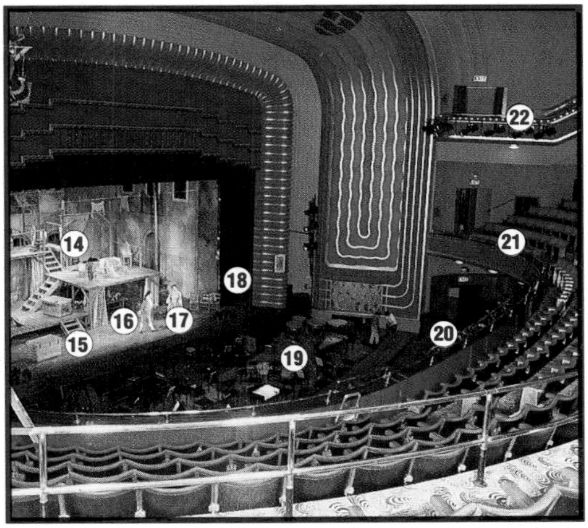

| | |
|---|---|
| **Música** | **Music** |
| orquesta | **1** orchestra |
| músico | **2** musician |
| piano | **3** piano |
| director | **4** conductor |
| batuta | **5** baton |
| hoja de música | **6** sheet music |
| grupo pop | **7** pop group |
| guitarra (eléctrica) | **8** (electric) guitar |
| cantante/vocalista | **9** singer/vocalist |
| batería | **10** drum |
| batería | **11** drummer |
| teclista | **12** keyboard player |
| sintetizador | **13** synthesizer |
| **El Teatro** | **The Theatre (*US* Theater)** |
| decorado | **14** scenery |
| escenario | **15** stage |
| actor | **16** actor |
| actriz | **17** actress |
| bastidores | **18** wings |
| foso de la orquesta | **19** orchestra pit |
| patio de butacas | **20** stalls (*US* orchestra seats) |
| primer piso | **21** circle/balcony (*US* mezzanine) |
| segundo piso | **22** gallery (*US* balcony) |
| **El Cine** | **The Cinema (*US* Movie Theater)** |
| pantalla | **23** screen |
| estrella de cine | **24** film star (*US* movie star) |
| acomodador | **25** usher |
| acomodadora | **26** usher (*Brit also* usherette) |
| pasillo | **27** aisle |
| público | **28** audience |

# Sports 1 page 77

| | | |
|---|---|---|
| patinaje sobre hielo | **1** | ice-skating |
| patinar | **2** | skate (*verb*) |
| patinadora | **3** | skater |
| patín | **4** | ice-skate |
| pista de hielo | **5** | ice-rink (*esp US* rink) |
| esquí | **6** | skiing |
| esquiar | **7** | ski (*verb*) |
| bastón | **8** | pole |
| esquí | **9** | ski |
| esquí acuático | **10** | water-skiing |
| hacer esquí acuático | **11** | water-ski (*verb*) |
| esquiador acuático | **12** | water-skier |
| surf | **13** | surfing |
| ola | **14** | wave |
| hacer surf | **15** | surf (*verb*) |
| surfista | **16** | surfer |
| tabla de surf | **17** | surfboard |
| wind-surf | **18** | windsurfing |
| windsurfista | **19** | windsurfer |
| tabla de wind-surf | **20** | sailboard |
| submarinismo | **21** | scuba-diving |
| bombona de aire | **22** | (air)tank |
| bucear | **23** | snorkelling (*US* snorkeling) |
| tubo de bucear | **24** | snorkel |
| natación | **25** | swimming |
| nadar | **26** | swim (*verb*) |
| nadador | **27** | swimmer |
| piscina | **28** | swimming-pool |
| saltar | **29** | dive (*verb*) |
| saltador | **30** | diver |

| | | |
|---|---|---|
| béisbol | **1** | baseball |
| casco de bateador | **2** | batting helmet |
| bateador | **3** | batter |
| guante de béisbol | **4** | baseball glove/mitt |
| protección del apañador | **5** | face mask/catcher's mask |
| apañador | **6** | catcher |
| multitud/público | **7** | crowd |
| balconcesto | **8** | basketball |
| red | **9** | net |
| tirar | **10** | shoot (*verb*) |
| fútbol americano | **11** | American football (*US* football) |
| pelota de fútbol | **12** | football |
| lanzar | **13** | throw (*verb*) |
| rugby | **14** | rugby |
| bloquear | **15** | tackle (*verb*) |
| hockey sobre hierba | **16** | hockey (*US* field hockey) |
| jugador de hockey | **17** | hockey player |
| palo de hockey | **18** | hockey stick |
| pelota de hockey | **19** | hockey ball |
| voleibol | **20** | volleyball |
| saltar | **21** | jump (*verb*) |
| squash | **22** | squash |
| raqueta | **23** | racket (*also* racquet) |
| badminton | **24** | badminton |
| pelota de badminton | **25** | shuttlecock |
| ping-pong | **26** | table tennis (*esp US* ping-pong) |
| pala de ping-pong | **27** | table tennis bat (*US* paddle) |
| dar | **28** | hit (*verb*) |

# Sports 3 page 79

dardos **1** darts
diana **2** dartboard
apuntar **3** aim (*verb*)
billar **4** snooker
taco **5** cue
mesa **6** table
tronera **7** pocket
bolos **8** bowling
bolera **9** bowling-alley
bolos **10** pins
golf **11** golf
caddy **12** caddy
calle **13** fairway
green **14** green
palo **15** club
agujero **16** hole

boxeo **17** boxing
rincón **18** corner
ring **19** ring
cuerdas **20** ropes
guante de boxeo **21** boxing glove
golpear **22** punch (*verb*)
lucha **23** wrestling
hacer lucha **24** wrestle (*verb*)
árbitro **25** referee
judo **26** judo
karate **27** karate
partir **28** chop (*verb*)

# Sports 4

gimnasia **1** gymnastics
gimnasta **2** gymnast
ciclismo **3** cycling
hacer ciclismo **4** cycle (*verb*)
automovilismo **5** motor-racing (*US* auto racing)
circuito de carreras **6** racetrack
coche de carreras **7** racing car (*US* race car)
piloto **8** racing driver (*US* race car driver)
equitación **9** riding (*US* horseback riding)
montar **10** ride (*verb*)
jinete **11** rider
silla **12** saddle
estribos **13** stirrups
riendas **14** reins

atletismo **15** athletics (*US* track and field)
campo **16** field
pista **17** track
espectadores **18** spectators
calle **19** lane
atleta **20** athlete
correr **21** run (*verb*)
taco de salida **22** starting-block
carreras de caballos **23** horse-racing
correr **24** race (*verb*)
caballo de carreras **25** racehorse
jockey **26** jockey
puerta de salida **27** starting-gate
hipódromo **28** racecourse (*esp US* racetrack)

# Sports 5 page 81

| Tenis | Tennis |
|---|---|
| partido individual | **1** singles match |
| sacar | **2** serve (*verb*) |
| servicio | **3** server |
| línea de fondo | **4** baseline |
| línea de saque | **5** service line |
| líneas laterales | **6** tramlines (*US* sidelines) |
| red | **7** net |
| partido de dobles | **8** doubles match |
| recogepelotas | **9** ballboy |
| pista de tenis | **10** tennis-court |
| juez | **11** umpire |

| Criquet | Cricket |
|---|---|
| partido de criquet | **12** cricket match |
| guardameta | **13** wicket-keeper |
| bateador | **14** batsman |
| rodilleras | **15** pads |
| pista | **16** pitch |
| boleador/lanzador | **17** bowler |
| lanzar | **18** bowl (*verb*) |
| palos | **19** wicket/stumps |
| juez | **20** umpire |
| servidor | **21** fielder |
| campo | **22** field |
| **Fútbol** | **Football (*esp US* Soccer)** |
| marcar un gol | **23** scoring a goal |
| tribuna | **24** stand |
| linier | **25** linesman |
| marcar | **26** score (*verb*) |
| poste | **27** goalpost |
| gol | **28** goal |
| fallar | **29** miss (*verb*) |
| portero | **30** goalkeeper |

page 82

# Keeping Fit (*US* Keeping in Shape)

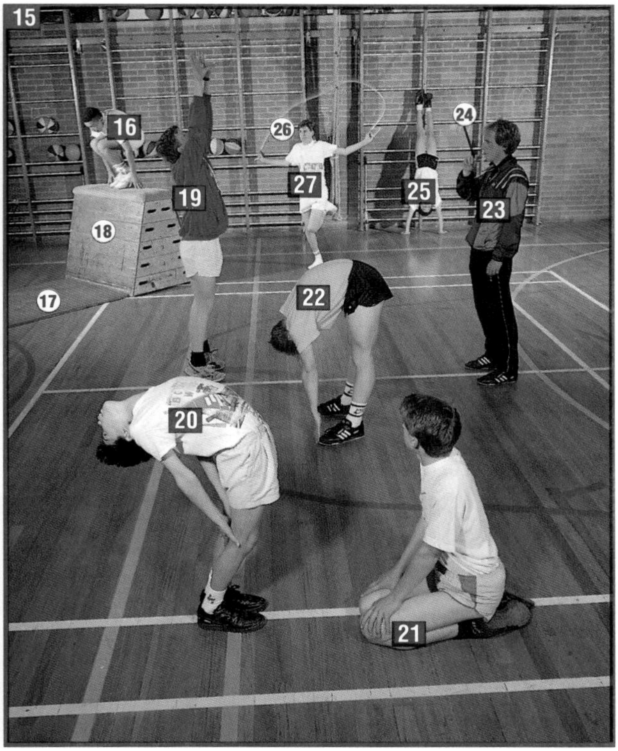

andar **1** walk (*verb*)
correr **2** jog (*verb*)
corredor **3** jogger
saltos/cama elástica **4** trampolining
caer **5** fall (*verb*)
cama elástica **6** trampoline
instructor **7** instructor
botar **8** bounce (*verb*)
lanzar **9** throw (*verb*)
coger **10** catch (*verb*)
columpiarse **11** swing (*verb*)
cuerda **12** rope
trepar **13** climb (*verb*)
espalderas **14** wall bars
gimnasio **15** gym/gymnasium
saltar **16** vault (*verb*)
colchoneta **17** mat
plinto **18** vaulting-horse
estirarse **19** stretch (*verb*)
doblarse hacia atrás **20** bend over backwards (*verb*) (*US* bend over backward)
arrodillarse **21** kneel (*verb*)
hacer flexiones **22** bend over (*verb*)
tocar el pito **23** blow a whistle (*verb*)
pito **24** whistle
hacer el pino **25** do a handstand (*verb*)
comba **26** skipping-rope (*US* jump rope)
saltar a la comba **27** skip (*verb*)

# Verbs 1 page 83

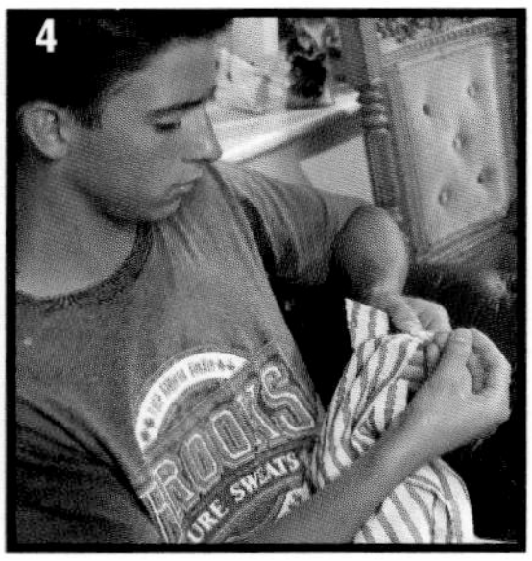


| | |
|---|---|
| Está planchando/Está planchando una camisa. | **1** He is **ironing**/He's **ironing** a shirt. |
| Está guisando/Está guisando la comida. | **2** He is **cooking**/He's **cooking** a meal. |
| Está limpiando/Está limpiando una ventana. | **3** He is **cleaning**/He's **cleaning** a window. |
| Está cosiendo. | **4** He is **sewing**. |

| | |
|---|---|
| Está barriendo/Está barriendo el camino. | **5** He is **sweeping**/He's **sweeping** the path (*US also* walk). |
| Está atando una bolsa. | **6** He is **tying up** a bag/He's **tying** a bag **up**. |
| Está cavando/Está cavando la tierra. | **7** He is **digging**/He's **digging** the soil. |
| Está enrollando una manguera. | **8** He is **winding up** a hose/He's **winding** a hose **up**. |

| | |
|---|---|
| Está llenando la hervidora. | **9** She is **filling** a kettle (*US* an electric teakettle). |
| El agua está hirviendo. | **10** The water is **boiling**. |
| Está echando el agua en la tetera. | **11** She is **pouring** the water into a teapot. |
| Está dándole vueltas al té. | **12** She is **stirring** her tea. |

page 84

# Verbs 2

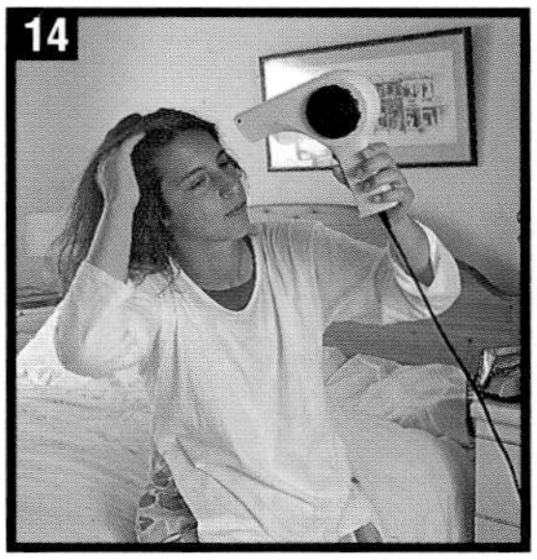

Se está lavando el pelo. **13** She is **washing** her hair.
Se está secando el pelo. **14** She is **drying** her hair.
Se está peinando. **15** She is **combing** her hair.
Se está cepillando el pelo. **16** She is **brushing** her hair.

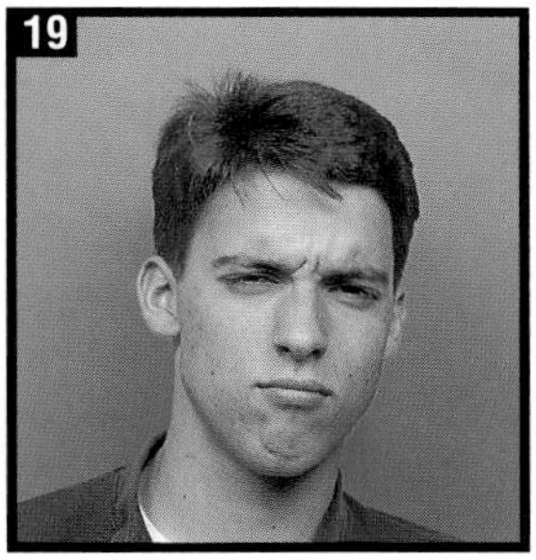
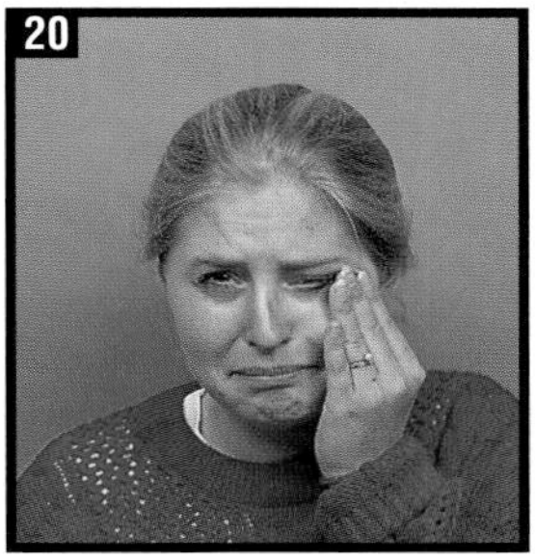

Está sonriendo. **17** He is **smiling**.
Se está riendo. **18** She is **laughing**.
Está frunciendo el ceño. **19** He is **frowning**.
Está llorando. **20** She is **crying**.

Está sentado. **21** He is **sitting**.
Está de pie. **22** He is **standing**.
Está tumbado. **23** He is **lying down**.
Está dormido. **24** He is **sleeping**.

# Verbs 3 page 85

| | |
|---|---|
| Se están dando la mano. | **1** They are **shaking** hands. |
| Está besando a la niña. | **2** She is **kissing** the child. |
| Está abrazando a la niña. | **3** She is **hugging** the child. |
| Está despidiéndose de la niña. | **4** She is **waving** to the child. |

| | |
|---|---|
| Le está hablando a él. | **5** She is **speaking** to him/She is **talking** to him. |
| Están cantando. | **6** They are **singing**. |
| Están bailando. | **7** They are **dancing**. |
| Están aplaudiendo. | **8** They are **clapping**. |

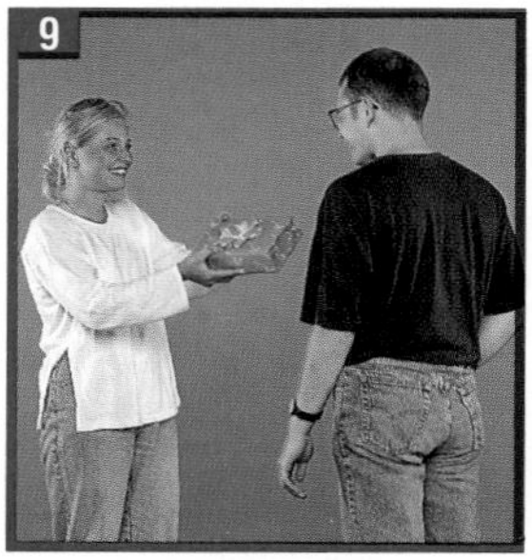

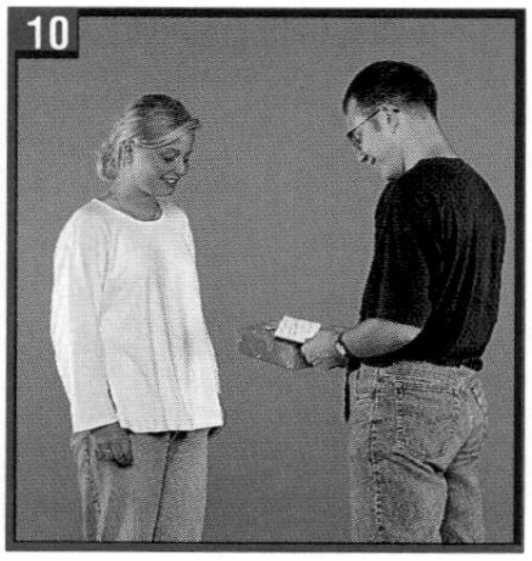

| | |
|---|---|
| Le está dando un regalo. | **9** She is **giving** him a present. |
| Está cogiendo el regalo. | **10** He is **taking** the present from her. |
| Está abriendo el regalo. | **11** He is **opening** the present. |
| Está leyendo el libro. | **12** He is **reading** the book. |

Está levantando la maleta. **13** She is **lifting** the suitcase.
Está llevando la maleta. **14** She is **carrying** the suitcase.
Está agarrando la maleta. **15** She is **holding** the suitcase.
Está dejando la maleta en el suelo. **16** She is **putting** the suitcase **down**.

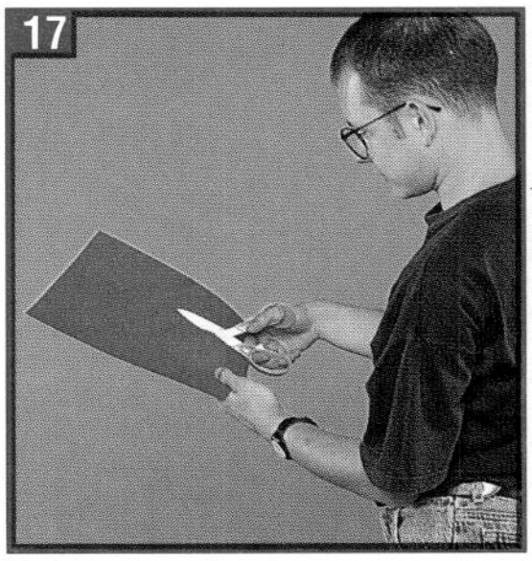


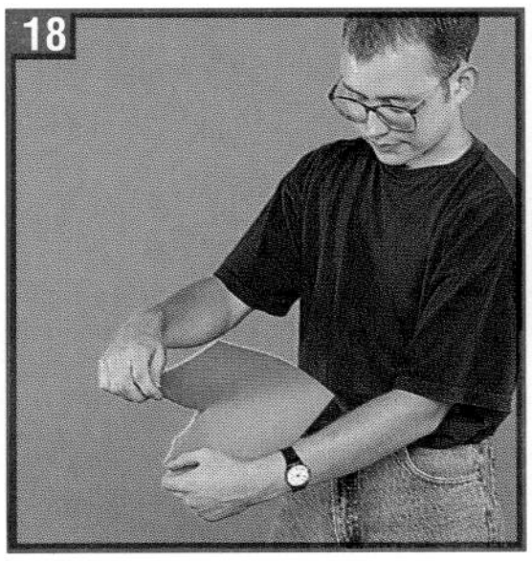

Está cortando un trozo de papel. **17** He is **cutting** a piece of paper.
Está rasgando un trozo de papel. **18** He is **tearing** a piece of paper.
Está doblando un trozo de papel. **19** He is **folding** a piece of paper.
Está partiendo una tableta de chocolate. **20** He is **breaking** a bar of chocolate.

Está empujando un carro. **21** She is **pushing** a trolley (*US* cart).
Está tirando de un carro. **22** She is **pulling** a trolley (*US* cart).
Está encendiendo una vela. **23** He is **lighting** a candle.
La vela se está quemando. **24** The candle is **burning**.

# Contrastive Adjectives 1 page 87

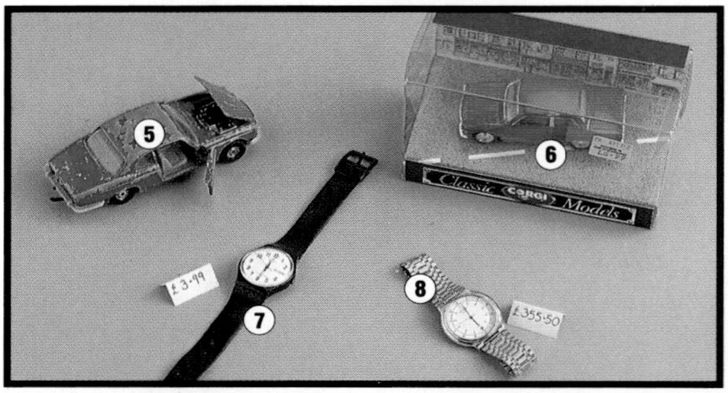

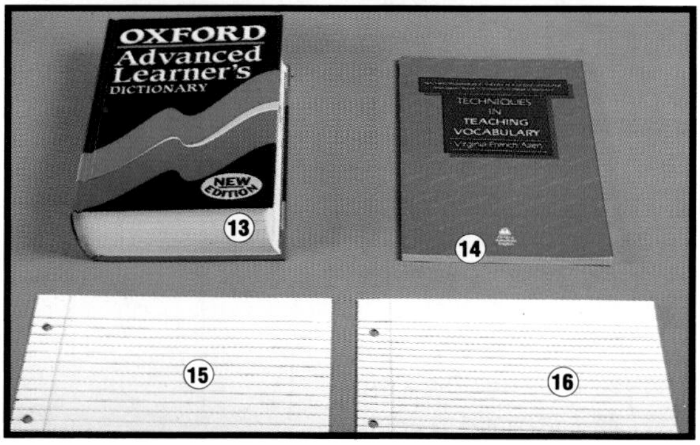

derecho **1** straight
torcido **2** crooked
grande **3** big/large
pequeño **4** little/small
viejo **5** old
nuevo **6** new
barato **7** cheap
caro **8** expensive
abierto **9** open
cerrado **10** closed
fácil **11** easy
difícil **12** difficult
gordo **13** thick
delgado **14** thin
ancho **15** wide
estrecho **16** narrow
alto **17** high
bajo **18** low
profundo **19** deep
poco profundo **20** shallow
débil **21** weak
fuerte **22** strong
rápido **23** fast
lento **24** slow

page 88

# Contrastive Adjectives 2

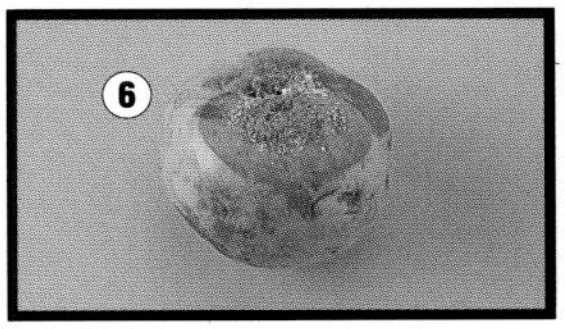

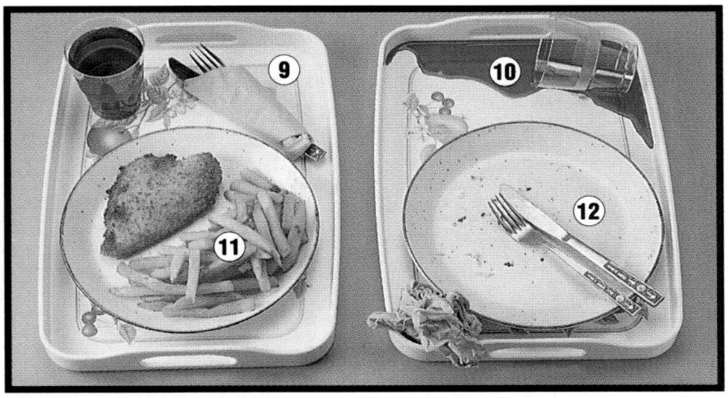

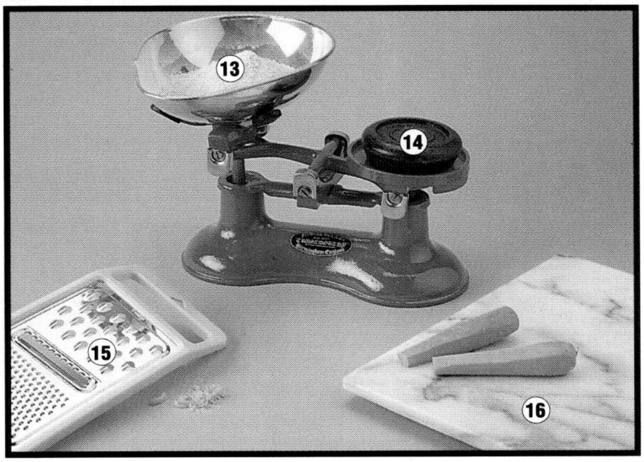

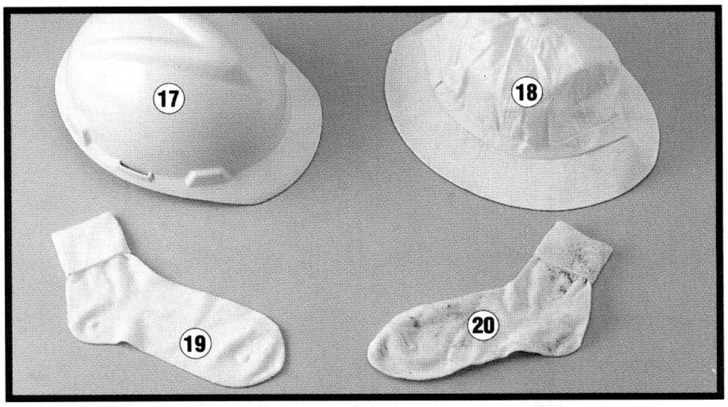

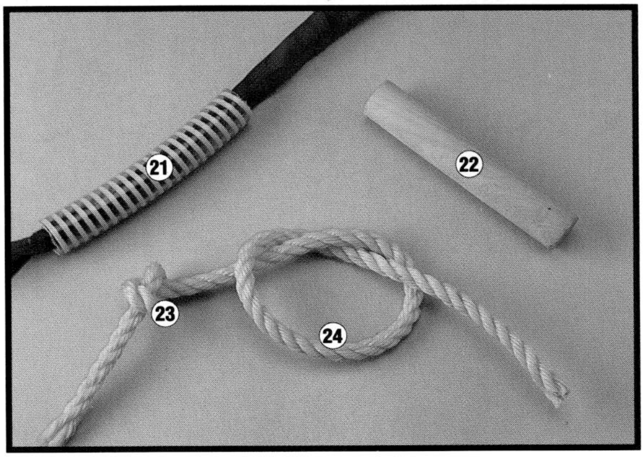


| | | |
|---|---|---|
| feliz | **1** | happy |
| triste/desgraciado | **2** | sad/unhappy |
| alto | **3** | loud |
| bajo | **4** | quiet |
| bueno | **5** | good |
| malo | **6** | bad |
| ordenado | **7** | tidy (*esp US* neat) |
| desordenado | **8** | untidy (*esp US* messy) |
| seco | **9** | dry |
| mojado | **10** | wet |
| lleno | **11** | full |
| vacío | **12** | empty |
| ligero | **13** | light |
| pesado | **14** | heavy |
| áspero | **15** | rough |
| suave | **16** | smooth |
| duro | **17** | hard |
| blando | **18** | soft |
| limpio | **19** | clean |
| sucio | **20** | dirty |
| hueco | **21** | hollow |
| macizo | **22** | solid |
| apretado | **23** | tight |
| flojo | **24** | loose |

# Animals 1 page 89

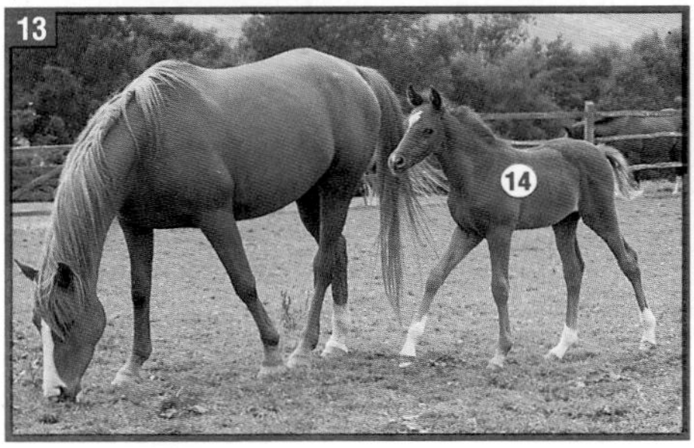


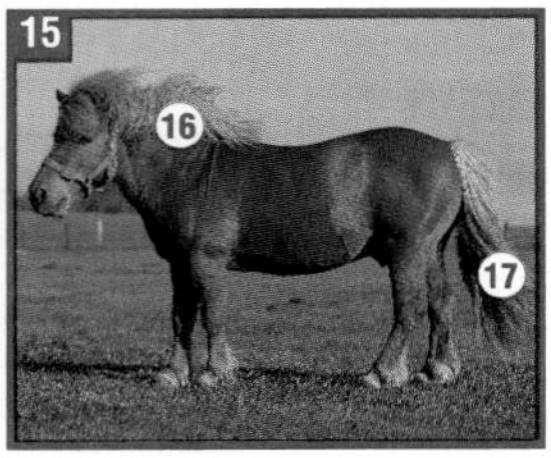


| | | |
|---|---|---|
| vaca | **1** | cow |
| ternero | **2** | calf |
| toro | **3** | bull |
| murciélago | **4** | bat |
| erizo | **5** | hedgehog |
| ardilla | **6** | squirrel |
| zorro | **7** | fox |
| cabra | **8** | goat |
| oveja | **9** | sheep |
| cordero | **10** | lamb |
| burro | **11** | donkey |
| casco | **12** | hoof |
| caballo | **13** | horse |
| potro | **14** | foal |
| poni | **15** | pony |
| crin | **16** | mane |
| cola | **17** | tail |

## Pets Animales Domésticos

| | | |
|---|---|---|
| gato | **18** | cat |
| bigotes | **19** | whiskers |
| piel | **20** | fur |
| gatito | **21** | kitten |
| perro | **22** | dog |
| cachorro | **23** | puppy |
| garra | **24** | paw |
| hámster | **25** | hamster |
| conejo | **26** | rabbit |

page 90

# Animals 2

| | | |
|---|---|---|
| ciervo | **1** | deer |
| cornamenta | **2** | antler |
| lobo | **3** | wolf |
| oso | **4** | bear |
| zarpa | **5** | claw |
| oso polar | **6** | polar bear |
| panda | **7** | panda |
| canguro | **8** | kangaroo |
| bolsa | **9** | pouch |
| camello | **10** | camel |
| joroba | **11** | hump |
| llama | **12** | llama |
| mono | **13** | monkey |
| gorila | **14** | gorilla |
| cebra | **15** | zebra |
| león | **16** | lion |
| tigre | **17** | tiger |
| leopardo | **18** | leopard |
| búfalo | **19** | buffalo |
| cuerno | **20** | horn |
| rinoceronte | **21** | rhinoceros |
| hipopótamo | **22** | hippopotamus |
| jirafa | **23** | giraffe |
| elefante | **24** | elephant |
| colmillo | **25** | tusk |
| trompa | **26** | trunk |
| foca | **27** | seal |
| aleta | **28** | flipper |
| delfín | **29** | dolphin |
| ballena | **30** | whale |

# Fish and Reptiles page 91

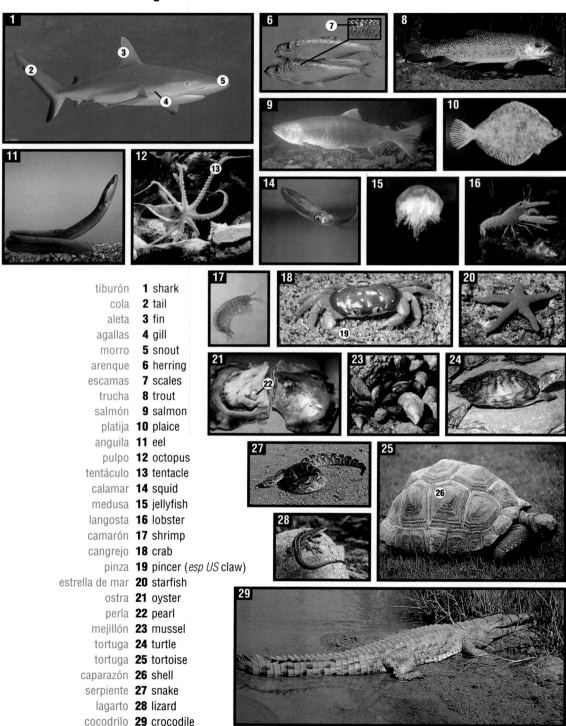

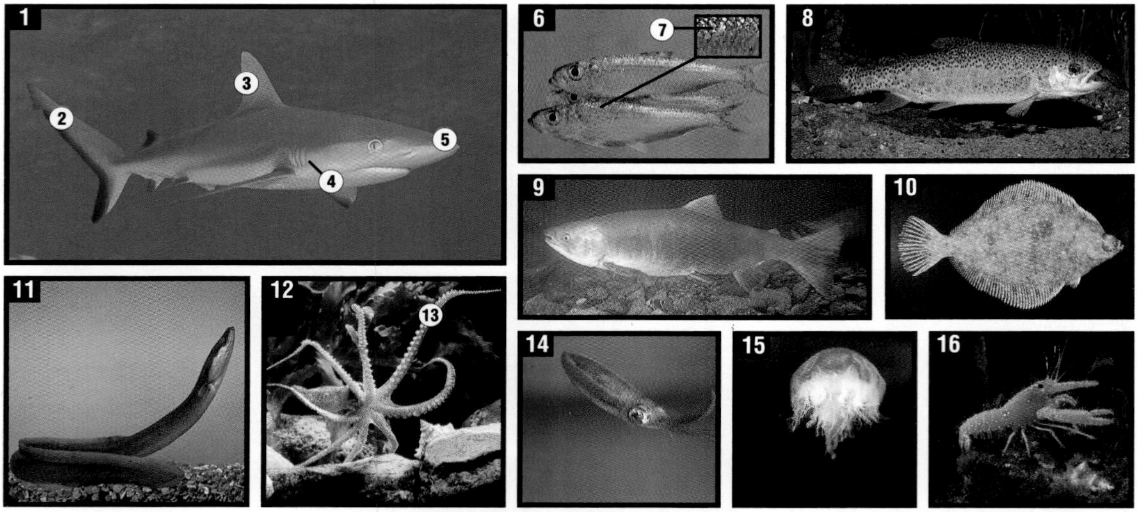

| | |
|---|---|
| tiburón | **1** shark |
| cola | **2** tail |
| aleta | **3** fin |
| agallas | **4** gill |
| morro | **5** snout |
| arenque | **6** herring |
| escamas | **7** scales |
| trucha | **8** trout |
| salmón | **9** salmon |
| platija | **10** plaice |
| anguila | **11** eel |
| pulpo | **12** octopus |
| tentáculo | **13** tentacle |
| calamar | **14** squid |
| medusa | **15** jellyfish |
| langosta | **16** lobster |
| camarón | **17** shrimp |
| cangrejo | **18** crab |
| pinza | **19** pincer (*esp US* claw) |
| estrella de mar | **20** starfish |
| ostra | **21** oyster |
| perla | **22** pearl |
| mejillón | **23** mussel |
| tortuga | **24** turtle |
| tortuga | **25** tortoise |
| caparazón | **26** shell |
| serpiente | **27** snake |
| lagarto | **28** lizard |
| cocodrilo | **29** crocodile |

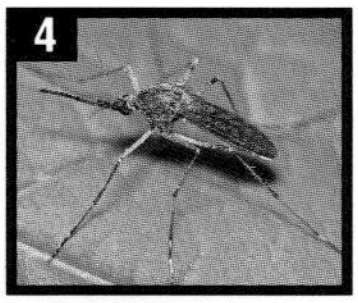


page 92

# Insects and Other Animals

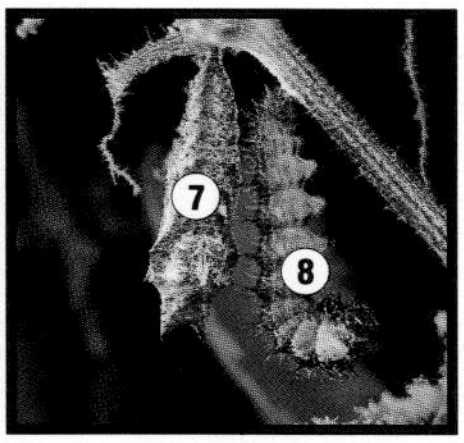

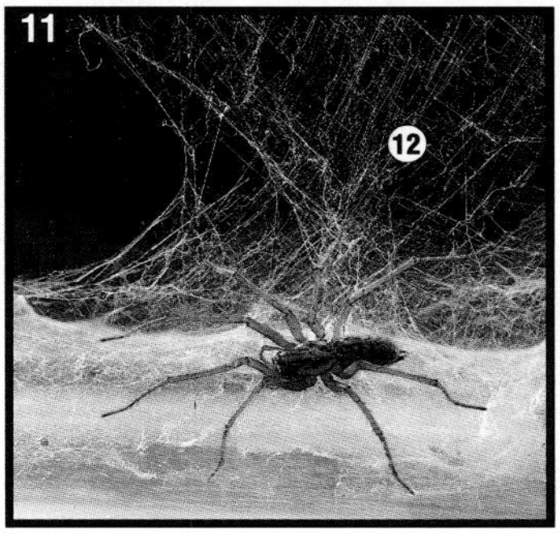


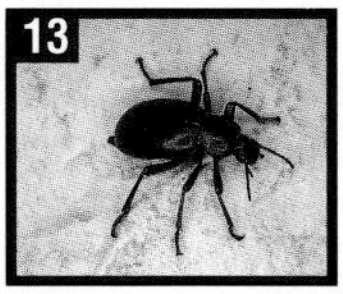

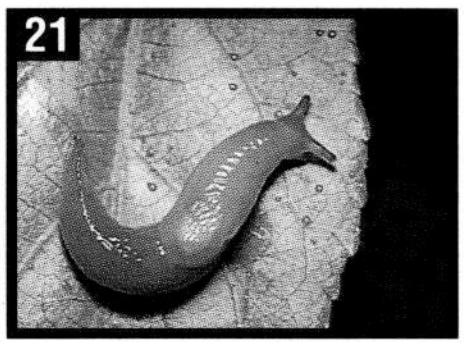


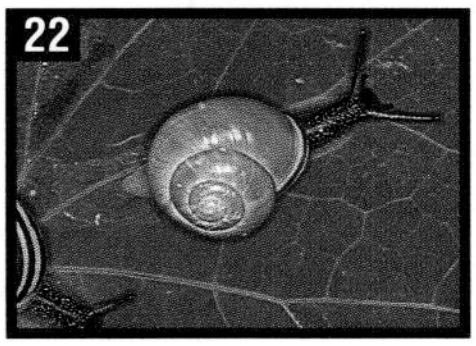


mosca **1** fly
abeja **2** bee
avispa **3** wasp
mosquito **4** mosquito
libélula **5** dragonfly
mariposa **6** butterfly
capullo **7** cocoon
gusano **8** caterpillar
mariposa **9** moth
antena **10** antenna
araña **11** spider
tela de araña **12** (cob)web
escarabajo **13** beetle
mariquita **14** ladybird (*US* ladybug)
hormiga **15** ant
cucaracha **16** cockroach (*also* roach)
saltamontes **17** grasshopper
grillo **18** cricket
mantis religiosa **19** praying mantis
lombriz **20** worm
babosa **21** slug
caracol **22** snail
escorpión **23** scorpion
aguijón **24** sting
rana **25** frog

# Birds page 93

pollo **1** chicken
gallina **2** hen
pollito **3** chick
gallo **4** cock (*US* rooster)
pluma **5** feather
pavo **6** turkey
faisán **7** pheasant
águila **8** eagle
pico **9** beak
halcón **10** hawk
cuervo **11** crow
búho **12** owl
nido **13** nest
paloma **14** pigeon
gorrión **15** sparrow
colibrí **16** hummingbird
ala **17** wing
canario **18** canary
loro **19** parrot
periquito **20** budgerigar (*US* parakeet)
golondrina **21** swallow
avestruz **22** ostrich
pingüino **23** penguin
pavo real **24** peacock
flamenco **25** flamingo
pico **26** bill
ganso **27** goose
pato **28** duck
pata palmípeda **29** webbed foot
gaviota **30** (sea)gull
cisne **31** swan

# Etiquetas para inglés británico y americano

*Brit* motorway (*Brit*)
se usa para mostrar que una palabra se usa sólo en el inglés británico

*US* zip code (*US*)
se usa para mostrar que una palabra se usa sólo en el inglés americano

jug (*US* pitcher)
se usa para mostrar que una palabra (jug) que se usa sólo en el inglés británico significa lo mismo que otra palabra (pitcher) que se usa sólo en el inglés americano

*Brit also* red (*Brit also* ginger)
se usa para mostrar que una palabra (red) que se usa tanto en el inglés británico como en el americano significa lo mismo que otra palabra (ginger) que se usa sólo en el inglés británico

*US also* blackboard (*US also* chalkboard)
se usa para mostrar que una palabra (blackboard) que se usa tanto en el inglés británico como en el americano significa lo mismo que otra palabra (chalkboard) que se usa sólo en el inglés americano

*esp US* sofa (*esp US* couch)
se usa para mostrar que una palabra que se usa principalmente en el inglés británico pero se puede usar también en el inglés americano (sofa) significa lo mismo que otra palabra (couch) que es la más común en el inglés americano

# Explicación de los símbolos fonéticos 

## Vocales y diptongos

| | | | | | | | |
|---|---|---|---|---|---|---|---|
| 1 | i: | como en | **see** / si: / | 11 | ɜ: | como en | **fur** / fɜ:(r) / |
| 2 | ɪ | como en | **sit** / sɪt / | 12 | ə | como en | **ago** / ə'gəʊ / |
| 3 | e | como en | **ten** / ten / | 13 | eɪ | como en | **page** / peɪdʒ / |
| 4 | æ | como en | **hat** / hæt / | 14 | əʊ | como en | **home** / həʊm / |
| 5 | ɑ: | como en | **arm** / ɑ:m / | 15 | aɪ | como en | **five** / faɪv / |
| 6 | ɒ | como en | **got** / gɒt / | 16 | aʊ | como en | **now** / naʊ / |
| 7 | ɔ: | como en | **saw** / sɔ: / | 17 | ɔɪ | como en | **join** / dʒɔɪn / |
| 8 | ʊ | como en | **put** / pʊt / | 18 | ɪə | como en | **near** / nɪə(r) / |
| 9 | u: | como en | **too** / tu: / | 19 | eə | como en | **hair** / heə(r) / |
| 10 | ʌ | como en | **cup** / kʌp / | 20 | ʊə | como en | **pure** / pjʊə(r) / |

## Consonantes

| | | | | | | | |
|---|---|---|---|---|---|---|---|
| 1 | p | como en | **pen** / pen / | 13 | s | como en | **so** / səʊ / |
| 2 | b | como en | **bad** / bæd / | 14 | z | como en | **zoo** / zu: / |
| 3 | t | como en | **tea** / ti: / | 15 | ʃ | como en | **she** / ʃi: / |
| 4 | d | como en | **did** / dɪd / | 16 | ʒ | como en | **vision** / 'vɪʒn / |
| 5 | k | como en | **cat** / kæt / | 17 | h | como en | **how** / haʊ / |
| 6 | g | como en | **got** / gɒt / | 18 | m | como en | **man** / mæn / |
| 7 | tʃ | como en | **chin** / tʃɪn / | 19 | n | como en | **no** / nəʊ / |
| 8 | dʒ | como en | **June** / dʒu:n / | 20 | ŋ | como en | **sing** / sɪŋ / |
| 9 | f | como en | **fall** / fɔ:l / | 21 | l | como en | **leg** / leg / |
| 10 | v | como en | **voice** / vɔɪs / | 22 | r | como en | **red** / red / |
| 11 | θ | como en | **thin** / θɪn / | 23 | j | como en | **yes** / jes / |
| 12 | ð | como en | **then** / ðen / | 24 | w | como en | **wet** / wet / |

/'/ representa un *acento primario* como en **about** / ə'baʊt /
/ˌ/ representa un *acento secundario* como en **academic** / ˌækə'demɪk /

(r) Una 'r' entre paréntesis es sonora en la pronunciación británica cuando va seguida por un sonido vocálico. En los demás casos se omite.
En la pronunciación americana no se omite ninguna 'r', ni de la transcripción fonética ni de la ortografía normal.

# Index


**Aberdeen** /ˌæbəˈdiːn/ **56**
**above** /əˈbʌv/ **58**/15
**accelerator** /əkˈseləreɪtə(r)/ **64**/28, **65**/26
**accident** /ˈæksɪdənt/ **6, 38**/13
**accordion** /əˈkɔːdɪən/ **75**/23
**ace** /eɪs/ **74**/34
**across** /əˈkrɒs/ **57**/2
**actor** /ˈæktə(r)/ **76**/16
**actress** /ˈæktrɪs/ **76**/17
**acute angle** /əˌkjuːt ˈæŋgl/ **47**/19
**address** /əˈdres; *US* ˈædres/ **32**/10, 18, 19
**adhesive tape** /ədhiːsɪv ˈteɪp/ **7**/10
**adjective** /ˈædʒɪktɪv/ **87/88**
**adult** /ˈædʌlt, *also* əˈdʌlt/ **5**/4, 5
**advertisement** /ədˈvɜːtɪsmənt; *US* ˌædvərˈtaɪzmənt/ **59**/20
**Afghanistan** /æfˈgænɪstɑːn; *US* æfˈgænɪstæn/ **54**
**Africa** /ˈæfrɪkə/ **53**/3
**after** /ˈɑːftə(r); *US* ˈæftər/ **37**/6, 7, 8, 14
**after-shave lotion** /ˈæftərʃeɪv ˌləʊʃn/ **17**/21
**afternoon** /ɑːftəˈnuːn; *US* æf-/ **37**/16
**aftershave** /ˈɑːftəʃeɪv/ **17**/21
**against** /əˈgenst, əˈgeɪnst/ **58**/4
**age** /eɪdʒ/ **5**
**aim (verb)** /eɪm/ **79**/3
**air filter** /ˈeə fɪltə(r)/ **64**/16
**air traffic controller** /ˌeə træfɪk kənˈtrəʊlə(r)/ **68**/5
**airline ticket** /ˈeəlaɪn tɪkɪt/ **67**/2
**airmail** /ˈeəmeɪl/ **32**/17
**airport** /ˈeəpɔːt/ **67/68**
**(air)tank** /ˈeətæŋk/ **77**/22
**aisle** /aɪl/ **76**/27
**Alabama** /ˌæləˈbæmə/ **55**
**alarm clock** /əˈlɑːm klɒk/ **18**/14
**Alaska** /əˈlæskə/ **55**
**Albania** /ælˈbeɪnɪə/ **54**
**Albuquerque** /ˈælbəˌkɜːrkɪ/ **55**
**Algeria** /ælˈdʒɪərɪə/ **54**
**alligator clip** /ˈælɪgeɪtər klɪp/ **46**/7
**almond** /ˈɑːmənd/ **28**/17
**along** /əˈlɒŋ/ **57**/12
**am** (*US* **A.M.**) /eɪˈem/ **37**/15
**AM/FM** /ˈeɪ em, ˌef em/ **30**/8
**ambulance** /ˈæmbjʊləns/ **38**/14
**ambulance service** /ˈæmbjʊləns sɜːvɪs/ **38**
**American** /əˈmerɪkən/ **32, 33, 35**
**American football** /əmerɪkən ˈfʊtbɔːl/ **78**/11
**amplifier** /ˈæmplɪfaɪə(r)/ **30**/16
**anchor** /ˈæŋkə(r)/ **70**/16
**Anchorage** /ˈæŋkərɪdʒ/ **55**
**angler** /ˈæŋglə(r)/ **72**/14
**Anglesey** /ˈæŋglsɪ/ **56**
**Angola** /æŋˈgəʊlə/ **54**
**animal** /ˈænɪml/ **89/90**
**ankle** /ˈæŋkl/ **3**/16, **6**/14
**answering machine** /ˈɑːnsərɪŋ (*US* ˈænsərɪŋ) məˌʃiːn/ **44**/5
**answerphone** /ˈɑːnsəfəʊn; *US* ˈænsər/ **44**/5
**ant** /ænt/ **92**/15
**Antarctic** /æntˈɑːktɪk/ **53**/11
**Antarctica** /æntˈɑːktɪkə/ **53**/7
**antenna** /ænˈtenə/ **14**/20, **92**/10
**antler** /ˈæntlə(r)/ **90**/2
**Antrim** /ˈæntrɪm/ **56**
**apartment house** /əˈpɑːrtməntˌhaʊs/ **13**/10
**apex** /ˈeɪpeks/ **47**/14
**Appalachian Mountains** /æpəˌleɪʃn ˈmaʊntnz/ **55**
**appetizer** /ˈæpɪtaɪzə(r)/ **28**
**apple** /ˈæpl/ **24**/4
**apple pie** /æpl ˈpaɪ/ **28**/8
**appointment** /əˈpɔɪntmənt/ **43**/8
**appointment book** /əˈpɔɪntmənt bʊk/ **44**/21
**April** /ˈeɪprəl/ **52**
**Arabian Sea** /əˌreɪbɪən ˈsiː/ **54**/29
**arc** /ɑːk/ **47**/7
**arch** /ɑːtʃ/ **14**/10
**architect** /ˈɑːkɪtekt/ **40**/1
**Arctic** /ˈɑːktɪk/ **53**/8
**Ards** /ɑːdz/ **56**
**area code** /ˈeərɪə kəʊd/ **38**/20
**Argentina** /ˌɑːdʒənˈtiːnə/ **53**
**Arizona** /ˌærɪˈzəʊnə/ **55**
**Arkansas** /ˈɑːrkənsɔː/ **55**
**arm** /ɑːm/ **3**/7
**Armagh** /ɑːˈmɑː/ **56**
**armchair** /ˈɑːmtʃeə(r)/ **16**/22
**Armenia** /ɑːˈmiːnɪə/ **54**
**around** /əˈraʊnd/ **58**/2
**arrangement** /əˈreɪndʒmənt/ **25**/10
**artist** /ˈɑːtɪst/ **39**/1
**Asia** /ˈeɪʃə/ **53**/5
**asparagus** /əˈspærəgəs/ **23**/5
**astronaut** /ˈæstrənɔːt/ **50**/6
**at the bottom of** /æt ðə ˈbɒtəm əv/ **58**/14
**at the top of** /æt ðə ˈtɒp əv/ **58**/12
**athlete** /ˈæθliːt/ **80**/20
**athletics** /æθˈletɪks/ **80**/15
**Atlanta** /atˈlæntə/ **55**
**aubergine** /ˈəʊbəʒiːn/ **23**/20
**audience** /ˈɔːdɪəns/ **76**/28
**August** /ˈɔːgəst/ **52**
**aunt** /ɑːnt; *US* ænt/ **1**/3
**Austin** /ˈɒstɪn/ **55**
**Australia** /ɒˈstreɪlɪə; *US* ɔːˈstreɪljə/ **53**/6
**Austria** /ˈɒstrɪə/ **54**
**auto racing** /ˈɔːtəʊ ˌreɪsɪŋ/ **80**/5
**automatic teller** /ˌɔːtəmætɪk ˈtelər/ **34**/16
**autumn** /ˈɔːtəm/ **52**/11
**avocado** /ˌævəˈkɑːdəʊ/ **24**/13
**Avon** /ˈeɪvən/ **56**
**away from** /əˈweɪ frɒm/ **57**/9
**Azerbaijan** /ˌæzəbaɪˈdʒɑːn/ **54**

**baby** /ˈbeɪbɪ/ **5**/1
**baby carriage** /ˈbeɪbɪ kærɪdʒ/ **60**/3
**back** /bæk/ **3**/9, **48**/10
**back garden** /ˌbæk ˈgɑːdn/ **22**/1
**back teeth** /ˌbæk ˈtiːθ/ **8**/12
**backbone** /ˈbækbəʊn/ **4**/14
**backgammon** /ˈbækgæmən/ **74**/24
**backhoe** /ˈbækhəʊ/ **61**/18
**backpack** /ˈbækpæk/ **66**/16, **71**/25
**backward** /ˈbækwərd/ **82**/20
**backwards** /ˈbækwədz/ **82**/20
**backyard** /ˌbækˈjɑːrd/ **22**/1
**bad** /bæd/ **88**/6
**badminton** /ˈbædmɪntən/ **78**/24
**bag** /bæg/ **24**/12, **26**/10, 16, **66**/13, **83**/6
**baggage reclaim** /ˌbægɪdʒ rɪˈkleɪm/ **67**/16
**Bahamas** /bəˈhɑːməz/ **53**
**Bahrain** /bɑːˈreɪn/ **54**
**baked potato** /ˌbeɪkt pəˈteɪtəʊ/ **28**/25
**baker** /ˈbeɪkə(r)/ **39**/7
**balance** /ˈbæləns/ **46**/23
**balcony** /ˈbælkənɪ/ **13**/12, **57**/14, **76**/21, 22
**bald** /bɔːld/ **5**/7
**ball** /bɔːl/ **26**/2, **78**/19
**ballboy** /ˈbɔːlbɔɪ/ **81**/9
**ballooning** /bəˈluːnɪŋ/ **72**/20
**Ballymena** /ˌbælɪˈmiːnə/ **56**
**Ballymoney** /ˌbælɪˈmʌnɪ/ **56**
**Baltic Sea** /ˌbɔːltɪk ˈsiː/ **54**/22
**Baltimore** /ˈbɒltɪmɔːr/ **55**
**banana** /bəˈnɑːnə; *US* bəˈnænə/ **24**/3
**Banbridge** /ˈbænbrɪdʒ/ **56**
**Band-Aid** /ˈbændeɪd/ **7**/3
**bandage** /ˈbændɪdʒ/ **7**/2
**Bangladesh** /ˌbæŋgləˈdeʃ/ **54**
**bangs** /bæŋz/ **5**/14
**bank** /bæŋk/ **34, 60**/18, **62**/13
**(bank) account number** /bæŋk əˈkaʊnt ˌnʌmbə(r)/ **34**/7
**(bank) balance** /bæŋk ˈbæləns/ **34**/6
**bank statement** /ˈbæŋk steɪtmənt/ **34**/5
**bar** /bɑː(r)/ **17**/8, **26**/11, **86**/20
**barbecue** /ˈbɑːbɪkjuː/ **22**/16
**Barents Sea** /ˌbɑːrənts ˈsiː/ **54**/41
**barge** /bɑːdʒ/ **69**/9
**bark** /bɑːk/ **25**/8
**barn** /bɑːn/ **73**/22
**barrier** /ˈbærɪə(r)/ **66**/22
**base** /beɪs/ **47**/16
**baseball** /ˈbeɪsbɔːl/ **78**/1
**baseball glove** /ˈbeɪsbɔːl glʌv/ **78**/4
**baseball mitt** /ˈbeɪsbɔːl mɪt/ **78**/4
**baseline** /ˈbeɪslaɪn/ **81**/4
**basement window** /ˈbeɪsmənt wɪndəʊ/ **13**/9
**basin** /ˈbeɪsn/ **8**/5
**basket** /ˈbɑːskɪt; *US* ˈbæskɪt/ **24**/2, 22, **25**/6, **58**/2
**basketball** /ˈbɑːskɪtbɔːl/ **78**/8
**bassoon** /bəˈsuːn/ **75**/15
**bat** /bæt/ **78**/27, **89**/4
**bath** /bɑːθ; *US* bæθ/ **17**/15
**bath-towel** /ˈbɑːθtaʊəl/ **17**/11
**bathing suit** /ˈbeɪðɪŋ suːt/ **11**/1, 2
**bathroom** /ˈbɑːθruːm, rʊm; *US* ˈbæθruːm, rʊm/ **17**
**bathroom cabinet** /ˌbɑːθruːm, rʊm ˈkæbɪnɪt/ **17**/1
**bathtub** /ˈbæθtʌb/ **17**/15
**baton** /ˈbætn, ˈbætɒn; *US* bəˈtɒn/ **76**/5
**batsman** /ˈbætsmən/ **81**/14
**batter** /ˈbætə(r)/ **78**/3
**battery** /ˈbætərɪ/ **46**/14
**batting helmet** /ˈbætɪŋ helmɪt/ **78**/2
**bay** /beɪ/ **53**
**Bay of Bengal** /ˌbeɪ əv beŋˈgɔːl/ **54**/30
**bay window** /ˌbeɪ ˈwɪndəʊ/ **14**/11
**be (verb)** /biː/ **6**/1–3
**beach** /biːtʃ/ **72**/1, 3, **73**/10
**beak** /biːk/ **93**/9
**bear** /beə(r)/ **90**/4
**beard** /bɪəd/ **4**/24
**Beaufort Sea** /ˌbəʊfət ˈsiː/ **53**/15
**bed** /bed/ **18**/3, **41**/2, **42**/24
**bed-linen** /ˈbedlɪnɪn/ **18**/2
**Bedfordshire** /ˈbedfədʃə(r)/ **56**
**bedroom** /ˈbedruːm, rʊm/ **18**
**bedside cabinet** /ˌbedsaɪd ˈkæbɪnɪt/ **18**/10
**bedspread** /ˈbedspred/ **18**/4
**bee** /biː/ **92**/2
**beet** /biːt/ **23**/8
**beetle** /ˈbiːtl/ **92**/13

# Index 


**beetroot** /ˈbiːtruːt/ **23**/8
**behind** /bɪˈhaɪnd/ **58**/19
**Belarus** /ˈbelərʊs/ **54**
**Belfast** /ˈbelfɑːst/ **56**
**Belgium** /ˈbeldʒəm/ **54**
**Belize** /beˈliːz/ **53**
**bell** /bel/ **65**/18
**bellhop** /ˈbelhɒp/ **71**/2
**below** /bɪˈləʊ/ **52**/8, **58**/16
**belt** /belt/ **12**/11
**bench** /bentʃ/ **22**/14
**bend over (verb)**/ bend ˈəʊvə(r)/ **82**/22
**bend to right** /ˌbend tʊ ˈraɪt/ **61**/8
**Benin** /ˈbenɪn/ **54**
**Bering Sea** /ˌberɪŋ ˈsiː/ **54**/38
**Berkeley** /ˈbɜːrklɪ/ **55**
**Berkshire** /ˈbɑːkʃə(r)/ **56**
**Bermuda** /bəˈmjuːdə/ **53**
**beside** /bɪˈsaɪd/ **58**/17
**between** /bɪˈtwiːn/ **58**/8
**Bhutan** /buːˈtɑːn/ **54**
**bicycle** /ˈbaɪsɪkl/ **65**/1
**bicyclist** /ˈbaɪsɪklɪst/ **60**/20
**big** /bɪg/ **87**/3
**bike** /baɪk/ **65, 65**/1
**bike and pedestrian path** /baɪk ənd pəˈdestrɪən pæθ/ **61**/9
**bill** /bɪl/ **35**/6, **93**/26
**Billings** /ˈbɪlɪŋz/ **55**
**bin** /bɪn/ **57**/4
**binoculars** /bɪˈnɒkjʊləz/ **29**/7
**bird** /bɜːd/ **93**
**Birmingham** /ˈbɜːrmɪŋhæm/ **55**
**Birmingham** /ˈbɜːmɪŋəm/ **56**
**biscuit** /ˈbɪskɪt/ **27**/15, 16
**biscuit tin** /ˈbɪskɪt tɪn/ **16**/10
**Bismarck** /ˈbɪzmɑːk/ **55**
**black** /blæk/ **9**/13
**black and white print** /ˌblæk ənd waɪt ˈprɪnt/ **29**/14
**black eye** /blæk ˈaɪ/ **6**/20
**Black Sea** /ˌblæk ˈsiː/ **54**/26
**blackboard** /ˈblækbɔːd/ **49**/1
**blanket** /ˈblæŋkɪt/ **18**/5
**blazer** /ˈbleɪzə(r)/ **10**/3
**blind** /blaɪnd/ **17**/19
**block of flats** /blɒk əv ˈflæts/ **13**/10
**blonde** /blɒnd/ **5**/15
**blood** /blʌd/ **6**/19
**blood pressure gauge** /ˈblʌd preʃə ˌgeɪdʒ/ **7**/23
**blouse** /blaʊz; *US* blaʊs/ **10**/9
**blow (verb)** /bləʊ/ **82**/23
**blue** /bluː/ **9**/7
**board** /bɔːd/ **74**/25
**boarding** /ˈbɔːdɪŋ/ **68**/1
**boarding pass** /ˈbɔːdɪŋ pɑːs; *US* pæs/ **67**/3
**boat** /bəʊt/ **60**/11
**boating** /ˈbəʊtɪŋ/ **72**/11
**boil (verb)** /bɔɪl/ **83**/10
**boiled potatoes** /ˌbɔɪld pəˈteɪtəʊz/ **28**/26
**Bolivia** /bəˈlɪvɪə/ **53**
**bolt** /bəʊlt/ **21**/24
**bongos** /ˈbɒŋgəʊz/ **75**/20
**bonnet** /ˈbɒnɪt/ **64**/14
**bonsai** /ˈbɒnsaɪ; *US also* bəʊnˈsaɪ/ **25**/12
**book** /bʊk/ **31**/20, **58**/4, 14, 15, **85**/12
**bookcase** /ˈbʊkkeɪs/ **58**/11–14
**boot** /buːt/ **10**/13, **64**/9
**Borders** /ˈbɔːdəz/ **56**
**Bosnia-Herzegovina** /ˌbɒznɪə ˌhɜːtsəgəˈviːnə/ **54**
**Boston** /ˈbɒstən/ **55**
**Botswana** /bɒtˈswɑːnə/ **54**
**bottle** /ˈbɒtl/ **27**/25
**bottom** /ˈbɒtəm/ **3**/11, **48**/8
**bounce (verb)** /baʊns/ **82**/8
**boundary** /baʊndrɪ/ **53, 56**
**bow** /baʊ/ **69**/16
**bow** /bəʊ/ **75**/2
**bowl (verb)** /bəʊl/ **81**/18
**bowl** /bəʊl/ **15**/13
**bowler** /ˈbəʊlə(r)/ **81**/17
**bowling** /ˈbəʊlɪŋ/ **79**/8
**bowling-alley** /ˈbəʊlɪŋ ælɪ/ **79**/9
**box** /bɒks/ **18**/9, **26**/9, **27**/1
**boxer** /ˈbɒksə(r)/ **12**/9
**boxing** /ˈbɒksɪŋ/ **79**/17
**boxing glove** /ˈbɒksɪŋ glʌv/ **79**/21
**boy** /bɔɪ/ **5**/2
**bra** /brɑː/ **11**/9
**brace** /breɪs/ **21**/15
**bracelet** /ˈbreɪslɪt/ **12**/23
**Bradford** /ˈbrædfəd/ **56**
**braid** /breɪd/ **5**/17
**brake lever** /ˈbreɪk liːvə(r)/ **65**/16
**branch** /brɑːntʃ; *US* bræntʃ/ **25**/7
**brass** /brɑːs; *US* bræs/ **75**
**Brazil** /brəˈzɪl/ **53**
**bread** /bred/ **27**/2
**breadboard** /ˈbredbɔːd/ **20**/18
**break (verb)** /breɪk/ **6**/13, **86**/20
**breakfast** /ˈbrekfəst/ **41**/9
**breastbone** /ˈbrestbəʊn/ **4**/12
**brick** /brɪk/ **13**/7, 16
**bricklayer** /ˈbrɪkleɪə(r)/ **40**/12
**bridge** /brɪdʒ/ **8**/17, **60**/15
**briefcase** /ˈbriːfkeɪs/ **10**/12
**bright** /braɪt/ **51**/13
**Brighton** /ˈbraɪtn/ **56**
**Bristol** /ˈbrɪstl/ **56**
**Britain** /ˈbrɪtn/ **56**
**British** /ˈbrɪtɪʃ/ **32, 33, 36**
**British Isles** /ˌbrɪtɪʃ ˈaɪls/ **56**
**broccoli** /ˈbrɒkəlɪ/ **23**/17
**brooch** /brəʊtʃ/ **12**/22
**broom** /bruːm/ **22**/13
**brother-in-law** /ˈbrʌðər ɪn lɔː/ **1**/10
**brown** /braʊn/ **9**/4
**bruise** /bruːz/ **6**/15
**Brunei** /ˈbruːnaɪ/ **54**
**brush (verb)** /brʌʃ/ **84**/16
**brush** /brʌʃ/ **19**/5
**Brussels sprout** (*US* **brussels sprout**) /ˌbrʌslz ˈspraʊt/ **23**/15
**bucket** /ˈbʌkɪt/ **19**/6
**Buckinghamshire** /ˈbʌkɪŋəmʃə(r)/ **56**
**buckle** /ˈbʌkl/ **11**/19
**bud** /bʌd/ **25**/27
**budgerigar** /ˈbʌdʒərɪgɑː(r)/ **93**/20
**Buffalo** /ˈbʌfələʊ/ **55**
**buffalo** /ˈbʌfələʊ/ **90**/19
**buffet** /bəˈfeɪ/ **15**/18
**building** /ˈbɪldɪŋ/ **13**/**14**, **60**/1
**building material** /ˈbɪldɪŋ məˌtɪərɪəl/ **13**
**built-in flash** /ˌbɪltɪn ˈflæʃ/ **29**/20
**bulb** /bʌlb/ **25**/13
**Bulgaria** /bʌlˈgeərɪə/ **54**
**bull** /bʊl/ **89**/3
**bulletin board** /ˈbʊlətɪn bɔːrd/ **44**/1
**bumper** /ˈbʌmpə(r)/ **64**/7
**bunch** /bʌntʃ/ **24**/3, **24**/10, **25**/9
**bungalow** /ˈbʌŋgələʊ/ **14**/19
**Bunsen burner** /ˌbʌnsn ˈbɜːnə(r)/ **45**/5
**bureau** /bjʊˈrəʊ/ **18**/19
**burette** /bjʊəˈret/ **46**/25
**Burkina** /bɜːˈkiːnə/ **54**
**Burma** /ˈbɜːmə/ **54**
**burn (verb)** /bɜːn/ **86**/24
**burner** /ˈbɜːnə(r)/ **20**/27
**Burundi** /bʊˈrʊndɪ/ **54**
**bus** /bʌs/ **63**/2
**bus shelter** /ˈbʌs ʃeltə(r)/ **59**/21
**bus stop** /ˈbʌs stɒp/ **59**/22
**bush** /bʊʃ/ **22**/9, **58**/1
**butcher** /ˈbʊtʃə(r)/ **39**/8
**butter** /ˈbʌtə(r)/ **27**/29
**butterfly** /ˈbʌtəflaɪ/ **92**/6
**buttocks** /ˈbʌtəks/ **3**/11
**button** /ˈbʌtən/ **74**/15
**buy (verb)** /baɪ/ **41**/11
**by** /baɪ/ **58**/6

**cab** /kæb/ **60**/6
**cabbage** /ˈkæbɪdʒ/ **23**/21
**cabin** /ˈkæbɪn/ **69**/5
**cabin cruiser** /ˈkæbɪn ˌkruːzə(r)/ **69**/13
**cabinet** /ˈkæbɪnɪt/ **17**/1, **18**/10, **20**/20
**cable** /ˈkeɪbl/ **65**/15, **69**/6
**cactus** /ˈkæktəs/ **25**/21
**caddy** /ˈkædɪ/ **79**/12
**café** /ˈkæfeɪ; *US* kæˈfeɪ/ **59**/4
**cake** /keɪk/ **28**/13
**calculator** /ˈkælkjʊleɪtə(r)/ **49**/5
**calendar** /ˈkælɪndə(r)/ **44**/2
**calf** /kɑːf; *US* kæf/ **89**/2
**California** /ˌkælɪˈfɔːnɪə/ **55**
**Cambodia** /kæmˈbəʊdɪə/ **54**
**Cambridge** /ˈkeɪmbrɪdʒ/ / **56**
**Cambridgeshire** /ˈkeɪmbrɪdʒʃə(r)/ **56**
**camcorder** /ˈkæmkɔːdə(r)/ **30**/1
**camel** /ˈkæml/ **90**/10
**camera** /ˈkæmərə/ **29**/16, 19, 23
**camera case** /ˈkæmərə keɪs/ **29**/21
**camera shop** /ˈkæmərə ʃɒp/ **29**
**camera store** /ˈkæmərə stɔːr/ **29**
**Cameroon** /ˌkæməˈruːn/ **54**
**camp stove** /ˈkæmp stəʊv/ **71**/22
**camping** /ˈkæmpɪŋ/ **71**/18
**camping stove** /ˈkæmpɪŋ stəʊv/ **71**/22
**can** /kæn/ **27**/6, 26
**can opener** /ˈkæn əʊpənər/ **20**/10
**Canada** /ˈkænədə/ **53**
**canal** /kəˈnæl/ **72**/12
**canary** /kəˈneərɪ/ **93**/18
**Canary Islands** /kəˈneərɪ ˌaɪləndz/ **54**
**candle** /ˈkændl/ **15**/3, **58**/8, 9, **86**/23, 24
**candy** /ˈkændɪ/ **26**/10, 14, 15, 18
**canoe** /kəˈnuː/ **69**/19
**cap** /kæp/ **10**/2
**capacity** /kəˈpæsətɪ/ **48**/26
**capital city** /ˌkæpɪtl ˈsɪtɪ/ **56**
**capsule** /ˈkæpsjuːl; *US* ˈkæpsl/ **7**/6
**car** /kɑː(r)/ **60**/24, **64**
**car accident** /ˈkɑːr ˌæksɪdənt/ **38**/13
**car-park** /ˈkɑːpɑːk/ **13**/15
**caravan** /ˈkærəvæn/ **63**/9, **71**/27

**caravan site** /ˈkærəvæn saɪt/ **71**/26
**card file** /ˈkɑːd faɪl/ **44**/8
**card index** /ˈkɑːd ɪndeks/ **44**/8
**Cardiff** /ˈkaːdɪf/ **56**
**cardigan** /ˈkɑːdɪgən/ **12**/7
**cargo** /ˈkɑːgəʊ/ **70**/4
**Caribbean Sea** /kærɪˌbiːən ˈsiː/ **53**/19
**Carlow** /ˈkɑːləʊ/ **56**
**carnation** /kɑːˈneɪʃn/ **25**/24
**carpenter** /ˈkɑːpəntə(r)/ **40**/8
**carpet** /ˈkɑːpɪt/ **16**/7
**Carrickfergus** /ˌkærɪkˈfɜːgəs/ **56**
**carrot** /ˈkærət/ **23**/14
**carry (verb)** /ˈkærɪ/ **86**/14
**cart** /kɑːrt/ **28**/6, **46**/15, **67**/18, **68**/3, **86**/21
**carton** /ˈkɑːtən/ **27**/21
**cash (verb)** /kæʃ/ **34**/10, 14
**cash** /kæʃ/ **34**/15, **35**
**cash dispenser** /ˈkæʃ dɪspensə(r)/ **34**/16
**cash machine** /ˈkæʃ məʃiːn/ **34**/16
**cash register** /ˈkæʃ ˌredʒɪstə(r)/ **29**/3
**cashier** /kæˈʃɪə(r)/ **34**/9
**cashpoint** /ˈkæʃpɔɪnt/ **34**/16
**Caspian Sea** /ˌkæspɪən ˈsiː/ **54**/27
**casserole** /ˈkæsərəʊl/ **20**/1
**cassette** /kəˈset/ **30**/6, **58**/3
**cassette deck** /kəˈset dek/ **30**/18
**cast** /kæst/ **7**/13
**castle** /ˈkɑːsl; *US* ˈkæsl/ **71**/13
**Castlereagh** /ˈkɑːslreɪ/ **56**
**cat** /kæt/ **89**/18
**catch (verb)** /kætʃ/ **42**/13, **82**/10
**catcher** /ˈkætʃə(r)/ **78**/6
**catcher's mask** /ˈkætʃərz mæsk/ **78**/5
**caterpillar** /ˈkætəpɪlə(r)/ **92**/8
**cauliflower** /ˈkɒlɪflaʊər; *US* ˈkɔːlɪ-/ **23**/4
**Cavan** /ˈkævən/ **56**
**CD** /ˌsiː ˈdiː/ **30**/7
**CD player** /ˌsiː ˈdiː ˌpleɪə(r)/ **30**/19
**ceiling** /ˈsiːlɪŋ/ **16**/1
**celery** /ˈselərɪ/ **23**/16
**cello** /ˈtʃeləʊ/ **75**/3
**Celsius** /ˈselsɪəs/ **52**/2
**cement truck** /sɪˈment trʌk/ **63**/6
**cement-mixer** /sɪˈmentmɪksə(r)/ **63**/6
**cent** /sent/ **35**/13
**center** /ˈsentər/ **47**/4
**center lane** /ˈsentər leɪn/ **62**/16
**centigrade** /ˈsentigreɪd/ **52**/2
**centimetre** /ˈsentɪmiːtə(r)/ **48**/30
**Central** /ˈsentrəl/ **56**
**Central African Republic** /ˌsentrəl ˌæfrɪkən rɪˈpʌblɪk/ **54**
**central reservation** /ˌsentrəl rezəˈveɪʃn/ **62**/8
**centre** /ˈsentə(r)/ **47**/4
**centre lane** /ˈsentə leɪn/ **62**/6
**century** /ˈsentʃərɪ/ **37**
**cereal** /ˈsɪərɪəl/ **27**/1
**certified mail** /ˌsɜːrtɪfaɪd ˈmeɪl/ **32**/21
**Chad** /tʃæd/ **54**
**chain** /tʃeɪn/ **12**/25, **65**/8
**chain-wheel** /ˈtʃeɪnwiːl; *US also* hwiːl/ **65**/10
**chair** /tʃeə(r)/ **49**/10
**chalk** /tʃɔːk/ **49**/24
**chalkboard** /ˈtʃɔːkbɔːrd/ **49**/1
**change (verb)** /tʃeɪndʒ/ **34**/10, 12, **35**/16
**Charleston** /tʃɑːrlstən/ **55**
**Charlotte** /ʃɑːrlət/ **55**
**cheap** /tʃiːp/ **87**/7
**check** /tʃek/ **9**/19
**check-in** /ˈtʃekɪn/ **67**/1
**check-in counter** /ˈtʃekɪn ˌkaʊntər/ **67**/4
**check-in desk** /ˈtʃekɪn ˌdesk/ **67**/4
**checked** /tʃekt/ **9**/19
**checkers** /ˈtʃekərz/ **74**/26
**cheek** /tʃiːk/ **4**/19
**cheese** /tʃiːz/ **27**/22
**cheesecake** /ˈtʃiːzkeɪk/ **28**/9
**cheque** (*US* **check**) /tʃek/ **34**/14, **43**/4
**cheque book** (*US* **checkbook**) /ˈtʃek bʊk/ **34**/1
**cheque card** /ˈtʃek kɑːd/ **34**/3
**cheque stub** (*US* **check stub**) /ˈtʃek stʌb/ **34**/2
**cherry** /ˈtʃerɪ/ **28**/1
**Cheshire** /ˈtʃeʃə(r)/ **56**
**chess** /tʃes/ **74**/29
**chest** /tʃest/ **3**/26
**chest of drawers** /ˈtʃest əv drɔːz/ **18**/19
**Chicago** /ʃɪˈkɑːgəʊ/ **55**
**chick** /tʃɪk/ **93**/3
**chicken** /ˈtʃɪkɪn/ **27**/10, **93**/1
**child** /tʃaɪld/ **5**/2, **85**/2–4
**children** /ˈtʃɪldrən/ **1**/19
**Chile** /ˈtʃɪlɪ/ **53**
**chimney** /ˈtʃɪmnɪ/ **14**/7
**chin** /tʃɪn/ **3**/28
**China** /ˈtʃaɪnə/ **54**
**chips** /tʃɪps/ **28**/27
**chisel** /ˈtʃɪzl/ **21**/14
**chocolate** /ˈtʃɒklət/ **26**/9, 11, 17, **28**/13
**chop (verb)** /tʃɒp/ **79**/28
**Christmas tree** /ˈkrɪsməs triː/ **25**/1
**chrysanthemum** /krɪˈsænθəməm/ **25**/15
**Cincinnati** /ˌsɪnsɪˈnætɪ/ **55**
**cinema** /ˈsɪnəmɑː, ˈsɪnəmə/ **76**
**circle** /ˈsɜːkl/ **47**/1, **76**/21
**circumference** /səˈkʌmfərəns/ **47**/2
**city** /ˈsɪtɪ/ **55**, **56**, **59**/**60**
**clamp stand** /ˈklæmp stænd/ **45**/20
**clap (verb)** /klæp/ **85**/8
**Clare** /kleə(r)/ **56**
**clarinet** /klærɪˈnet/ **75**/14
**classroom** /ˈklɑːsruːm, rʊm; *US* ˈklæs-/ **49**
**claw** /klɔː/ **90**/5, **91**/19
**clean (verb)** /kliːn/ **83**/3
**clean** /kliːn/ **88**/19
**Cleveland** /ˈkliːvlənd/ **55**, **56**
**cliff** /klɪf/ **73**/11
**climb (verb)** /klaɪm/ **82**/13
**climber** /ˈklaɪmə(r)/ **72**/25
**climbing** /ˈklaɪmɪŋ/ **72**/24
**clock** /klɒk/ **15**/26, **58**/8
**clock-face** /ˈklɒkfeɪs/ **37**/2
**closed** /kləʊzd/ **87**/10
**closet** /ˈklɒzɪt/ **18**/17
**clothes** /kləʊðz; *US* kləʊz/ **9**/**11**
**clothes-line** /ˈkləʊðzlaɪn; *US* ˈkləʊz-/ **19**/22
**clothes-peg** /ˈkləʊðzpeg/ **19**/10
**clothespin** /ˈkləʊzpin/ **19**/10
**cloudy** /ˈklaʊdɪ/ **51**/8
**club** /klʌb/ **74**/31, **79**/15
**clutch** /klʌtʃ/ **64**/26
**Clwyd** /ˈkluːɪd/ **56**
**coach** /kəʊtʃ/ **63**/2, **66**/4
**coat** /kəʊt/ **10**/17
**coat-hanger** /ˈkəʊthæŋə(r)/ **18**/18
**(cob)web** /ˈkɒbweb/ **92**/12
**cock** /kɒk/ **93**/4
**cockpit** /ˈkɒkpɪt/ **68**/14
**cockroach** /ˈkɒkrəʊtʃ/ **92**/16
**cocktail** /ˈkɒkteɪl/ **28**/11
**coconut** /ˈkəʊkənʌt/ **24**/7
**cocoon** /kəˈkuːn/ **92**/7
**coffee-pot** /ˈkɒfɪˌpɒt; *US* ˈkɔːfɪˌpɒt/ **15**/21
**coffee-table** /ˈkɒfɪˌteɪbl; *US* ˈkɔːfɪ-/ **16**/8
**coin** /kɔɪn/ **35**/1, **36**/1
**colander** /ˈkʌləndə(r)/ **20**/9
**cold** /kəʊld/ **6**/7, **52**/6
**cold water faucet** /ˈkəʊld wɔːtər ˌfɔːsɪt/ **19**/19
**cold(-water) tap** /ˌkəʊldˈwɔːtə ˌtæp/ **19**/19
**Coleraine** /ˈkəʊləˌreɪn/ **56**
**collar** /ˈkɒlə(r)/ **11**/15
**collection** /kəˈlekʃn/ **31**/6
**Colombia** /kəˈlʌmbɪə/ **53**
**Colorado** /ˌkɒləˈrɑːdəʊ/ **55**
**colour** (*US* **color**) /ˈkʌlə(r)/ **9**
**colour print** (*US* **color print**) /ˈkʌlə prɪnt/ **29**/13
**coloured pens** (*US* **colored pens**) /ˈkʌləd penz/ **26**/5
**Columbia** /kəˈlʌmbɪə/ **55**
**comb (verb)** /kəʊm/ **84**/15
**comb** /kəʊm/ **17**/27
**combine harvester** (*US* **combine**) /ˌkɒmbaɪn ˈhɑːvɪstə(r)/ **73**/25
**come (verb)** /kʌm/ **57**/7
**come back (verb)** /kʌm ˈbæk/ **41**/5
**compact camera** /ˌkɒmpækt ˈkæmərə/ **29**/19
**compact disc** /ˌkɒmpækt ˈdɪsk/ **30**/7
**compact disc player** /ˌkɒmpækt ˈdɪsk ˌpleɪə(r)/ **30**/19
**compass** /ˈkʌmpəs/ **49**/19
**compasses** /ˈkʌmpəsɪz/ **49**/19
**computer programmer** /kəmˈpjuːtə ˌprəʊgræmə(r)/ **40**/5
**concrete** /ˈkɒŋkriːt/ **13**/18
**concrete wall** /ˌkɒŋkriːt ˈwɔːl/ **14**/12
**condenser** /kənˈdensə(r)/ **45**/23
**conductor** /kənˈdʌktə(r)/ **76**/4
**cone** /kəʊn/ **47**/22, **61**/17
**confectionery** /kənˈfekʃənərɪ/ **26**
**conga** /ˈkɒŋgə/ **75**/22
**Congo** /ˈkɒŋgəʊ/ **54**
**conical flask** /ˈkɒnɪkl flɑːsk; *US* flæsk/ **45**/17
**Connecticut** /kəˈnetɪkət/ **55**
**constellation** /ˌkɒnstəˈleɪʃn/ **50**/25
**construction worker** /kənˈstrʌkʃn ˌwɜːkə(r)/ **61**/15
**contact lens** /ˌkɒntækt ˈlenz/ **8**/20
**contact lens cleaner** /ˌkɒntækt ˈlenz kliːnə(r)/ **8**/22
**container** /kənˈteɪnər/ **27**/19
**continent** /ˈkɒntɪnənt/ **53**
**contrastive adjective** /kənˈtrɑːstɪv ˌædʒɪktɪv/ **87**/**88**
**control tower** /kənˈtrəʊl taʊə(r)/ **68**/4
**convertible** /kənˈvɜːtəbl/ **63**/13
**cook (verb)** /kʊk/ **83**/2
**cookbook** /ˈkʊkbʊk/ **20**/4
**cooked meat** /ˌkʊkd ˈmiːt/ **27**/7
**cookery book** /ˈkʊkərɪ bʊk/ **20**/4
**cookie** /ˈkʊkɪ/ **27**/15, 16

**cookie tin** /ˈkʊkɪ tɪn/ **16**/10
**Cookstown** /ˈkʊksˌtaʊn/ **56**
**cool** /kuːl/ **52**/5
**coping saw** /ˈkəʊpɪŋ ˌsɔː/ **21**/20
**copy** /ˈkɒpɪ/ **43**/11
**Coral Sea** /ˌkɒrəl ˈsiː/ **54**/32
**cord** /kɔːd/ **19**/11
**Cork** /kɔːk/ **56**
**corn** /kɔːn/ **28**/20
**corner** /ˈkɔːnə(r)/ **48**/5, **79**/18
**cornfield** /ˈkɔːnfiːld/ **73**/26
**Cornwall** /ˈkɔːnwəl/ **56**
**correction fluid** /kəˈrekʃn fluːɪd/ **44**/9
**Costa Rica** /ˌkɒstə ˈriːkə/ **53**
**Côte d'Ivoire** /ˌkəʊt diːˈvwɑː/ **54**
**cottage** /ˈkɒtɪdʒ/ **14**/13
**cotton** /ˈkɒtn/ **74**/11
**cotton ball** /ˈkɒtn bɔːl/ **7**/4
**cotton wool** /ˌkɒtn ˈwʊl/ **7**/4
**couch** /kaʊtʃ/ **16**/17
**cough** /kɒf; *US* kɔːf/ **6**/9
**counter** /ˈkaʊntə(r)/ **20**/13, **31**/3
**counter assistant** /ˌkaʊntər əˈsɪstənt/ **31**/4
**counterfoil** /ˈkaʊntəfɔɪl/ **34**/2
**country** /ˈkʌntrɪ/ **53**
**country code** /ˈkʌntrɪ kəʊd/ **38**/19
**country house** /ˌkʌntrɪ ˈhaʊs/ **71**/14
**countryside** /ˈkʌntrɪsaɪd/ **71**/16
**county** /ˈkaʊntɪ/ **56**
**courgette** /kɔːˈʒet/ **23**/12
**courier** /ˈkʊrɪə(r)/ **31**/15
**courtyard** /ˈkɔːtjɑːd/ **57**/2
**cousin** /ˈkʌzn/ **1**/9
**Coventry** /ˈkɒvəntrɪ/ **56**
**cow** /kaʊ/ **89**/1
**crab** /kræb/ **91**/18
**Craigavon** /kreɪgˈævən/ **56**
**crane** /kreɪn/ **70**/2
**crank** /kræŋk/ **65**/5
**crash barrier** /ˈkræʃ bærɪə(r)/ **62**/9
**cream** /kriːm/ **9**/6, **28**/12
**credit card** /ˈkredɪt kɑːd/ **34**/4
**crescent** /ˈkresnt/ **50**/1
**cricket** /ˈkrɪkɪt/ **81, 92**/18
**cricket match** /ˈkrɪkɪt mætʃ/ **81**/12
**crisps** /krɪsps/ **26**/16, 19
**Croatia** /krəʊˈeɪʃə/ **54**
**crocodile** /ˈkrɒkədaɪl/ **91**/29
**crocodile clip** /ˈkrɒkədaɪl ˌklɪp/ **46**/7
**crooked** /ˈkrʊkɪd/ **87**/2
**crossroads** /ˈkrɒsrəʊds/ **60**/21
**crosswalk** /ˈkrɒswɔːk/ **59**/24
**crow** /krəʊ/ **93**/11
**crowd** /kraʊd/ **78**/7
**crucible** /ˈkruːsɪbl/ **46**/26
**cruise** /kruːz/ **72**/6
**crutch** /krʌtʃ/ **7**/14
**cry (verb)** /kraɪ/ **84**/20
**Cuba** /ˈkjuːbə/ **53**
**cube** /kjuːb/ **47**/21
**cucumber** /ˈkjuːkʌmbə(r)/ **23**/10
**cue** /kjuː/ **79**/5
**cuff** /kʌf/ **11**/17
**Cumbria** /ˈkʌmbrɪə/ **56**
**cup** /kʌp/ **16**/14, **42**/16, **58**/16
**cupboard** /ˈkʌbəd/ **20**/20
**curb** /kɜːrb/ **59**/9
**curly** /ˈkɜːlɪ/ **5**/10
**curtains** /ˈkɜːtnz/ **16**/20
**curve** /kɜːv/ **47**/27
**curve to right** /ˌkɜːrv tʊ ˈraɪt/ **61**/8
**cushion** /ˈkʊʃn/ **16**/18
**customer** /ˈkʌstəmə(r)/ **29**/1
**customs** /ˈkʌstəms/ **67**/19
**customs officer** /ˈkʌstəmz ˌɒfɪsə(r)/ **67**/20
**cut (verb)** /kʌt/ **86**/17
**cut** /kʌt/ **6**/18
**cutting board** /ˈkʌtɪŋ bɔːrd/ **20**/18
**cycle (verb)** /ˈsaɪkl/ **80**/4
**cycle and pedestrian route** /ˌsaɪkl ənd pəˈdestrɪən ruːt/ **61**/9
**cycling** /ˈsaɪklɪŋ/ **80**/3
**cyclist** /ˈsaɪklɪst/ **60**/20
**cylinder** /ˈsɪlɪndə(r)/ **47**/24
**cylinder head** /ˈsɪlɪndə(r) hed/ **64**/17
**cymbals** /ˈsɪmblz/ **75**/21
**Cyprus** /ˈsaɪprəs/ **54**
**Czech Republic** /ˌtʃek rɪˈpʌblɪk/ **54**

**daffodil** /ˈdæfədɪl/ **25**/14
**daily routine** /ˌdeɪlɪ ruːˈtiːn/ **41/42**
**daisy** /ˈdeɪzɪ/ **25**/23
**Dallas** /ˈdæləs/ **55**
**dam** /dæm/ **73**/14
**dance (verb)** /dɑːns; *US* dæns/ **85**/7
**dark** /dɑːk/ **5**/8, **9**/12, **51**/14
**dartboard** /ˈdɑːtbɔːd/ **79**/2
**darts** /dɑːts/ **79**/1
**dashboard** /ˈdæʃbɔːd/ **64**/20
**date** /deɪt/ **33**
**daughter** /ˈdɔːtə(r)/ **1**/17
**day** /deɪ/ **37**
**Dayton** /ˈdeɪtn/ **55**
**December** /dɪˈsembə(r)/ **52**
**deck** /dek/ **69**/4
**deep** /diːp/ **87**/19
**deer** /dɪə(r)/ **90**/1
**degrees** /dɪˈgriːz/ **52**/1, 2, 8
**Delaware** /ˈdeləweə(r)/ **55**
**delicatessen** /ˌdelɪkəˈtesn/ **27**
**delivery** /dɪˈlɪvərɪ/ **31**/12, 15
**Denmark** /ˈdenmɑːk/ **54**
**dental assistant** /ˈdentl əˌsɪstənt/ **8**/6
**dental nurse** /ˈdentl ˌnɜːs/ **8**/6
**dentist** /ˈdentɪst/ **8**/1
**dentist's chair** /ˈdentɪsts ˌtʃeə(r)/ **8**/4
**Denver** /ˈdenvər/ **55**
**department store** /dɪˈpɑːtmənt stɔː(r)/ **59**/18
**departures board** /dɪˈpɑːtʃəz bɔːd/ **66**/17
**departures lounge** /dɪˈpɑːtʃəz ˌlaʊndʒ/ **67**/12
**deposit slip** /dɪˈpɒzɪt slɪp/ **34**/18
**depth** /depθ/ **48**/1
**Derby** /ˈdɑːbɪ/ **56**
**Derbyshire** /ˈdɑːbɪʃə(r)/ **56**
**Derry** /ˈderɪ/ **56**
**Des Moines** /də ˈmɔɪn/ **55**
**describe (verb)** /dɪˈskraɪb/ **9**
**description** /dɪˈskrɪpʃn/ **5**
**desert** /ˈdezət/ **73**/15
**desk** /desk/ **44**/6
**despatch-rider** /dɪˈspætʃ raɪdə(r)/ **31**/16
**dessert** /dɪˈzɜːt/ **28, 28**/6
**detached house** /dɪˌtætʃt ˈhaʊs/ **14**/1
**detergent** /dɪtɜːdʒənt/ **19**/1
**Detroit** /dɪˈtrɔɪt/ **55**
**Devon** /ˈdevən/ **56**
**diagonal** /daɪˈægənl/ **47**/12
**dial** /ˈdaɪəl/ **38**/26
**diameter** /daɪˈæmɪtə(r)/ **47**/5
**diamond** /ˈdaɪəmənd/ **74**/33
**diary** /ˈdaɪərɪ/ **44**/21
**dice** /daɪs/ **74**/28
**Dictaphone** /ˈdɪktəfəʊn/ **43**/2
**dictate (verb)** /dɪkˈteɪt/ **43**/1
**dictating machine** /dɪkˈteɪtɪŋ məˌʃiːn/ **43**/2
**difficult** /ˈdɪfɪkəlt/ **87**/12
**dig (verb)** /dɪg/ **83**/7
**dime** /daɪm/ **35**/4
**dining-room** /ˈdaɪnɪŋruːm, rʊm/ **15**
**dinner** /ˈdɪnə(r)/ **42**/22
**dirty** /ˈdɜːtɪ/ **88**/20
**disc jockey** /ˈdɪsk dʒɒkɪ/ **39**/3
**dish** /dɪʃ/ **15**/6
**dish towel** /ˈdɪʃ taʊəl/ **20**/7
**dishwashing liquid** /ˈdɪʃwɒʃɪŋ ˌlɪkwɪd/ **20**/5
**disk drive** /ˈdɪsk draɪv/ **44**/24
**disk jockey** /ˈdɪsk dʒɒkɪ/ **39**/3
**District of Columbia** /ˌdɪstrɪkt əv kəˈlʌmbɪə/ **55**
**dive (verb)** /daɪv/ **77**/29
**diver** /ˈdaɪvə(r)/ **77**/30
**divided by** /dɪˈvaɪdɪd baɪ/ **48**/14
**Djibouti** /dʒɪˈbuːtɪ/ **54**
**do a handstand (verb)** /ˌduː ə ˈhændstænd/ **82**/25
**do not enter** /ˌduː nɒt ˈentə(r)/ **61**/3
**dock** /dɒk/ **70**/1
**doctor** /ˈdɒktə(r)/ **7**/19
**doctor's office** /ˈdɒktərz ˌɒfɪs/ **7**
**doctor's surgery** /ˈdɒktəz ˌsɜːdʒərɪ/ **7**
**dog** /dɒg/ **89**/22
**dollar** /ˈdɒlər/ **35**/12, 13
**dollar bill** /ˌdɒlər ˈbɪl/ **35**/7
**dolphin** /ˈdɒlfɪn/ **90**/29
**Dominican Republic** /dəˌmɪnɪkən rɪˈpʌblɪk/ **53**
**Donegal** /ˈdɒnɪgɔːl/ **56**
**donkey** /ˈdɒŋkɪ/ **89**/11
**doormat** /dɔːmæt/ **18**/21
**doorstep** /ˈdɔːstep/ **13**/6
**dormer** /ˈdɔːmə(r)/ **14**/15
**Dorset** /ˈdɔːsɪt/ **56**
**double room** /ˌdʌbl ˈruːm, ˈrʊm/ **71**/7
**double yellow lines** /ˌdʌbl ˌjeləʊ ˈlaɪnz/ **60**/22
**(double-)bass** /ˌdʌblˈbeɪs/ **75**/5
**double-decker bus** /ˌdʌblˌdekə ˈbʌs/ **60**/25
**doubles match** /ˈdʌblz mætʃ/ **81**/8
**Douglas** /ˈdʌgləs/ **56**
**Dover** /ˈdəʊvə(r)/ **56**
**Down** /daʊn/ **56**
**down** /daʊn/ **57**/13
**downstairs** /ˌdaʊnˈsteəz/ **18**/23, **41**/3
**dozen** /ˈdʌzn/ **27**/13
**dragonfly** /ˈdrægənflaɪ/ **92**/5
**drainpipe** /ˈdreɪnpaɪp/ **14**/21
**drapes** /dreɪps/ **16**/20
**draughts** /drɑːfts/ **74**/26
**drawer** /drɔː(r)/ **15**/19, **58**/3
**drawing** /ˈdrɔːɪŋ/ **74**/2
**dress** /dres/ **12**/19
**dresser** /ˈdresər/ **18**/1
**dressing gown** /ˈdresɪŋ gaʊn/ **11**/13
**dressing table** /ˈdresɪŋ teɪbl/ **18**/1
**dressing up** /ˌdresɪŋ ˈʌp/ **12**
**dried flowers** /draɪd ˈflaʊəz/ **25**/9, **58**/7
**drill** /drɪl/ **8**/2, **21**/10, 18

**drink (verb)** /drɪŋk/ **42**/16
**drive (verb)** /draɪv/ **42**/19
**drive** /draɪv/ **22**/26
**driveway** /ˈdraɪvweɪ/ **22**/26
**dropper** /ˈdrɒpə(r)/ **46**/11
**drum** /drʌm/ **76**/10
**drummer** /ˈdrʌmə(r)/ **76**/11
**drumsticks** /ˈdrʌmstɪks/ **75**/19
**dry (verb)** /draɪ/ **84**/14
**dry** /draɪ/ **88**/9
**Dublin** /ˈdʌblɪn/ **56**
**duck** /dʌk/ **93**/28
**dull** /dʌl/ **51**/14
**Dumfries and Galloway** /dʌmˌfriːs ənd ˈgæləweɪ/ **56**
**dump truck** /ˈdʌmp trʌk/ **61**/14
**dumper (truck)** /ˈdʌmpə ˌtrʌk/ **61**/14
**Dundee** /dʌnˈdiː/ **56**
**Dungannon** /dʌŋˈgænən/ **56**
**Durham** /ˈdʌrəm/ **56**
**dust cloth** /ˈdʌst klɔːθ/ **19**/14
**dustbin** /dʌstbɪn/ **22**/20
**duster** /ˈdʌstə(r)/ **19**/14
**dustpan** /ˈdʌstpæn/ **19**/4
**duty-free shop** /djuːtɪˈfriː ˌʃɒp/ **67**/10
**Dyfed** /ˈdʌvɪd/ **56**

**eagle** /ˈiːgl/ **93**/8
**ear** /ɪə(r)/ **3**/3
**earring** /ˈɪərɪŋ/ **12**/27
**Earth** /ɜːθ/ **50**/21
**easel** /ˈiːzl/ **49**/13
**east** /iːst/ **56**
**East China Sea** /ˌiːst ˌtʃaɪnə ˈsiː/ **54**/34
**East Sussex** /ˌiːst ˈsʌsɪks/ **56**
**easy** /ˈiːzɪ/ **87**/11
**eat (verb)** /iːt/ **41**/9, **42**/17, 22
**Ecuador** /ˈekwədɔː(r)/ **53**
**edge** /edʒ/ **48**/4
**Edinburgh** /ˈedɪnbərə/ **56**
**eel** /iːl/ **91**/11
**egg** /eg/ **27**/13, 14
**eggplant** /ˈegplænt/ **23**/20
**Egypt** /ˈiːdʒɪpt/ **54**
**eight** /eɪt/ **33**/8
**eighteen** /ˌeɪˈtiːn/ **33**/18
**eighth** /eɪtθ/ **33**
**eighty** /ˈeɪtɪ/ **33**/80
**El Paso** /el ˈpæsəʊ/ **55**
**El Salvador** /el ˈsælvədɔː(r)/ **53**
**elbow** /ˈelbəʊ/ **3**/8
**elderly** /ˈeldəlɪ/ **5**/6
**electric drill** /ɪˌlektrɪk ˈdrɪl/ **21**/10
**(electric) guitar** /ɪˌlektrɪk gɪˈtɑː(r)/ **76**/8
**electric razor** /ɪˌlektrɪk ˈreɪzə(r)/ **17**/22
**electric teakettle** /ɪˌlektrɪk ˈtiːketl/ **20**/19
**electrician** /ɪˌlekˈtrɪʃn/ **40**/7
**electrode** /ɪˈlektrəʊd/ **46**/6
**electronics store** /ɪlekˈtrɒnɪks stɔːr/ **30**
**elephant** /ˈelɪfənt/ **90**/24
**eleven** /ɪˈlevn/ **33**/11
**eleventh** /ɪˈlevnθ/ **33**
**embankment** /ɪmˈbæŋkmənt/ **62**/3
**embroidery** /ɪmˈbrɔɪdərɪ/ **74**/18
**emergency services** /ɪˈmɜːdʒənsɪ ˌsɜːvɪsɪz/ **38**
**empty** /ˈemptɪ/ **88**/12
**engine** /ˈendʒɪn/ **64**/15, **65**/28, **66**/3
**England** /ˈɪŋglənd/ **56**
**English Channel** /ˌɪŋglɪʃ ˈtʃænl/ **56**
**entrance** /ˈentrəns/ **66**/21
**envelope** /ˈenvələʊp/ **26**/3, **32**/6
**environment** /ɪnˈvaɪərənmənt/ **73**
**equals** /ˈiːkwəlz/ **48**/15
**equator** /ɪˈkweɪtə(r)/ **53**/**54**
**Equatorial Guinea** /ekwəˌtɔːrɪəl ˈgɪnɪ/ **54**
**eraser** /ɪˈreɪzər/ **49**/26
**Eritrea** /ˌerɪˈtreɪə/ **54**
**Essex** /ˈesɪks/ **56**
**estate** /ɪsˈteɪt/ **63**/14
**Estonia** /eˈstəʊnɪə/ **54**
**Ethiopia** /ˌiːθɪˈəʊpɪə/ **54**
**Eugene** /jʊˈdʒiːn/ **55**
**Europe** /ˈjʊərəp/ **53**/4
**evening** /ˈiːvnɪŋ/ **37**/17
**examination couch** /ɪgˌzæmɪˈneɪʃn kaʊtʃ/ **7**/22
**examination table** /ɪgˌzæmɪˈneɪʃn teɪbl/ **7**/22
**examining table** /ɪgˈzæmɪnɪŋ teɪbl/ **7**/22
**exchange rate** /ɪksˈtʃeɪndʒ reɪt/ **34**/8
**exercise book** /ˈeksəsaɪz bʊk/ **49**/4
**exhaust-pipe** /ɪgˈzɔːstpaɪp/ **64**/6
**exit ramp** /ˈeksɪt ræmp/ **62**/12
**exit sign** /ˈeksɪt saɪŋ/ **66**/5
**expensive** /ɪkˈspensɪv/ **87**/8
**Express Mail** /ɪkˈspres meɪl/ **32**/25
**eye** /aɪ/ **4**/25, **6**/13
**eye drops** /ˈaɪ drɒps/ **8**/21
**eye test** /ˈaɪ test/ **8**/14
**eyebrow** /ˈaɪbraʊ/ **4**/26
**eyeglass case** /ˈaɪglæs ˌkeɪs/ **8**/19
**eyelash** /ˈaɪlæʃ/ **4**/28
**eyelid** /ˈaɪlɪd/ **4**/27
**eyepiece** /ˈaɪpiːs/ **46**/22

**face** /feɪs/ **4**/17
**face mask** /ˈfeɪs mæsk/ **78**/5
**factory** /ˈfæktərɪ/ **59**/23
**Faeroe Islands** /ˈfeərəʊ ˌaɪləndz/ **54**
**Fahrenheit** /ˈfærənhaɪt/ **52**/1
**fair** /feə(r)/ **5**/9
**fairway** /ˈfeəweɪ/ **79**/13
**Falkland Islands** /ˈfɔːlklənd ˌaɪləndz/ **53**
**fall (verb)** /fɔːl/ **57**/8, **82**/5
**fall** /fɔːl/ **52**/11
**fall over (verb)** /fɔːl ˈəʊvə(r)/ **6**/11
**family relationships** /ˌfæməlɪ rɪˈleɪʃnʃɪps/ **1**/**2**
**farm** /fɑːm/ **73**/20
**farmer** /ˈfɑːmə(r)/ **39**/9
**farmhouse** /ˈfɑːmhaʊs/ **73**/21
**fast** /fɑːst; *US* fæst/ **87**/23
**fast lane** /ˈfɑːst leɪn; *US* ˈfæst/ **62**/7, 17
**fat** /fæt/ **5**/21
**father** /ˈfɑːðə(r)/ **1**/6
**father-in-law** /ˈfɑːðər ɪn lɔː/ **1**/7
**faucet** /ˈfɔːsɪt/ **19**/19, 20
**fax (verb)** /fæks/ **43**/10
**fax** /fæks/ **43**/10
**feather** /ˈfeðə(r)/ **93**/5
**February** /ˈfebrʊərɪ; *US* ˈfebrʊerɪ/ **52**
**fence** /fens/ **22**/15
**fender** /ˈfendər/ **65**/22
**Fermanagh** /fəˈmænə/ **56**
**fern** /fɜːn/ **25**/5
**ferry** /ˈferɪ/ **70**/9
**field** /fiːld/ **73**/24, **80**/16, **81**/22
**field hockey** /ˈfiːld hɒkɪ/ **78**/16
**fielder** /ˈfiːldə(r)/ **81**/21
**Fife** /faɪf/ **56**
**fifteen** /ˌfɪfˈtiːn/ **33**/15
**fifth** /fɪfθ/ **33**
**fifty** /ˈfɪftɪ/ **33**/50
**Fiji** /ˈfiːˌdʒiː/ **54**
**file (verb)** /faɪl/ **43**/9
**file** /faɪl/ **21**/13, **44**/14
**file cabinet** /ˈfaɪl ˌkæbɪnɪt/ **44**/15
**filing cabinet** /ˈfaɪlɪŋ ˌkæbɪnɪt/ **44**/15
**fill (verb)** /fɪl/ **83**/9
**fill in (verb)** /fɪl ˈɪn/ **43**/5
**fill out (verb)** /fɪl ˈaʊt/ **43**/5
**filling** /ˈfɪlɪŋ/ **8**/9
**filling-station** /ˈfɪlɪŋsteɪʃn/ **64**/1
**film** /fɪlm/ **29**/11
**film star** /ˈfɪlm stɑː(r)/ **76**/24
**filter paper** /ˈfɪltə peɪpə(r)/ **45**/11
**fin** /fɪn/ **91**/3
**finger** /ˈfɪŋgə(r)/ **3**/20
**finish (verb)** /ˈfɪnɪʃ/ **42**/18
**Finland** /ˈfɪnlənd/ **54**
**fire** /ˈfaɪə(r)/ **16**/4, **38**/8
**fire brigade** /ˈfaɪə brɪˌgeɪd/ **38**
**fire department** /ˈfaɪər dɪˌpɑːrtmənt/ **38**
**fire extinguisher** /ˈfaɪər ɪkˌstɪŋgwɪʃə(r)/ **38**/9
**fire fighter** /ˈfaɪər faɪtər/ **38**/10
**fire-engine** /ˈfaɪərendʒɪn/ **38**/4
**fireman** /ˈfaɪəmən/ **38**/10
**fireplace** /ˈfaɪəpleɪs/ **16**/3, **58**/6, 7
**first** /fɜːst/ **33**
**first class mail** /ˌfɜːrst klæs ˈmeɪl/ **32**/14
**first floor** /ˌfɜːst ˈflɔː(r)/ **13**/13, 14
**first quarter** /ˌfɜːrst ˈkwɔːrtər/ **50**/2
**first-class post** /ˌfɜːstklɑːs ˈpəʊst/ **32**/11
**fish** /fɪʃ/ **91**
**fisherman** /ˈfɪʃəmən/ **39**/10
**fishing** /ˈfɪʃɪŋ/ **72**/13
**fishing boat** /ˈfɪʃɪŋ bəʊt/ **69**/14
**fishing-rod** /ˈfɪʃɪŋrɒd/ **72**/15
**fist** /fɪst/ **3**/10
**five** /faɪv/ **33**/5
**fizzy drink** /ˌfɪzɪ ˈdrɪŋk/ **27**/26
**flag** /flæg/ **59**/19
**flame** /fleɪm/ **45**/3
**flamingo** /fləˈmɪŋgəʊ/ **93**/25
**flannel** /ˈflænl/ **17**/13
**flap** /flæp/ **32**/7
**flash (gun)** /ˈflæʃ gʌn/ **29**/18
**flashlight** /ˈflæʃlaɪt/ **19**/17
**flat bottom flask** /ˌflæt bɒtəm ˈflɑːsk; *US* flæsk/ **45**/9
**flex** /fleks/ **19**/11
**flight attendant** /flaɪt əˈtendənt/ **67**/14
**flipper** /ˈflɪpə(r)/ **90**/28
**floor** /flɔː(r)/ **13**/11, 13, 14, **49**/9
**floppy disk** /ˌflɒpɪ ˈdɪsk/ **44**/23
**Florida** /ˈflɒrɪdə/ **55**
**florist** /ˈflɒrɪst/ **25**
**flower** /ˈflaʊə(r)/ **57**/12
**flower-bed** /ˈflaʊəbed/ **22**/24
**flowerpot** /ˈflaʊəpɒt/ **22**/10
**flute** /fluːt/ **75**/12
**fly** /flaɪ/ **92**/1
**flyover** /ˈflaɪəʊvə(r)/ **62**/10
**foal** /fəʊl/ **89**/14
**focusing control** /ˈfəʊkəsɪŋ kənˌtrəʊl/ **46**/18
**focusing knob** /ˈfəʊkəsɪŋ nɒb/ **46**/18
**foggy** /ˈfɒgɪ/ **51**/7

**fold (verb)** /fəʊld/ **86**/19
**food processor** /ˈfuːd ˌprəʊsesə(r); *US* ˈfuːd ˌprɒsesər/ **20**/25
**foot** /fʊt/ **3**/13
**football** /ˈfʊtbɔːl/ **78**/11, 12, **81**
**footbrake** /ˈfʊtbreɪk/ **64**/27
**footbridge** /ˈfʊtbrɪdʒ/ **62**/22
**forehead** /ˈfɒrɪd, *also* ˈfɔːhed; *US* ˈfɔːrɪd/ **4**/18
**foreign currency** /ˌfɒrən ˈkʌrənsɪ/ **34**/13
**forest** /ˈfɒrɪst; *US* ˈfɔːrɪst/ **73**/5
**fork** /fɔːk/ **15**/12, **22**/18
**fork-lift truck** /ˈfɔːklɪft trʌk/ **63**/8
**form** /fɔːm/ **43**/5
**Fort Worth** /ˌfɔːrt ˈwɜːrθ/ **55**
**forty** /ˈfɔːtɪ/ **33**/40
**four** /fɔː(r)/ **33**/4
**fourteen** /ˌfɔːˈtiːn/ **33**/14
**fourth** /fɔːθ/ **33**
**fox** /fɒks/ **89**/7
**fraction** /ˈfrækʃn/ **48**/18
**frame** /freɪm/ **8**/18, **15**/24, **65**/4
**France** /frɑːns; *US* fræns/ **54**
**freesia** /ˈfriːzɪə; *US* ˈfriːʒər/ **25**/20
**freeway** /ˈfriːweɪ/ **62**/11
**freezer** /ˈfriːzə(r)/ **20**/15
**freezing** /ˈfrɪzɪŋ/ **52**/7
**French fries** /ˈfrentʃ fraɪz/ **28**/27
**French Guiana** /ˌfrentʃ gɪˈɑːnə, gɪˈænə/ **53**
**French horn** /ˌfrentʃ ˈhɔːn/ **75**/6
**Friday** /ˈfraɪdɪ/ **33**
**fridge** /frɪdʒ/ **20**/14
**friend** /frend/ **42**/20
**fringe** /frɪndʒ/ **5**/14
**frog** /frɒg/ **92**/25
**from** /frɒm/ **57**/7
**front** /frʌnt/ **48**/7
**front desk** /ˌfrʌnt ˈdesk/ **71**/1
**front door** /ˌfrʌnt ˈdɔː(r)/ **14**/3
**front garden** /ˌfrʌnt ˈgɑːdn/ **22**/21
**front teeth** /ˌfrʌnt tiːθ/ **8**/11
**front walk** /ˈfrʌnt wɔːk/ **22**/23
**front yard** /ˌfrʌnt ˈjɑːrd/ **22**/21
**frown (verb)** /fraʊn/ **84**/19
**fruit** /fruːt/ **24, 28**/7
**fruit cocktail** /ˌfruːt ˈkɒkteɪl/ **28**/11
**frying-pan** /ˈfraɪɪŋ pæn/ **20**/24
**fuel gauge** /ˈfjuːəl geɪdʒ/ **64**/23
**fuel truck** /ˈfjuːəl trʌk/ **63**/3
**full** /fʊl/ **50**/3, **88**/11
**full slip** /ˈfʊl slɪp/ **11**/5
**funnel** /ˈfʌnl/ **45**/10, **70**/10
**fur** /fɜː(r)/ **89**/20
**furrow** /ˈfʌrəʊ/ **73**/30
**fuselage** /ˈfjuːzəlɑːʒ/ **68**/17

**Gabon** /ˈgæbɒn/ **54**
**Galapagos Islands** /gəˈlæpəgɒs ˌaɪləndz/ **53**
**galaxy** /ˈgæləksɪ/ **50**/24
**gall-bladder** /ˈgɔːl blædə(r)/ **4**/5
**gallery** /ˈgælərɪ/ **76**/22
**Galway** /ˈgɔːlweɪ/ **56**
**Gambia** /ˈgæmbɪə/ **54**
**garage** /ˈgærɑːʒ, ˈgærɪdʒ; *US* gəˈrɑːʒ/ **14**/2
**garbage can** /ˈgɑːrbɪdʒ ˌkæn/ **22**/20, **59**/14
**garden** /ˈgɑːdn/ **22**
**gardener** /ˈgɑːdnə(r)/ **39**/2
**garlic** /ˈgɑːlɪk/ **23**/2
**gas gauge** /ˈgæs geɪdʒ/ **64**/23
**gas pedal** /ˈgæs pedl/ **64**/28
**gas pump** /ˈgæs pʌmp/ **64**/11
**gas station** /ˈgæs steɪʃn/ **64**/1
**gate** /geɪt/ **22**/22, **66**/22, **67**/15
**gateau** /ˈgætəʊ; *US* gæˈtəʊ/ **28**/13
**gauze** /gɔːz/ **45**/25
**gauze pad** /ˈgɔːz pæd/ **7**/9
**gear changer** /ˈgɪər tʃeɪndʒər/ **65**/13
**gear lever** /ˈgɪə liːvə(r)/ **64**/21, **65**/13
**gearshift** /ˈgɪərʃɪft/ **64**/21
**Georgia** /ˈdʒɔːdʒə/ **54**
**Georgia** /ˈdʒɔːrdʒə/ **55**
**Germany** /ˈdʒɜːmənɪ/ **54**
**get dressed (verb)** /get ˈdrest/ **41**/8
**get out (verb)** /get ˈaʊt/ **41**/2
**get up (verb)** /get ˈʌp/ **41**/2
**Ghana** /ˈgɑːnə/ **54**
**gill** /gɪl/ **91**/4
**ginger** /ˈdʒɪndʒə(r)/ **5**/12
**giraffe** /dʒɪˈrɑːf; *US* dʒəˈræf/ **90**/23
**girl** /gɜːl/ **5**/3
**give (verb)** /gɪv/ **85**/9
**give way** /ˌgɪv ˈweɪ/ **61**/1
**Glasgow** /ˈglɑːzgəʊ, ˈglæzgəʊ/ **56**
**glass** /glɑːs; *US* glæs/ **13**/23, **15**/14
**glass rod** /ˌglɑːs ˈrɒd; *US* ˌglæs-/ **46**/2
**glasses** /ˈglɑːsɪz; *US* ˈglæsɪz/ **8**/15
**glasses case** /ˈglɑːsɪz ˌkeɪs; *US* ˈglæsɪz/ **8**/19
**globe** /gləʊb/ **49**/11
**Gloucester** /ˈglɒstə(r)/ **56**
**Gloucestershire** /ˈglɒstəʃə(r)/ **56**
**glove** /glʌv/ **10**/15
**glue** /gluː/ **49**/23
**go (verb)** /gəʊ/ **41**/3, 4, **42**/24, **57**/6
**goal** /gəʊl/ **81**/23, 28
**goal-post** /ˈgəʊlpəʊst/ **81**/27
**goalkeeper** /ˈgəʊlkiːpə(r)/ **81**/30
**goat** /gəʊt/ **89**/8
**goggles** /ˈgɒglz/ **45**/1
**golf** /gɒlf/ **79**/11
**good** /gʊd/ **88**/5
**goose** /guːs/ **93**/27
**gorilla** /gəˈrɪlə/ **90**/14
**grade crossing** /ˈgreɪd ˌkrɒsɪŋ/ **66**/2
**graduated beaker** /ˌgrædʒʊeɪtɪd ˈbiːkər/ **45**/24
**graduated cylinder** /ˌgrædʒʊeɪtɪd ˈsɪlɪndər/ **46**/3
**grain** /greɪn/ **73**/27
**gram** /græm/ **48**/24
**Grampian** /ˈgræmpɪən/ **56**
**granddaughter** /ˈgrænˌdɔːtə(r)/ **1**/23
**grandfather** /ˈgrændˌfɑːðə(r)/ **1**/2
**grandmother** /ˈgrændˌmʌðə(r)/ **1**/1
**grandparent** /ˈgrændˌpeərənt/ **1**/21
**grandson** /ˈgrændsʌn/ **1**/22
**grape** /greɪp/ **24**/10
**grapefruit** /ˈgreɪpfruːt/ **24**/21
**graphic equalizer** /ˌgræfɪk ˈiːkwəlaɪzə(r)/ **30**/17
**grass** /grɑːs; *US* græs/ **22**/3
**grass verge** /grɑːs ˈvɜːdʒ/ **62**/23
**grasshopper** /ˈgrɑːshɒpə(r); *US* ˈgræshɒpər/ **92**/17
**gray** /greɪ/ **9**/15
**Great Britain** /ˌgreɪt ˈbrɪtn/ **56**
**Great Falls** /ˌgreɪt ˈfɔːlz/ **55**
**Greater London** /ˌgreɪtə ˈlʌndən/ **56**
**Greater Manchester** /ˌ- ˈmæntʃəstə(r)/ **56**
**Greece** /griːs/ **54**
**green** /griːn/ **9**/11, 12, **79**/14
**green pepper** /ˌgriːn ˈpepə(r)/ **23**/3
**Greenland** /ˈgriːnlənd/ **53**
**greetings card** /ˈgriːtɪŋz kɑːd/ **32**/4
**grey** /greɪ/ **9**/15
**ground** /graʊnd/ **57**/5
**ground floor** /ˌgraʊnd ˈflɔː(r)/ **13**/14
**groundsheet** /ˈgraʊnd ʃiːt/ **71**/20
**grow (verb)** /grəʊ/ **57**/3, 12
**guarantee** /ˌgærənˈtiː/ **34**/3
**guardrail** /ˈgɑːrdˌreɪl/ **62**/19
**Guatemala** /ˌgwɑːtəˈmɑːlə/ **53**
**guest** /gest/ **71**/3
**Guinea** /ˈgɪnɪ/ **54**
**Guinea-Bissau** /ˌgɪnɪ bɪˈsəʊ/ **54**
**gulf** /gʌlf/ **53**
**Gulf of Alaska** /ˌgʌlf əv əˈlæskə/ **53**/16
**Gulf of Guinea** /ˌgʌlf əv ˈgɪnɪ/ **54**/24
**Gulf of Mexico** /ˌgʌlf əv ˈmeksɪkəʊ/ **53**/18
**gum** /gʌm/ **8**/7
**gutter** /ˈgʌtə(r)/ **14**/22, **59**/8
**Guyana** /gaɪˈænə/ **53**
**Gwent** /gwent/ **56**
**Gwynedd** /ˈgwɪneð/ **56**
**gym** /dʒɪm/ **82**/15
**gymnasium** /dʒɪmˈneɪzɪəm/ **82**/15
**gymnast** /ˈdʒɪmnæst/ **80**/2
**gymnastics** /dʒɪmˈnæstɪks/ **80**/1
**gypsy** /ˈdʒɪpsɪ/ **12**/5

**hair** /heə(r)/ **3**/2, **5**, **84**/13–16
**hair-drier** (*or* **-dryer**) /ˈheədraɪə(r)/ **18**/20
**hairbrush** /ˈheəbrʌʃ/ **18**/8
**hairdresser** /ˈheədresə(r)/ **39**/5
**Haiti** /ˈheɪtɪ/ **53**
**half** /hɑːf; *US* hæf/ **27**/14, **37**/9, **48**/21, **50**/2, 4
**half moon** /hɑːf ˈmuːn; *US* hæf/ **50**/2, 4
**half slip** /ˈhɑːf slɪp; *US* ˈhæf slɪp/ **11**/8
**hammer** /ˈhæmə(r)/ **21**/16
**hamper** /ˈhæmpər/ **17**/16
**Hampshire** /ˈhæmpʃə(r)/ **56**
**hamster** /ˈhæmstə(r)/ **89**/25
**hand** /hænd/ **3**/19, **85**/1
**hand drill** /ˈhænd drɪl/ **21**/18
**hand-towel** /ˈhændtaʊəl/ **17**/10
**handbag** /ˈhændbæg/ **10**/10
**handkerchief** /ˈhæŋkətʃɪf, *also* -tʃiːf/ **10**/21
**handle** /ˈhændl/ **30**/9
**handlebar** /ˈhændlbɑː(r)/ **65**/19
**handsaw** /ˈhændsɔː/ **21**/22
**hang-glider** /ˈhæŋˌglaɪdə(r)/ **72**/23
**hang-gliding** /ˈhæŋˌglaɪdɪŋ/ **72**/22
**hanger** /ˈhæŋər/ **18**/18
**happy** /ˈhæpɪ/ **88**/1
**hard** /hɑːd/ **88**/17
**hard shoulder** /ˌhɑːd ˈʃəʊldə(r)/ **62**/4
**harmonica** /hɑːˈmɒnɪkə/ **75**/25
**harness** /ˈhɑːnɪs/ **72**/26
**hat** /hæt/ **12**/17
**hatchback** /ˈhætʃbæk/ **63**/15
**hatchet** /ˈhætʃɪt/ **21**/17
**have (verb)** /hæv/ **6**/4–14, **41**/7, 9, **42**/16
**Hawaii** /həˈwaɪiː/ **55**
**Hawaiian Islands** /həˈwaɪən ˌaɪləndz/ **53**
**hawk** /hɔːk/ **93**/10
**head** /hed/ **3**/1, **5**/7
**headache** /ˈhedeɪk/ **6**/6

**headboard** /ˈhedbɔ:d/ **18**/13
**headlight** /ˈhedlaɪt/ **64**/4
**headphones** /ˈhedfəʊnz/ **30**/12
**health care** /ˈhelθ keə(r)/ **7**/**8**
**health club** /ˈhelθ klʌb/ **42**/19
**heart** /hɑ:t/ **4**/4, **74**/32
**heavy** /ˈhevɪ/ **88**/14
**hedge** /hedʒ/ **22**/27
**hedgehog** /ˈhedʒhɒg/ **89**/5
**heel** /hi:l/ **3**/15, **11**/20
**height** /haɪt/ **48**/2
**helicopter** /ˈhelɪkɒptə(r)/ **68**/9
**helmet** /ˈhelmɪt/ **12**/2
**hen** /hen/ **93**/2
**Hereford and Worcester** /ˌherɪfəd ənd ˈwʊstə(r)/ **56**
**herring** /ˈherɪŋ/ **91**/6
**Hertfordshire** /ˈhɑ:tfədʃə(r)/ **56**
**hi-fi** /ˈhaɪfaɪ/ **30**/13
**hi-fi shop** /ˈhaɪfaɪ ˌʃɒp/ **30**
**high** /haɪ/ **87**/17
**Highland** /ˈhaɪlənd/ **56**
**highway** /ˈhaɪweɪ/ **62**/24
**hiker** /ˈhaɪkə(r)/ **71**/24
**hiking** /ˈhaɪkɪŋ/ **71**/23
**hill** /hɪl/ **73**/12
**hip-bone** /ˈhɪpbəʊn/ **4**/15
**hippopotamus** /ˌhɪpəˈpɒtəməs/ **90**/22
**hit (verb)** /hɪt/ **78**/28
**hobby** /ˈhɒbɪ/ **74**
**hockey** /ˈhɒkɪ/ **78**/16
**hockey ball** /ˈhɒkɪ bɔ:l/ **78**/19
**hockey player** /ˈhɒkɪ pleɪə(r)/ **78**/17
**hockey stick** /ˈhɒkɪ stɪk/ **78**/18
**hold (verb)** /həʊld/ **86**/15
**hole** /həʊl/ **79**/16
**hole-punch** /ˈhəʊlpʌntʃ/ **44**/7
**holiday** /ˈhɒlɪdeɪ/ **71**/**72**
**holiday resort** /hɒlɪdeɪ rɪˌzɔ:t/ **72**/2
**hollow** /ˈhɒləʊ/ **88**/21
**Hollywood** /ˈhɒlɪwʊd/ **55**
**home** /həʊm/ **41**/10
**Honduras** /hɒnˈdjʊərəs; *US* - dʊərəs/ **53**
**Honolulu** /ˌhɒnəˈlu:lu:/ **55**
**hood** /hʊd/ **64**/14
**hoof** /hu:f/ **89**/12
**hook** /hʊk/ **19**/16
**Hoover** /ˈhu:və(r)/ **19**/7
**horn** /hɔ:n/ **90**/20
**horse** /hɔ:s/ **89**/13
**horse-racing** /ˈhɔ:sreɪsɪŋ/ **80**/23
**horseback riding** /ˈhɔ:rsbæk ˌraɪdɪŋ/ **72**/16, **80**/9
**hose** /həʊz/ **38**/12, **64**/12, **83**/8
**hospital room** /ˈhɒspɪtl ru:m, rʊm/ **7**
**hospital ward** /ˈhɒspɪtl wɔ:d/ **7**
**hot** /hɒt/ **52**/3
**hot water faucet** /ˈhɒt wɔ:tər ˌfɔ:sɪt/ **19**/20
**hot-air balloon** /ˌhɒtˈeə bəˌlu:n/ **72**/21
**hot(-water) tap** /ˌhɒtˈwɔ:tə ˌtæp/ **19**/20
**hotel reception** /həʊˌtel rɪˈsepʃn/ **71**/1
**hour** /ˈaʊə(r)/ **37**
**hour-hand** /ˈaʊəhænd/ **37**/4
**Houston** /ˈhju:stən/ **55**
**hovercraft** /ˈhɒvəkrɑ:ft; *US* -kræft/ **70**/8
**hub** /hʌb/ **65**/12
**Hudson** /ˈhʌdsn/ **55**
**Hudson Bay** /ˌhʌdsn ˈbeɪ/ **53**/17
**hug (verb)** /hʌg/ **85**/3
**Hull** /hʌl/ **56**
**human body** /ˌhju:mən ˈbɒdɪ/ **3**/**4**
**Humberside** /ˈhʌmbəsaɪd/ **56**
**hummingbird** /ˈhʌmɪŋbɜ:d/ **93**/16
**hump** /hʌmp/ **90**/11
**hundred** /ˈhʌndrəd/ **33**/100
**Hungary** /ˈhʌŋgərɪ; *US* ˈhʌŋgrɪ/ **54**
**hungry** /ˈhʌŋgrɪ/ **6**/2
**hurt (verb)** /hɜ:t/ **6**/12
**husband** /ˈhʌzbənd/ **1**/18
**hydrant** /haɪdrənt/ **38**/11
**hydrofoil** /haɪdrəfɔɪl/ **70**/7
**hypotenuse** /haɪˈpɒtənju:z; *US* haɪˈpɒtnu:s/ **47**/17

**ice-cream** /ˌaɪsˈkri:m, *esp US* ˈaɪskri:m/ **28**/10
**ice-rink** /ˈɑɪsrɪŋk/ **77**/5
**ice-skating** /ˈaɪsskeɪtɪŋ/ **77**/1
**Iceland** /ˈaɪslənd/ **54**
**Idaho** /ˈaɪdəhəʊ/ **55**
**Idaho Falls** /ˌaɪdəhəʊ ˈfɔ:lz/ **55**
**ignition** /ɪgˈnɪʃn/ **64**/25
**Illinois** /ˌɪləˈnɔɪ/ **55**
**in** /ɪn/ **58**/3, 7
**in box** /ˈɪn bɒks/ **44**/3
**in front of** /ɪn ˈfrʌnt əv/ **58**/18
**in the middle of** /ɪn ðə ˈmɪdl əv/ **58**/13
**in-tray** /ˈɪntreɪ/ **44**/3
**India** /ˈɪndɪə/ **54**
**Indian** /ˈindɪən/ **53**/12
**Indiana** /ˌɪndɪˈænə/ **55**
**Indianapolis** /ˌɪndɪəˈnæpəlɪs/ **55**
**indicator** /ˈɪndɪkeɪtə(r)/ **64**/3
**Indonesia** /ˌɪndəˈni:zɪə; *US* ˌɪndəˈni:ʒə/ **54**
**inflatable dinghy** /ɪnˌfleɪtəbl ˈdɪŋgɪ/ **70**/14
**injection** /ɪnˈdʒekʃn/ **7**/21
**injured** /ˈɪndʒəd/ **38**/15
**insect** /ˈɪnsekt/ **92**
**inside** /ˈɪnsaɪd/ **58**/3
**inside lane** /ˈɪnsaɪd leɪn/ **62**/5
**instructor** /ɪnˈstrʌktə(r)/ **82**/7
**internal** /ɪnˈtɜ:nl/ **4**/1
**international boundary** /ˌɪntəˈnæʃnəl baʊndrɪ/ **56**
**international code** /ˌɪntəˈnæʃnəl kəʊd/ **38**/18
**intersection** /ˌɪntərˈsekʃn/ **60**/21, **62**/25
**interstate highway** /ˌɪntərsteɪt ˈhaɪweɪ/ **62**/11
**intestines** /ɪnˈtestɪnz/ **4**/9
**into** /ˈɪntu:/ **57**/4
**Inverness** /ˌɪnvəˈnes/ **56**
**Iowa** /ˈaɪəwə/ **55**
**Ipswich** /ˈɪpswɪtʃ/ **56**
**Iran** /ɪˈrɑ:n/ **54**
**Iraq** /ɪˈrɑ:k/ **54**
**iris** /ˈaɪərɪs/ **4**/29, **25**/28
**Irish Republic** /ˌaɪrɪʃ rɪˈpʌblɪk/ **56**
**Irish Sea** /ˌaɪrɪʃ ˈsi:/ **56**
**iron (verb)** /ˈaɪən; *US* aɪərn/ **83**/1
**iron** /ˈaɪən; *US* ˈaɪərn/ **19**/13
**ironing-board** /ˈaɪənɪŋ bɔ:d; *US* ˈaɪərnɪŋ bɔ:rd/ **19**/9
**island** /ˈaɪlənd/ **55**
**Isle of Man** /ˌaɪl əv ˈmæn/ **56**
**Isle of Wight** /ˌaɪl əv ˈwaɪt/ **56**
**Isles of Scilly** /ˌaɪlz əv ˈsɪlɪ/ **56**
**Israel** /ˈɪzreɪl/ **54**
**Italy** /ˈɪtəlɪ/ **54**
**Ivory Coast** /ˌaɪvərɪ ˈkəʊst/ **54**

**jack** /dʒæk/ **74**/31
**jacket** /ˈdʒækɪt/ **10**/8
**jacket potato** /ˌdʒækɪt pəˈteɪtəʊ/ **28**/25
**jackhammer** /ˈdʒækhæmər/ **61**/16
**Jackson** /ˈdʒæksən/ **55**
**Jacksonville** /ˈdʒæksənvɪl/ **55**
**jam** /dʒæm/ **27**/5, 17
**Jamaica** /dʒəˈmeɪkə/ **53**
**January** /ˈdʒænjʊərɪ; *US* ˈdʒænjʊerɪ/ **52**
**Japan** /dʒəˈpæn/ **54**
**jar** /dʒɑ:(r)/ **27**/5
**jaw** /dʒɔ:/ **3**/4
**JCB** /ˌdʒeɪ si: ˈbi:/ **61**/18
**jeans** /dʒi:nz/ **10**/7
**jeep** /dʒi:p/ **63**/10
**jellyfish** /ˈdʒelɪfɪʃ/ **91**/15
**jet engine** /ˌdʒet ˈendʒɪn/ **68**/19
**jewellery** *(esp US* **jewelry**) /ˈdʒu:əlrɪ/ **12**
**job** /dʒɒb/ **39**/**40**
**jockey** /ˈdʒɒkɪ/ **80**/26
**jog (verb)** /dʒɒg/ **82**/2
**jogger** /ˈdʒɒgə(r)/ **82**/3
**jogging suit** /ˈdʒɒgɪŋ ˌsu:t/ **12**/3
**joint** /dʒɔɪnt/ **27**/7
**Jordan** /ˈdʒɔ:dn/ **54**
**judo** /ˈdʒu:dəʊ/ **79**/26
**jug** /dʒʌg/ **15**/17
**July** /dʒu:ˈlaɪ/ **52**
**jump (verb)** /dʒʌmp/ **78**/21
**jump rope** /ˈdʒʌmp rəʊp/ **82**/26
**junction** /ˈdʒʌŋkʃn/ **62**/25
**June** /dʒu:n/ **52**
**Jupiter** /ˈdʒu:pɪtə(r)/ **50**/19

**Kampuchea** /ˌkæmpʊˈtʃɪə/ **54**
**kangaroo** /ˌkæŋgəˈru:/ **90**/8
**Kansas** /ˈkænzəs/ **55**
**Kansas City** /ˌkænzəs ˈsɪtɪ/ **55**
**Kara Sea** /ˌkɑ:rəˈsi:; *US* ˌkærə/ **54**/40
**karate** /kəˈrɑ:tɪ/ **79**/27
**kayak** /ˈkaɪæk/ **69**/19
**Kazakhstan** /ˌkæzækˈstɑ:n/ **54**
**keeping fit** /ˌki:pɪŋ ˈfɪt/ **82**
**keeping in shape** /ˌki:pɪŋ ɪn ˈʃeɪp/ **82**
**Kent** /kent/ **56**
**Kentucky** /kenˈtʌkɪ/ **55**
**Kenya** /ˈkenjə/ **54**
**kerb** /kɜ:b/ **59**/9
**Kerry** /ˈkerɪ/ **56**
**kettle** /ˈketl/ **20**/19, **83**/9
**kettledrum** /ˈketldrʌm/ **75**/17
**key** /ki:/ **44**/11, **75**/24
**keyboard** /ˈki:bɔ:d/ **44**/22
**keyboard player** /ˈki:bɔ:d ˌpleɪə(r)/ **76**/12
**kidney** /ˈkɪdnɪ/ **4**/7
**Kildare** /kɪlˈdeə(r)/ **56**
**Kilkenny** /kɪlˈkenɪ/ **56**
**kilogram** /ˈkɪləgræm/ **48**/25
**kilometre** /ˈkɪləmi:tə(r), kɪˈlɒmɪtə(r)/ **48**
**king** /kɪŋ/ **74**/33
**Kirgyzstan** /ˌkɪəgɪˈstɑ:n/ **54**
**kiss (verb)** /kɪs/ **85**/2
**kit** /kɪt/ **74**/7
**kitchen** /ˈkɪtʃɪn/ **20**

# Index 


**kitten** /ˈkɪtn/ **89**/21
**kiwi fruit** /ˈki:wi: fru:t/ **24**/18
**knave** /neɪv/ **74**/31
**knee** /ni:/ **3**/18
**kneecap** /ˈni:kæp/ **4**/16
**kneel (verb)** /ni:l/ **82**/21
**knife** /naɪf/ **15**/10
**knitting** /ˈnɪtɪŋ/ **74**/21
**knitting-needle** /ˈnɪtɪŋ ni:dl/ **74**/23
**knocker** /ˈnɒkə(r)/ **13**/4
**Kuwait** /kʊˈweɪt/ **54**

**lab coat** /ˈlæb kəʊt/ **46**/1
**label** /ˈleɪbl/ **32**/3
**ladder** /ˈlædə(r)/ **38**/5
**ladle** /ˈleɪdl/ **20**/11
**ladybird** /ˈleɪdɪbɜ:d/ **92**/14
**ladybug** /ˈleɪdɪbʌg/ **92**/14
**lake** /leɪk/ **55**, **73**/4
**Lake Erie** /ˌleɪk ˈɪərɪ/ **55**
**Lake Huron** /ˌleɪk ˈhjʊərɒn/ **55**
**Lake Michigan** /ˌleɪk ˈmɪʃɪgən/ **55**
**Lake Ontario** /ˌleɪk ɒnˈteərɪəʊ/ **55**
**Lake Superior** /ˌleɪk su:ˈpɪərɪər/ **55**
**lamb** /læm/ **89**/10
**lamb chop** /ˌlæm ˈtʃɒp; *US* ˈlæm tʃɒp/ **28**/19
**lamp** /læmp/ **15**/22
**lamppost** /ˈlæmppəʊst/ **60**/7
**lampshade** /ˈlæmpʃeɪd/ **15**/23
**Lancashire** /ˈlæŋkəʃə(r)/ **56**
**landing** /ˈlændɪŋ/ **68**/8
**lane** /leɪn/ **80**/19
**Laois** /li:ʃ/ **56**
**Laos** /ˈlɑ:ɒs/ **54**
**Laptev Sea** /ˌlæptev ˈsi:/ **54**/39
**Laramie** /ˈlærəmɪ/ **55**
**large** /lɑ:dʒ/ **87**/3
**Larne** /lɑ:n/ **56**
**Las Vegas** /lɒs ˈveɪgəs/ **55**
**last quarter** /ˌlɑ:st ˈkwɔ:rtər/ **50**/4
**Latvia** /ˈlætvɪə/ **54**
**laugh (verb)** /lɑ:f; *US* læf/ **84**/18
**launch pad** /ˈlɔ:ntʃ pæd/ **50**/12
**laundry basket** /ˈlɔ:ndrɪ bɑ:skɪt/ **17**/16
**laundry room** /ˈlɔ:ndrɪ ru:m, rʊm/ **19**
**lawn** /lɔ:n/ **22**/3
**lawnmower** /ˈlɔ:nməʊə(r)/ **22**/5
**leaf** /li:f/ **25**/11
**leave (verb)** /li:v/ **41**/10
**Lebanon** /ˈlebənən; *US* ˈlebənɒn/ **54**
**Leeds** /li:dz/ **56**
**left lane** /ˈleft leɪn/ **62**/17
**leg** /leg/ **3**/12, **6**/12, 13
**Leicester** /ˈlestə(r)/ **56**
**Leicestershire** /ˈlestəʃə(r)/ **56**
**Leitrim** /ˈli:trɪm/ **56**
**lemon** /ˈlemən/ **24**/6
**length** /leŋθ/ **48**/6
**lens** /lenz/ **8**/16, **29**/17
**leopard** /ˈlepəd/ **90**/18
**Lesotho** /leˈsu:tu:/ **54**
**letter** /ˈletə(r)/ **32**/5, **43**/1, 3, 4, 6, 10
**letter-box** /ˈletəbɒks/ **13**/5, **31**/11, 14, **59**/3
**lettuce** /ˈletɪs/ **23**/7
**level** /ˈlevəl/ **21**/7
**level crossing** /ˌlevl ˈkrɒsɪŋ/ **66**/2
**Liberia** /laɪˈbɪrɪə/ **54**
**library** /ˈlaɪbrərɪ; *US* ˈlaɪbrerɪ/ **57**/6, 7
**Libya** /ˈlɪbɪə/ **54**
**license plate** /ˈlaɪsns pleɪt/ **64**/5
**lid** /lɪd/ **15**/5
**lie down (verb)** /ˌlaɪ ˈdaʊn/ **84**/23
**lifeboat** /ˈlaɪfbəʊt/ **69**/18
**lift (verb)** /lɪft/ **86**/13
**light (verb)** /laɪt/ **86**/23
**light** /laɪt/ **9**/11, **18**/16, **88**/13
**light switch** /ˈlaɪt swɪtʃ/ **18**/27
**light-bulb** /ˈlaɪtbʌlb/ **19**/15
**lighthouse** /ˈlaɪthaʊs/ **70**/12
**lightning** /ˈlaɪtnɪŋ/ **51**/11
**lily** /ˈlɪlɪ/ **25**/26
**Limavady** /ˌlɪməˈvædɪ/ **56**
**lime** /laɪm/ **24**/17
**Limerick** /ˈlɪmərɪk/ **56**
**Lincoln** /ˈlɪŋkən/ **55**
**Lincolnshire** /ˈlɪŋkənʃə(r)/ **56**
**line** /laɪn/ **47**/25, 26, 29, 30, **66**/7, 12, **69**/6
**liner** /ˈlaɪnə(r)/ **70**/11
**linesman** /ˈlaɪnzmən/ **81**/25
**lion** /ˈlaɪən/ **90**/16
**lip** /lɪp/ **4**/23
**lipstick** /ˈlɪpstɪk/ **12**/21
**Lisburn** /ˈlɪzbən/ **56**
**listen (verb)** /ˈlɪsn/ **41**/12
**Lithuania** /ˌlɪθju:ˈeɪnɪə/ **54**
**litre** /ˈli:tə(r)/ **48**/28
**litter-bin** /ˈlɪtəbɪn/ **59**/14
**little** /ˈlɪtl/ **87**/4
**Little Rock** /ˈlɪtl rɒk/ **55**
**liver** /ˈlɪvə(r)/ **4**/6
**Liverpool** /ˈlɪvəpu:l/ **56**
**living-room** /ˈlɪvɪŋ ru:m, rʊm/ **16**
**lizard** /ˈlɪzəd/ **91**/28
**llama** /ˈlɑ:mə/ **90**/12
**loaf** /ləʊf/ **27**/2
**lobster** /ˈlɒbstə(r)/ **91**/16
**lock** /lɒk/ **18**/26, **65**/6
**log** /lɒg/ **16**/5
**London** /ˈlʌndən/ **56**
**long** /lɒŋ/ **5**/12, 15
**Longford** /ˈlɒŋfəd/ **56**
**look (verb)** /lʊk/ **57**/1, 14
**loose** /lu:s/ **88**/24
**lorry** /ˈlɒrɪ/ **63**/4
**lorry driver** /ˈlɒrɪ draɪvə(r)/ **40**/2
**Los Angeles** /lɒs ˈændʒəlɪz/ **55**
**Lothian** /ˈləʊðɪən/ **56**
**lotion** /ˈləʊʃn/ **17**/21
**loud** /laʊd/ **88**/3
**Louisiana** /lu:ˌi:zɪˈænə/ **55**
**Louisville** /ˈlu:ɪvɪl/ **55**
**Louth** /lu:θ/ **56**
**low** /ləʊ/ **87**/18
**luggage** /ˈlʌgɪdʒ/ **67**/17
**luggage reclaim** /ˈlʌgɪdʒ rɪˌkleɪm/ **67**/16
**lunar module** /ˌlu:nə ˈmɒdju:l; *US* ˈmɒdʒu:l/ **50**/5
**lunar vehicle** /ˌlu:nə ˈvɪəkl; *US* ˈvi:hɪkl/ **50**/8
**lunch** /lʌntʃ/ **42**/17
**lung** /lʌŋ/ **4**/3
**lychee (*also* litchi)** /ˌlaɪˈtʃi:, ˈlaɪtʃi:; *US* ˈli:tʃi:/ **24**/15

**Macedonia** /ˌmæsɪˈdəʊnjə/ **54**
**Madagascar** /ˌmædəˈgæskə(r)/ **54**
**magazine** /mægəˈzi:n; *US* ˈmægəzi:n/ **26**/7
**Magherafelt** /ˈmækerəfelt/ **56**
**magnet** /ˈmægnɪt/ **46**/8
**magnifying glass** /ˈmægnɪfaɪɪŋ glɑ:s; *US* -glæs/ **45**/14
**mail** /meɪl/ **31**/10, **41**/6
**mail truck** /ˈmeɪl trʌk/ **31**/7
**mailbag** /ˈmeɪlbæg/ **31**/9, 13
**mailbox** /ˈmeɪlbɒks/ **13**/5, **31**/11, 14, **59**/3
**mailman** /ˈmeɪlmæn/ **31**/8
**main course** /ˈmeɪn kɔ:s/ **28**
**main river** /meɪn rɪvə(r)/ **55**
**Maine** /meɪn/ **55**
**make (verb)** /meɪk/ **74**/6
**make a deposit (verb)** /ˌmeɪk ə dɪˈpɒzɪt/ **34**/17
**make a note (verb)** /ˌmeɪk ə ˈnəʊt/ **43**/8
**make-up** /ˈmeɪkʌp/ **12**/20
**Malawi** /məˈlɑ:wɪ/ **54**
**Malaysia** /məˈleɪzɪə; *US* məˈleɪʒə/ **54**
**Mali** /ˈmɑ:lɪ/ **54**
**mallet** /ˈmælɪt/ **21**/2
**man** /mæn/ **5**/5, 6, **38**/15
**Manchester** /ˈmæntʃɪstə(r)/ **56**
**mane** /meɪn/ **89**/16
**mango** /ˈmæŋgəʊ/ **24**/19
**manhole cover** /ˈmænhəʊl kʌvə(r)/ **59**/7
**mantel** /ˈmæntl/ **16**/2, **58**/9, 10
**mantelpiece** /ˈmæntlpi:s/ **16**/2, **58**/9, 10
**map** /mæp/ **49**/18
**March** /mɑ:tʃ/ **52**
**margarine** /ˌmɑ:dʒəˈri:n; *US* ˈmɑ:rdʒərɪn/ **27**/20, 28
**marina** /məˈri:nə/ **69**/10
**market** /ˈmɑ:kɪt/ **23**/24, **23**/1
**Mars** /mɑ:z/ **50**/20
**Maryland** /ˈmeərɪlənd/ **55**
**mask** /mɑ:sk; *US* mæsk/ **7**/17
**Massachusetts** /ˌmæsəˈtʃu:sɪts/ **55**
**mast** /mɑ:st; *US* mæst/ **69**/2
**mat** /mæt/ **82**/17
**match** /mætʃ/ **81**/1, 8, 12
**matter** /ˈmætə(r)/ **6**
**mattress** /ˈmætrɪs/ **18**/11
**Mauritania** /ˌmɒrɪˈteɪnɪə; *US* ˌmɔ:r-/ **54**
**Mauritius** /məˈrɪʃəs; *US* mɔ:ˈrɪʃəs/ **54**
**May** /meɪ/ **52**
**Mayo** /ˈmeɪəʊ/ **56**
**meal** /mi:l/ **83**/2
**measurement** /ˈmeʒəmənt/ **48**
**measuring beaker** /ˈmeʒərɪŋ bi:kə(r)/ **45**/24
**measuring cylinder** /ˈmeʒərɪŋ sɪlɪndə(r)/ **46**/3
**meat** /mi:t/ **27**/8
**Meath** /mi:θ/ **56**
**mechanic** /mɪˈkænɪk/ **40**/11
**median strip** /ˈmi:dɪən strɪp/ **62**/18
**medicine** /ˈmedsn; *US* ˈmedɪsn/ **7**/1
**medicine chest** /ˈmedɪsn tʃest/ **17**/1
**Mediterranean Sea** /ˌmedɪtəˌreɪnɪən ˈsi:/ **54**/23
**meet (verb)** /mi:t/ **42**/20
**melon** /ˈmelən/ **24**/1, **28**/2
**Memphis** /ˈmemfɪs/ **55**
**menu** /ˈmenju:/ **28**/15
**Mercury** /ˈmɜ:kjʊrɪ/ **50**/23
**Merseyside** /ˈmɜ:zɪsaɪd/ **56**
**message** /ˈmesɪdʒ/ **32**/9
**messenger** /ˈmesɪndʒər/ **31**/15, 16

**messy** /'mesɪ/ **88**/8
**metal detector** /'metl dɪˌtektə(r)/ **67**/8
**Mexico** /'meksɪkəʊ/ **53**
**mezzanine** /'mezəni:n/ **76**/21
**Miami** /maɪ'æmɪ/ **55**
**Michigan** /'mɪʃɪgən/ **55**
**microbalance** /'maɪkrəʊbæləns/ **46**/27
**microphone** /'maɪkrəfəʊn/ **30**/2
**microscope** /'maɪkrəskəʊp/ **46**/17
**Mid Glamorgan** /ˌmɪd glə'mɔ:gən/ **56**
**midday** /ˌmɪd'deɪ/ **37**/13
**middle lane** /'mɪdl leɪn/ **62**/6, 16
**Middlesbrough** /'mɪdlzbərə/ **56**
**midnight** /'mɪdnaɪt/ **37**/13
**milk** /mɪlk/ **27**/24
**millilitre** /'mɪlɪli:tə(r)/ **48**/27
**millimetre** /'mɪlɪmi:tə(r)/ **48**/29
**million** /'mɪljən/ **33**/1000000
**Milwaukee** /mɪl'wɔ:kɪ/ **55**
**mineral water** /'mɪnərəl wɔ:tə(r)/ **27**/25
**Minneapolis** /ˌmɪnɪ'æpəlɪs/ **55**
**Minnesota** /ˌmɪnə'səʊtə/ **55**
**minus** /'maɪnəs/ **48**/12, **52**/8
**minute** /'mɪnɪt/ **37**/14
**minute-hand** /'mɪnɪt hænd/ **37**/3
**mirror** /'mɪrə(r)/ **15**/1
**miss (verb)** /mɪs/ **81**/29
**Mississippi** /ˌmɪsɪ'sɪpɪ/ **55**
**Missouri** /mɪ'zʊərɪ/ **55**
**misty** /'mɪstɪ/ **51**/6
**mitt** /mɪt/ **78**/4
**mixer** /'mɪksə(r)/ **20**/8
**mixing bowl** /'mɪksɪŋ bəʊl/ **20**/3
**Mobile** /'məʊbi:l/ **55**
**model** /'mɒdl/ **74**/6, 8
**Moldova** /mɒl'dəʊvə/ **54**
**Monaghan** /'mɒnəhən/ **56**
**Monday** /'mʌndɪ/ **33**
**money** /'mʌnɪ/ **34**/12, **35/36**
**money order** /'mʌnɪ ɔ:rdər/ **32**/23
**Mongolia** /mɒŋ'gəʊlɪə/ **54**
**monkey** /'mʌŋkɪ/ **90**/13
**monster** /'mɒnstə(r)/ **12**/13
**Montana** /mɒn'tænə/ **55**
**month** /mʌnθ/ **52**
**monthly statement** /ˌmʌnθlɪ 'steɪtmənt/ **34**/5
**moon** /mu:n/ **50**/1, 2, 3, 4
**mooring** /'mɔ:rɪŋ/ **69**/15
**mop** /mɒp/ **19**/8
**morning** /'mɔ:nɪŋ/ **37**/15
**Morocco** /mə'rɒkəʊ/ **54**
**mortar** /'mɔ:tə(r)/ **45**/8
**mosquito** /məs'ki:təʊ, *Brit also* mɒs-/ **92**/4
**moth** /mɒθ/ **92**/9
**mother** /'mʌðə(r)/ **1**/5
**mother-in-law** /'mʌðər ɪn lɔ:/ **1**/8
**motor bike** /'məʊtə baɪk/ **65**/25
**motor boat** /'məʊtə bəʊt/ **69**/11
**motor cycle** /'məʊtə ˌsaɪkl/ **65**/25
**motor-racing** /'məʊtəˌreɪsɪŋ/ **80**/5
**motorway** /'məʊtəweɪ/ **62**/1
**mountain** /'maʊntɪn; *US* 'maʊntn/ **55**, **73**/1
**moustache** /mə'stɑ:ʃ; *US* 'mʌstæʃ/ **4**/21
**mouth** /maʊθ/ **3**/29
**movie star** /'mu:vɪ stɑ:r/ **76**/24
**movie theater** /'mu:vɪ θɪətər/ **76**
**Moyle** /mɔɪl/ **56**
**Mozambique** /ˌməʊzæm'bi:k/ **54**
**mudguard** /'mʌdgɑ:d/ **65**/22
**mug** /mʌg/ **20**/16, **58**/5
**multiplied by** /'mʌltɪplaɪd baɪ/ **48**/13
**mushroom** /'mʌʃrʊm, 'mʌʃru:m/ **28**/21
**music** /'mju:zɪk/ **41**/12, **76**
**musical instrument** /mju:zɪkl 'ɪnstrʊmənt/ **75**
**musician** /mju:'zɪʃn/ **76**/2
**mussel** /'mʌsl/ **91**/23
**Myanmar** /ˌmɪən'mɑ:(r)/ **54**

**nail** /neɪl/ **3**/17, **21**/23
**nail-brush** /'neɪlbrʌʃ/ **17**/5
**Namibia** /nə'mɪbɪə/ **54**
**napkin** /'næpkɪn/ **15**/7
**narrow** /'nærəʊ/ **87**/16
**Nashville** /'næʃvɪl/ **55**
**national boundary** /'næʃnəl baʊndərɪ/ **56**
**navy** /'neɪvɪ/ **9**/9
**near** /nɪə(r)/ **58**/6
**neat** /ni:t/ **88**/7
**Nebraska** /nə'bræskə/ **55**
**neck** /nek/ **3**/5
**necklace** /'neklɪs/ **12**/26
**needle** /'ni:dl/ **74**/19
**negative** /'negətɪv/ **29**/10
**Nepal** /nɪ'pɔ:l; *US* nə'pɑ:l/ **54**
**nephew** /'nevju:; *US* 'nefju:/ **1**/15
**Neptune** /'neptju:n; *US* 'neptu:n/ **50**/16
**nest** /nest/ **93**/13
**net** /net/ **78**/9, **81**/7
**Netherlands** /'neðələndz/ **54**
**Nevada** /nə'vɑ:də/ **55**
**new** /nju:; *US* nu:/ **87**/6
**New Caledonia** /ˌnu: kælə'dəʊnjə/ **54**
**New Hampshire** /ˌnu: 'hæmpʃər/ **55**
**New Haven** /ˌnu: 'heɪvn/ **55**
**New Jersey** /ˌnu: 'dʒɜ:rzɪ/ **55**
**New Mexico** /ˌnu: 'meksɪkəʊ/ **55**
**new moon** /nju: 'mu:n/ **50**/1
**New Orleans** /ˌnu: 'ɔ:rli:nz/ **55**
**New York** /ˌnu: 'jɔ:rk/ **55**
**New Zealand** /ˌnju: (*US* ˌnu:) 'zi:lənd/ **54**
**Newcastle** /'nju:kɑ:sl/ **56**
**Newry and Mourne** /ˌnjʊərɪ ənd 'mɔ:n/ **56**
**news-stand** /'nju:zstænd/ **59**/15
**news-vendor** /'nju:zvendə(r)/ **59**/17
**newsagent** /'nju:zeɪdʒənt/ **26**
**newscaster** /'nu:zkæstər/ **39**/4
**newspaper** /'nju:zpeɪpə(r); *US* 'nu:zpeɪpər/ **26**/8, **41**/11, **42**/14, **59**/16
**newsreader** /'nju:zri:də(r)/ **39**/4
**newsstand** /'nu:zstænd/ **26**
**Newtownabbey** /ˌnju:tn'æbɪ/ **56**
**next to** /nekst tʊ/ **58**/17
**Niagara Falls** /naɪˌægrə 'fɔ:lz/ **55**
**Nicaragua** /nɪkə'rægjʊə; *US* ˌnɪkə'rɑ:gwə/ **53**
**nickel** /'nɪkl/ **35**/3
**niece** /ni:s/ **1**/14
**Niger** /'naɪdʒə(r)/ **54**
**Nigeria** /naɪ'dʒɪərɪə/ **54**
**night** /naɪt/ **37**/18
**night table** /'naɪt teɪbl/ **18**/10
**night-dress** /'naɪtdres/ **11**/11
**nightgown** /'naɪtgaʊn/ **11**/11
**nine** /naɪn/ **33**/9
**nineteen** /ˌnaɪn'ti:n/ **33**/19
**ninety** /'naɪntɪ/ **33**/90
**ninth** /naɪnθ/ **33**
**no entry** /ˌnəʊ 'entrɪ/ **61**/3
**no left turn** /ˌnəʊ ˌleft 'tɜ:n/ **61**/7
**no U-turn** /ˌnəʊ ˌju:'tɜ:n/ **61**/5
**noon** /nu:n/ **37**/13
**Norfolk** /'nɔ:fək/ **56**
**north** /nɔ:θ/ **56**
**North America** /ˌnɔ:θ ə'merɪkə/ **53**/1
**North Atlantic** /ˌnɔ:θ ət'læntɪk/ **53**/9
**North Carolina** /ˌnɔ:rθ kærə'laɪnə/ **55**
**North Dakota** /ˌnɔ:rθ də'kəʊtə/ **55**
**North Down** /ˌnɔ:θ 'daʊn/ **56**
**North Korea** /ˌnɔ:θ kə'rɪə/ **54**
**North Pacific** /ˌnɔ:θ pə'sɪfɪk/ **53**/14
**North Sea** /ˌnɔ:θ 'si:/ **54**/21
**North Yorkshire** /ˌnɔ:θ 'jɔ:kʃə(r)/ **56**
**Northamptonshire** /nɔ:θ'æmptənʃə(r)/ **56**
**Northern Ireland** /ˌnɔ:ðən 'aɪələnd/ **56**
**Northumberland** /nɔ:θ'ʌmbələnd/ **56**
**Norway** /'nɔ:weɪ/ **54**
**Norwegian Sea** /nɔ:ˌwi:dʒən 'si:/ **54**/20
**Norwich** /'nɒrɪtʃ/ **56**
**nose** /nəʊz/ **4**/20, **68**/13
**note** /nəʊt/ **36**/9
**notebook** /'nəʊtbʊk/ **44**/13, **49**/4
**notice** /'nəʊtɪs/ **57**/9, 10
**notice-board** /'nəʊtɪsbɔ:d/ **44**/1
**Nottingham** /'nɒtɪŋəm/ **56**
**Nottinghamshire** /'nɒtɪŋəmʃə(r)/ **56**
**November** /nəʊ'vembə(r)/ **52**
**nozzle** /'nɒzl/ **64**/13
**number** /'nʌmbə(r)/ **33**
**number-plate** /'nʌmbə pleɪt/ **64**/5
**nurse** /nɜ:s/ **7**/12
**nut** /nʌt/ **21**/25, **24**/12

**o'clock** /ə'klɒk/ **37**/1, 13, 15, 16, 17
**oar** /ɔ:(r)/ **69**/8
**objective lens** /əb'dʒektɪv lenz/ **46**/21
**oboe** /'əʊbəʊ/ **75**/13
**obtuse angle** /ɒbˌtju:s 'æŋgl; *US* ɒbˌtu:s -/ **47**/18
**ocean** /'əʊʃn/ **53**
**ocean liner** /'əʊʃn laɪnər/ **70**/11
**October** /ɒk'təʊbə(r)/ **52**
**octopus** /'ɒktəpəs/ **91**/12
**off** /ɒf/ **57**/8
**Offaly** /'ɒfəlɪ/ **56**
**office** /'ɒfɪs; *US* 'ɔ:fɪs/ **43/44**
**Ohio** /əʊ'haɪəʊ/ **55**
**(oil-)tanker** /ɔɪl'tæŋkə(r)/ **70**/6
**ointment** /'ɔɪntmənt/ **7**/8
**Oklahoma** /ˌəʊklə'həʊmə/ **55**
**Oklahoma City** /ˌəʊkləˌhəʊmə 'sɪtɪ/ **55**
**old** /əʊld/ **5**/6, **50**/4, **87**/5
**Omagh** /əʊ'mɑ:/ **56**
**Omaha** /'əʊməhɑ:/ **55**
**Oman** /əʊ'mɑ:n/ **54**
**on** /ɒn/ **58**/9
**on top of** /ɒn 'tɒp əv/ **58**/11
**one** /wʌn/ **33**/1
**one-family house** /'wʌnˌfæməlɪ ˌhaʊs/ **14**/1
**one-way street** /ˌwʌnweɪ 'stri:t/ **61**/10
**onion** /'ʌnɪən/ **23**/11
**onto** /'ɒntu:/ **57**/5
**open (verb)** /'əʊpən/ **85**/11
**open** /'əʊpən/ **87**/9
**operating room** /'ɒpəreɪtɪŋ ru:m, rʊm/ **7**/16
**operating theatre** /'ɒpəreɪtɪŋ θɪətə(r)/ **7**/16
**operation** /ˌɒpə'reɪʃn/ **7**
**optician** /ɒp'tɪʃn/ **8**/13

**orange** /ˈɒrɪndʒ; *US* ˈɔ:rɪndʒ/ 9/3, 24/9
**orange juice** /ˈɒrɪndʒ dʒu:s; *US* ˈɔ:-/ 27/21
**orbit** /ˈɔ:bɪt/ 50/13
**orchestra** /ˈɔ:kɪstrə/ 76/1
**orchestra pit** /ˈɔ:kɪstrə pɪt/ 76/19
**orchestra seats** /ˈɔ:rkɪstrə si:ts/ 76/20
**orchid** /ˈɔ:kɪd/ 25/18
**Oregon** /ˈɒrɪgən/ 55
**organ** /ˈɔ:gən/ 4/1
**Orkney Islands** /ˈɔ:knɪ aɪləndz/ 56
**Orlando** /ɔ:ˈlændəʊ/ 55
**ornament** / ˈɔ:nəmənt/ 58/12
**ostrich** /ˈɒstrɪtʃ/ 93/22
**out box** /ˈaʊt bɒks/ 44/4
**out of** /ˈaʊt əv/ 57/1
**out-tray** /ˈaʊtreɪ/ 44/4
**outboard motor** /ˌaʊtbɔ:d ˈməʊtə(r)/ 70/15
**outer space** /ˌaʊtə ˈspeɪs/ 50
**outlet** /ˈaʊtlet/ 19/21
**outside** /ˈaʊtsaɪd/ 58/1
**outside lane** /ˈaʊtsaɪd leɪn/ 62/7
**oval** /ˈəʊvl/ 47/8
**oven** /ˈʌvn/ 20/22
**oven glove** /ˈʌvn glʌv/ 20/21
**over** /ˈəʊvə(r)/ 57/14, 58/10
**overpass** /ˈəʊvərpæs/ 62/20
**owl** /aʊl/ 93/12
**Oxford** /ˈɒksfəd/ 56
**Oxfordshire** /ˈɒksfədʃə(r)/ 56
**oyster** /ˈɔɪstə(r)/ 91/21

**pack** /pæk/ 26/3, 14, 74/30
**package** /ˈpækɪdʒ/ 27/16, 32/1
**packet** /ˈpækɪt/ 26/3, 14, 15, 16, 27/16
**paddle** /ˈpædl/ 69/20, 78/27
**pads** /pædz/ 81/15
**pail** /peɪl/ 19/6
**paintbox** /ˈpeɪntbɒks/ 49/15
**paintbrush** /ˈpeɪntbrʌʃ/ 49/14
**painting** /ˈpeɪntɪŋ/ 15/25, 74/1
**pair of** /ˈpeər əv/ 8/15, 49/19
**Pakistan** /ˌpɑ:kɪˈstɑ:n; *US* ˈpækɪstæn/ 54
**palm** /pɑ:m/ 3/22, 25/16
**Panama** /ˈpænəmɑ:/ 53
**panda** /ˈpændə/ 90/7
**pants** /pænts/ 10/4, 11/10
**pantyhose** /ˈpæntɪhəʊz/ 11/7
**papaya** /pəˈpaɪə/ 24/14
**paper** /ˈpeɪpə(r)/ 57/4, 5, 8, 86/17-19
**paper bag** /ˌpeɪpə ˈbæg/ 23/22
**paper-clip** /ˈpeɪpəklɪp/ 44/10
**Papua New Guinea** /ˌpæpʊəˌnju: (*US* ˌnu:) ˈgɪnɪ/ 54
**parachute** /ˈpærəʃu:t/ 72/19
**parachuting** /ˈpærəʃu:tɪŋ/ 72/18
**Paraguay** /ˈpærəgwaɪ; *US* ˈpærəgweɪ/ 53
**parakeet** /ˈpærəki:t/ 93/20
**parallel** /ˈpærəlel/ 47/30
**paramedic** /pærəˈmedɪk/ 38/17
**parcel** /ˈpɑ:sl/ 32/1
**parent** /ˈpeərənt/ 1/20
**park** /pɑ:k/ 60/2
**parking lot** /ˈpɑ:rkɪŋ lɒt/ 13/15
**parking notice** /ˈpɑ:kɪŋ nəʊtɪs/ 59/2
**parking sign** /ˈpɑ:rkɪŋ saɪn/ 59/2
**parrot** /ˈpærət/ 93/19
**part** /pɑ:rt/ 5/16
**parting** /ˈpɑ:tɪŋ/ 5/16
**party** /ˈpɑ:tɪ/ 71/11
**passenger** /ˈpæsɪndʒə(r)/ 66/20, 68/2
**passenger car** /ˈpæsɪndʒər kɑ:r/ 66/4
**passing lane** /ˈpæsɪŋ leɪn/ 62/17
**passport** /ˈpɑ:spɔ:t; *US* ˈpæspɔ:rt/ 67/6
**passport control** /ˌpɑ:spɔ:t kənˈtrəʊl; *US* ˌpæspɔ:rt/ 67/5
**past** /pɑ:st; *US* pæst/ 37/6–9, 14, 18
**pâté** /ˈpæteɪ; *US* pɑ:ˈteɪ/ 28/4
**path** /pɑ:θ; *US* pæθ/ 22/23, 83/5
**patient** /ˈpeɪʃnt/ 8/3
**patio** /ˈpætɪəʊ/ 22/11
**pattern** /ˈpætn/ 9
**patterned** /ˈpætnd/ 9/21
**pavement** /ˈpeɪvmənt/ 59/6
**paw** /pɔ:/ 89/24
**pawpaw** /ˈpɔ:pɔ:/ 24/14
**pay (verb)** /peɪ/ 35
**pay in (verb)** /ˌpeɪˈɪn/ 34/17
**paying-in slip** /peɪɪŋˈɪn slɪp/ 34/18
**PC** /ˌpi: ˈsi:/ 44/25
**pea** /pi:/ 28/24
**peach** /pi:tʃ/ 24/11
**peacock** /ˈpi:kɒk/ 93/24
**peak** /pi:k/ 73/2
**peanut** /ˈpi:nʌt/ 24/5
**pear** /peə(r)/ 24/16
**pearl** /pɜ:l/ 91/22
**pedal** /ˈpedl/ 65/9
**pedestrian** /pəˈdestrɪən/ 60/8
**pedestrian crossing** /pəˌdestrɪən ˈkrɒsɪŋ/ 59/24
**pelvis** /ˈpelvɪs/ 4/15
**pen** /pen/ 49/22
**pence** /pens/ 36/14–17
**pence piece** /ˌpens ˈpi:s/ 36/2–7
**pencil** /ˈpensl/ 49/20
**pencil-sharpener** /ˈpenslʃɑ:pnə(r)/ 49/25
**penguin** /ˈpeŋgwɪn/ 93/23
**penknife** /ˈpennaɪf/ 21/4
**Pennsylvania** /ˌpensɪlˈveɪnjə/ 55
**penny** /ˈpenɪ/ 35/2, 36/2
**pepper** /ˈpepə(r)/ 15/16
**per cent** /pəˈsent/ 48/17
**percussion** /pəˈkʌʃn/ 75
**perfume** /ˈpɜ:fju:m; *US also* pərˈfju:m/ 67/11
**perpendicular** /ˌpɜ:pənˈdɪkʊlə(r)/ 47/29
**personal computer** /ˌpɜ:sənl kəmˈpju:tə(r)/ 44/25
**personal stereo** /pɜ:sənl ˈsterɪəʊ/ 30/11
**Peru** /pəˈru:/ 53
**pestle** /ˈpesl; *US* ˈpestl/ 45/7
**pet** /pet/ 89
**petal** /ˈpetl/ 25/4
**Petri dish** (*US* **petri dish**) /ˈpetrɪ dɪʃ; *US* pi:trɪ dɪʃ/ 46/9
**petrol pump** /ˈpetrəl pʌmp/ 64/11
**pharmacist** /ˈfɑ:məsɪst/ 39/6
**pheasant** /ˈfeznt/ 93/7
**Philadelphia** /fɪləˈdelfɪə/ 55
**Philippines** /ˈfɪlɪpi:nz/ 54
**Phoenix** /ˈfi:nɪks/ 55
**phonecard** /ˈfəʊnkɑ:d/ 38/24
**photo album** /ˈfəʊtəʊ ælbəm/ 29/12
**photographer** /fəˈtɒgrəfə(r)/ 40/4
**physical** /ˈfɪzɪkl/ 5
**piano** /pɪˈænəʊ/ 76/3
**piccolo** /ˈpɪkələʊ/ 75/10
**pick up (verb)** /pɪk ˈʌp/ 41/6
**pick-up truck** /ˈpɪkʌp trʌk/ 63/7
**picnic** /ˈpɪknɪk/ 71/17
**picture** /ˈpɪktʃə(r)/ 49/17, 58/10
**pie** /paɪ/ 27/11
**piece** /pi:s/ 27/10, 12, 49/24, 86/17-19
**pier** /pɪə(r)/ 60/16
**pigeon** /ˈpɪdʒɪn/ 93/14
**pile** /paɪl/ 26/8
**pill** /pɪl/ 7/7
**pillar** /ˈpɪlə(r)/ 14/4
**pillar-box** /ˈpɪləbɒks/ 59/3
**pillow** /ˈpɪləʊ/ 18/12
**pillowcase** /ˈpɪləʊkeɪs/ 18/7
**pilot** /ˈpaɪlət/ 68/11
**pin** /pɪn/ 12/22, 74/16
**pincer** /ˈpɪnsə(r)/ 91/19
**pine cone** /ˈpaɪn kəʊn/ 25/22
**pine tree** /ˈpaɪn tri:/ 25/1
**pineapple** /ˈpaɪnæpl/ 24/8
**ping-pong** /ˈpɪŋpɒŋ/ 78/26
**pink** /pɪŋk/ 9/2
**pins** /pɪnz/ 79/10
**pint** /paɪnt/ 27/24
**pipette** /pɪˈpet/ 46/12
**pitch** /pɪtʃ/ 81/16
**pitcher** /ˈpɪtʃər/ 15/17
**Pittsburgh** /ˈpɪtsbɜ:rg/ 55
**plaice** /pleɪs/ 91/10
**plaid** /plæd/ 9/20
**plain** /pleɪn/ 9/16
**plait** /plæt/ 5/17
**plane** /pleɪn/ 21/8, 68/12
**planet** /ˈplænɪt/ 50
**plant** /plɑ:nt; *US* plænt/ 16/19, 58/11
**plaster cast** /ˌplɑ:stə ˈkɑ:st/ 7/13
**plate** /pleɪt/ 15/9, 58/13, 15, 17
**plateau** /ˈplætəʊ; *US* plætəʊ/ 73/18
**platform** /ˈplætfɔ:m/ 66/6
**platform number** /ˈplætfɔ:m nʌmbə(r)/ 66/18
**play (verb)** /pleɪ/ 42/21
**player** /ˈpleɪə(r)/ 78/17
**playing-card** /ˈpleɪɪŋkɑ:d/ 74/30
**pliers** /ˈplaɪəz/ 21/6
**plough** (*US* **plow**) /plaʊ/ 73/29
**plug** /plʌg/ 17/7, 19/12
**plum** /plʌm/ 24/20
**plumber** /ˈplʌmə(r)/ 40/10
**plunger** /ˈplʌndʒə(r)/ 45/15
**plus** /plʌs/ 48/11
**Pluto** /ˈplu:təʊ/ 50/15
**Plymouth** /ˈplɪməθ/ 56
**pm** (*US* P.M.) /pi:ˈem/ 37/16, 17, 18
**pneumatic drill** /nju:ˌmætɪk ˈdrɪl; *US* nu:ˌmætɪk ˈdrɪl/ 61/16
**pocket** /ˈpɒkɪt/ 11/18, 79/7
**pocketknife** /ˈpɒkɪtnaɪf/ 21/4
**point** /pɔɪnt/ 48/16
**Poland** /ˈpəʊlənd/ 54
**polar bear** /ˈpəʊlə beə(r)/ 90/6
**polaroid camera** /ˌpəʊlərɔɪd ˈkæmərə/ 29/23
**pole** /pəʊl/ 77/8
**police** /pəˈli:s/ 38
**police car** /pəˈli:s kɑ:(r)/ 38/2
**police officer** /pəˈli:s ɒfɪsə(r); *US* ɔ:fɪsər/ 38/3, 59/5
**police station** /pəˈli:s steɪʃn/ 38/1
**polka-dot** /ˈpɒlkədɒt; *US* ˈpəʊkədɒt/ 9/18

**pond** /pɒnd/ **73**/23
**pony** /'pəʊnɪ/ **89**/15
**pony tail** /'pəʊnɪ teɪl/ **5**/13
**pony-trekking** /'pəʊnɪtrekɪŋ/ **72**/16
**Poole** /pu:l/ **56**
**pop group** /'pɒp gru:p/ **76**/7
**porch** /pɔ:tʃ/ **14**/16
**port** /pɔ:t/ **69/70**
**porter** /'pɔ:tə(r)/ **71**/2
**portion** /'pɔ:ʃn/ **27**/10
**Portland** /'pɔ:rtlənd/ **55**
**Portsmouth** /'pɔ:tsməθ/ **56**
**Portugal** /'pɔ:tʃʊgl/ **54**
**post** /pəʊst/ **31**/10, **41**/6
**post office** /'pəʊst ɒfɪs; *US* ɔ:-/ **31**/1
**postal clerk** /'pəʊstl klɜ:rk/ **31**/4
**postal code** /'pəʊstl kəʊd/ **32**/13
**postal order** /'pəʊstl ɔ:də(r)/ **32**/22
**postal services** /'pəʊstl ˌsɜ:vɪsɪz/ **31/32**
**postbag** /'pəʊstbæg/ **31**/13
**postbox** /'pəʊstbɒks/ **31**/11
**postcard** /'pəʊstkɑ:d/ **32**/8
**postcode** /'pəʊstkəʊd/ **32**/13
**poster** /'pəʊstə(r)/ **18**/15
**postman** /'pəʊstmən/ **31**/8
**postmark** /'pəʊstmɑ:k/ **32**/12
**pot** /pɒt/ **20**/26, **27**/5, 19
**pot holder** /'pɒt həʊldər/ **20**/21
**potato** /pə'teɪtəʊ/ **23**/9
**potato chips** /pə'teɪtəʊ tʃɪps/ **26**/16, 19
**pottery** /'pɒtərɪ/ **74**/3
**pouch** /paʊtʃ/ **90**/9
**pound** /paʊnd/ **36**/17, 18
**pound coin** /ˌpaʊnd 'kɔɪn/ **36**/8
**pound note** /ˌpaʊnd 'nəʊt/ **36**/10–13
**pour (verb)** /pɔ:(r)/ **83**/11
**power saw** /'paʊə sɔ:/ **21**/9
**Powys** /'pəʊɪs/ **56**
**pram** /præm/ **60**/3
**praying mantis** /ˌpreɪɪŋ 'mæntɪs/ **92**/19
**preposition** /ˌprepə'zɪʃn/ **57/58**
**prescription** /prɪ'skrɪpʃn/ **7**/5
**present** /'preznt/ **85**/9, 10, 11
**Princeton** /'prɪnstən/ **55**
**print (verb)** /prɪnt/ **43**/11
**print** /prɪnt/ **9**/21, **29**/13, 14
**printer** /'prɪntə(r)/ **44**/19
**printout** /'prɪntaʊt/ **44**/18
**prism** /'prɪzm/ **45**/12
**promenade** /ˌprɒmə'nɑ:d; *US* 'neɪd/ **72**/5
**propeller** /prə'pelə(r); *US* prəʊ-/ **68**/15
**protractor** /prə'træktə(r); *US* prəʊ-/ **49**/7
**Providence** /'prɒvɪdəns/ **55**
**Puerto Rico** /ˌpwɜ:təʊ 'ri:kəʊ/ **53**
**pull (verb)** /pʊl/ **86**/22
**pump** /pʌmp/ **65**/3
**punch (verb)** /pʌntʃ/ **79**/22
**punnet** /'pʌnɪt/ **24**/2
**pupil** /'pju:pl/ **4**/30, **49**/2
**puppy** /'pʌpɪ/ **89**/23
**purple** /'pɜ:pl/ **9**/10
**purse** /pɜ:s/ **10**/10, **11**/22
**push (verb)** /pʊʃ/ **86**/21
**pushchair** /'pʊʃtʃeə(r)/ **60**/4
**put down (verb)** /ˌpʊt 'daʊn/ **86**/16
**pyjamas** (*US* **pajamas**) /pə'dʒɑ:məz; *US* pə'dʒæməz/ **11**/14
**pyramid** /'pɪrəmɪd/ **47**/23

**Qatar** /'kʌtɑ:(r)/ **54**
**quarter** /'kwɔ:tə(r)/ **35**/5, **37**/8, 11, **48**/19
**queen** /kwi:n/ **74**/32
**queue** /kju:/ **66**/12
**quiet** /'kwaɪət/ **88**/4

**rabbit** /'ræbɪt/ **89**/26
**race (verb)** /reɪs/ **80**/24
**race car** /'reɪs kɑ:r/ **80**/7
**race car driver** /reɪs kɑ:r draɪvər/ **12**/1, **80**/8
**racecourse** /'reɪskɔ:s/ **80**/28
**racehorse** /'reɪshɔ:s/ **80**/25
**racetrack** /'reɪstræk/ **80**/6, 28
**racing car** /'reɪsɪŋ kɑ:(r)/ **80**/7
**racing driver** /'reɪsɪŋ draɪvə(r)/ **12**/1, **80**/8
**rack** /ræk/ **45**/6
**racket** (*also* **racquet**) /'rækɪt/ **78**/23
**radiator** /'reɪdɪeɪtə(r)/ **15**/4
**radiator grille** /'reɪdɪeɪtə grɪl/ **64**/18
**radio** /'reɪdɪəʊ/ **30**/15
**radio cassette recorder** /reɪdɪəʊ kə'set rɪˌkɔ:də(r)/ **30**/8
**radish** /'rædɪʃ/ **23**/6
**radius** /'reɪdɪəs/ **47**/3
**railings** /'reɪlɪŋz/ **60**/9
**railroad** /'reɪlrəʊd/ **66**
**railway** /'reɪlweɪ/ **66**
**rain (verb)** /reɪn/ **51**/2
**rainbow** /'reɪnbəʊ/ **51**/12
**raincoat** /'reɪnkəʊt/ **10**/22
**rainy** /'reɪnɪ/ **51**/2
**rake** /reɪk/ **22**/7
**ranch house** /'ræntʃ haʊs/ **14**/19
**raspberry** /'rɑ:zbrɪ; *US* 'ræzberɪ/ **28**/10
**razor** /'reɪzə(r)/ **17**/23
**razor-blade** /'reɪzəbleɪd/ **17**/24
**read (verb)** /ri:d/ **42**/14, **85**/12
**Reading** /'redɪŋ/ **56**
**rear-light** /ˌrɪə'laɪt/ **64**/8
**receipt** /rɪ'si:t/ **29**/2, **35**/14
**receiver** /rɪ'si:və(r)/ **38**/23
**reception** /rɪ'sepʃn/ **71**/1
**receptionist** /rɪ'sepʃnɪst/ **71**/4
**record** /'rekɔ:d/ **30**/5
**recorder** /rɪ'kɔ:də(r)/ **75**/11
**rectangle** /'rektæŋgl/ **47**/11
**red** /red/ **5**/12, **9**/1
**Red Sea** /ˌred 'si:/ **54**/25
**reel** /ri:l/ **26**/1, **29**/11, **74**/11
**referee** /ˌrefə'ri:/ **79**/25
**reflector** /rɪ'flektə(r)/ **65**/14
**refrigerator** /rɪ'frɪdʒəreɪtər/ **20**/14
**region** /'ri:dʒən/ **56**
**registered post** /ˌredʒɪstəd 'pəʊst/ **32**/20
**reins** /reɪnz/ **80**/14
**remote control** /rɪˌməʊt kən'trəʊl/ **16**/9
**Reno** /'ri:nəʊ/ **55**
**reptile** /'reptaɪl/ **91**
**reservoir** /'rezəvwɑ:(r)/ **73**/13
**restaurant** /'restrɒnt; *US* 'restərənt/ **28**
**return address** /rɪ'tɜ:rn æˌdres/ **32**/19
**Réunion** /rɪ'ju:njən/ **54**
**rhinoceros** /raɪ'nɒsərəs/ **90**/21
**Rhode Island** /ˌrəʊd 'aɪlənd/ **55**
**rib** /rɪb/ **4**/13
**ribbon** /'rɪbən/ **58**/2, **74**/14
**Richmond** /'rɪtʃmənd/ **55**
**ride (verb)** /raɪd/ **80**/10
**rider** /'raɪdə(r)/ **80**/11
**riding** /'raɪdɪŋ/ **80**/9
**right angle** /'raɪt æŋgl/ **47**/15
**right lane** /'raɪt leɪn/ **62**/15
**ring** /rɪŋ/ **12**/24, **79**/19
**ring binder** /'rɪŋ baɪndə(r)/ **44**/16
**ring stand** /rɪŋ stænd/ **45**/20
**rink** /rɪŋk/ **77**/5
**Rio Grande** /ˌri:əʊ 'grænd/ **55**
**river** /'rɪvə(r)/ **60**/17
**roach** /rəʊtʃ/ **92**/16
**road** /rəʊd/ **61/62**, **62**/24
**road sign** /'rəʊd saɪn/ **59**/1, **61/62**
**road work** /'rəʊd wɜ:rk/ **61**/13
**roadworks** /'rəʊdwɜ:ks/ **61**/13
**roast** /'rəʊst/ **27**/7
**roast beef** /ˌrəʊst 'bi:f/ **28**/16
**roast chicken** /ˌrəʊst 'tʃɪkɪn/ **27**/9
**robe** /rəʊb/ **11**/13
**Rochester** /'rɒtʃɪstər/ **55**
**rock** /rɒk/ **70**/13, **73**/9
**rocket** /'rɒkɪt/ **50**/10
**Rocky Mountains** /ˌrɒkɪ 'maʊntnz/ **55**
**roll** /rəʊl/ **26**/1, 6, 15, **27**/4, **29**/11
**rolling-pin** /'rəʊlɪŋpɪn/ **20**/12
**Romania** /ru:'meɪnɪə/ **54**
**roof** /ru:f/ **13**/2, **14**/14, 23
**room key** /'ru:m ˌki:, 'rʊm/ **71**/5
**rooster** /'ru:stər/ **93**/4
**root** /ru:t/ **25**/3
**rope** /rəʊp/ **79**/20, **82**/12
**Roscommon** /rɒs'kɒmən/ **56**
**rose** /rəʊz/ **25**/17
**rotary** /'rəʊtərɪ/ **60**/26
**rotor** /'rəʊtə(r)/ **68**/11
**rough** /rʌf/ **88**/15
**round** /raʊnd/ **58**/2
**round bottom flask** /ˌraʊnd ˌbɒtəm 'flɑ:sk; *US* 'flæsk/ **45**/22
**roundabout** /'raʊndəbaʊt/ **60**/26
**row** /rəʊ/ **26**/7
**rowboat** /'rəʊbəʊt/ **69**/7
**rowing-boat** /'rəʊɪŋbəʊt/ **69**/7
**rubber** /'rʌbə(r)/ **49**/26
**rubber raft** /'rʌbər ræft/ **70**/14
**rubber tubing** /ˌrʌbə 'tju:bɪŋ; *US* ˌrʌbər 'tu:bɪŋ/ **45**/4
**rucksack** /'rʌksæk/ **66**/16, **71**/25
**rug** /rʌg/ **16**/6
**rugby** /'rʌgbɪ/ **78**/14
**ruler** /'ru:lə(r)/ **49**/21
**run (verb)** /rʌn/ **80**/21
**runner bean** /'rʌnə bi:n/ **28**/23
**runway** /'rʌnweɪ/ **68**/7
**Russia** /'rʌʃə/ **54**
**Russian Federation** /ˌrʌʃn fedə'reɪʃn/ **54**
**Rwanda** /rʊ'ændə/ **54**

**Sacramento** /ˌsækrə'mentəʊ/ **55**
**sad** /sæd/ **88**/2
**saddle** /'sædl/ **65**/2, **80**/12
**safari** /sə'fɑ:rɪ/ **72**/17
**sail** /seɪl/ **69**/3
**sailboard** /'seɪlbɔ:d/ **77**/20
**sailboat** /'seɪlbəʊt/ **69**/12
**sailing** /'seɪlɪŋ/ **72**/10
**sailing-ship** /'seɪlɪŋ ʃɪp/ **69**/1
**sailor** /'seɪlə(r)/ **39**/11

**Saint George's Channel** /snt ˌdʒɔ:dʒɪz 'tʃænl/ **56**
**salad** /'sæləd/ **28**/22
**salesperson** /'seɪlzpɜ:rsn/ **29**/6
**salmon** /'sæmən/ **91**/9
**saloon** /sə'lu:n/ **63**/12
**salt** /sɔ:lt/ **15**/15
**Salt Lake City** /ˌsɔ:lt ˌleɪk 'sɪtɪ/ **55**
**San Antonio** /ˌsæn æn'təʊnɪəʊ/ **55**
**San Diego** /ˌsæn dɪ'egəʊ/ **55**
**San Francisco** /ˌsæn fræn'sɪskəʊ/ **55**
**San Jose** /ˌsæn həʊ'zeɪ/ **55**
**sand** /sænd/ **73**/16
**sandal** /'sændl/ **12**/8
**sand-dune** /'sænddju:n; *US* du:n/ **73**/17
**sandpaper** /'sændpeɪpə(r)/ **21**/3
**sandwich** /'sænwɪdʒ; *US* -wɪtʃ/ **27**/3
**Santa Fe** /ˌsæntə'feɪ/ **55**
**sash window** /'sæʃ ˌwɪndəʊ/ **13**/8
**satellite** /'sætəlaɪt/ **50**/9
**Saturday** /'sætədɪ/ **33**
**Saturn** /'sætɜ:n/ **50**/18
**saucepan** /'sɔ:spən; *US* 'sɔ:spæn/ **20**/26
**saucer** /'sɔ:sə(r)/ **16**/13
**Saudi Arabia** /ˌsaʊdɪ ə'reɪbɪə/ **54**
**Savannah** /sə'vænə/ **55**
**saw** /sɔ:/ **21**/9, 12, 20
**saxophone** /'sæksəfəʊn/ **75**/16
**scale** /skeɪl/ **17**/14, **31**/2, **46**/23, **53–56**
**scales** /skeɪlz/ **17**/14, **31**/2, **46**/23, **91**/7
**scar** /skɑ:(r)/ **6**/21
**scarf** /skɑ:f/ **10**/14, **12**/6
**scenery** /'si:nərɪ/ **76**/14
**school bag** /'sku:l bæg/ **49**/8
**school uniform** /ˌsku:l 'ju:nɪfɔ:m/ **10**/1
**science laboratory** /'saɪəns ləˌbɒrətrɪ; *US* 'læbrətɔ:rɪ/ **45**/**46**
**scissors** /'sɪzəz/ **49**/12
**scooter** /'sku:tə(r)/ **65**/21
**score (verb)** /skɔ:(r)/ **81**/26
**scorpion** /'skɔ:pɪən/ **92**/23
**Scotch tape** /'skɒtʃ teɪp/ **26**/1
**Scotland** /'skɒtlənd/ **56**
**scourer** /'skaʊərə(r)/ **20**/6
**scouring pad** /'skaʊərɪŋ pæd/ **20**/6
**scratch** /skrætʃ/ **6**/17
**screen** /skri:n/ **44**/26, **76**/23
**screw** /skru:/ **21**/22
**screwdriver** /'skru:draɪvə(r)/ **21**/21
**scrub brush** /'skrʌb brʌʃ/ **19**/18
**scrubbing-brush** /'skrʌbɪŋbrʌʃ/ **19**/18
**scuba-diving** /'sku:bədaɪvɪŋ/ **77**/21
**sea** /si:/ **53, 73**/8
**Sea of Japan** /ˌsi: əv dʒə'pæn/ **54**/36
**Sea of Okhotsk** /ˌsi: əv əʊ'kɒtsk/ **54**/37
**sea wall** /ˌsi:'wɔ:l/ **72**/4
**seafront** /'si:frʌnt/ **72**/5
**(sea)gull** /'si:gʌl/ **93**/30
**seal** /si:l/ **90**/27
**seaside** /'si:saɪd/ **72**/1
**season** /'si:zn/ **52**
**seat** /si:t/ **57**/3, **65**/2, 23, **67**/13
**Seattle** /sɪ'ætl/ **55**
**second** /'sekənd/ **33**
**second floor** /ˌsekənd 'flɔ:r/ **13**/13
**second-class post** /ˌsekəndklɑ:s 'pəʊst/ **32**/15
**second-hand** /'sekəndhænd/ **37**/5
**secretary** /'sekrətrɪ; *US* 'sekrəterɪ/ **44**/20
**sector** /'sektə(r)/ **47**/6
**security** /sɪ'kjʊərətɪ/ **67**/7
**sedan** /sɪ'dæn/ **63**/12
**Sellotape** /'seləteɪp/ **26**/1
**semi-detached house** /ˌsemɪdɪˌtætʃt 'haʊs/ **14**/6
**send (verb)** /send/ **43**/10
**sender** /'sendə(r)/ **32**/18
**Senegal** /ˌsenɪ'gɔ:l/ **54**
**September** /sep'tembə(r)/ **52**
**serve (verb)** /sɜ:v/ **81**/2
**server** /'sɜ:və(r)/ **81**/3
**service area** /'sɜ:rvɪs eərɪə/ **61**/11
**service line** /'sɜ:vɪs laɪn/ **81**/5
**service station** /'sɜ:vɪs steɪʃn/ **61**/11
**set** /set/ **26**/5
**set square** /'set skweə(r)/ **49**/6
**seven** /'sevn/ **33**/7
**seventeen** /ˌsevn'ti:n/ **33**/17
**seventh** /'sevnθ/ **33**
**seventy** /'sevntɪ/ **33**/70
**sew (verb)** /səʊ/ **83**/4
**sewing** /'səʊɪŋ/ **74**/9
**sewing-machine** /'səʊɪŋməˌʃi:n/ **74**/10
**shade** /ʃeɪd/ **17**/19
**shake (verb)** /ʃeɪk/ **85**/1
**shaker** /'ʃeɪkə(r)/ **74**/27
**shallow** /'ʃæləʊ/ **87**/20
**shampoo** /ʃæm'pu:/ **17**/26
**shape** /ʃeɪp/ **47**
**shark** /ʃɑ:k/ **91**/1
**shaving cream** /'ʃeɪvɪŋ kri:m/ **17**/25
**shaving-foam** /'ʃeɪviŋfəʊm/ **17**/25
**shears** /ʃɪəʒ/ **22**/8
**sheep** /ʃi:p/ **89**/9
**sheet** /ʃi:t/ **18**/6, **31**/18
**sheet music** /'ʃi:t mju:zɪk/ **76**/6
**Sheffield** /'ʃefi:ld/ **56**
**shelf** /ʃelf/ **20**/23
**shell** /ʃel/ **91**/26
**Shetland Islands** /'ʃetlənd ˌaɪləndz/ **56**
**ship** /ʃɪp/ **70**/5
**shirt** /ʃɜ:t/ **10**/19
**shock absorber** /'ʃɒk əbˌzɔ:bə(r)/ **65**/29
**shoe** /ʃu:/ **10**/23
**shoelace** /'ʃu:leɪs/ **11**/23
**shoot (verb)** /ʃu:t/ **78**/10
**shop** /ʃɒp/ **59**/12
**shop assistant** /'ʃɒp əˌsɪstənt/ **29**/6
**short** /ʃɔ:t/ **5**/8, 9, 10, 11, 19
**shorts** /ʃɔ:ts/ **12**/12
**shoulder** /'ʃəʊldə(r)/ **3**/6, **62**/14, 23
**shower** /'ʃaʊə(r)/ **17**/20, **41**/7
**shrimp** /ʃrɪmp/ **91**/17
**Shropshire** /'ʃrɒpʃə(r)/ **56**
**shutter** /'ʃʌtə(r)/ **14**/5
**shuttlecock** /'ʃʌtlkɒk/ **78**/25
**side** /saɪd/ **47**/10, **48**/9
**side mirror** /'saɪd mɪrər/ **64**/2
**side street** /'saɪd stri:t/ **60**/5
**sideboard** /'saɪdbɔ:d/ **15**/18
**sideline** /'saɪdlaɪn/ **81**/6
**sidewalk** /'saɪdwɔ:k/ **59**/6
**Sierra Leone** /sɪˌerə lɪ'əʊn/ **54**
**Sierra Nevada** /sɪˌerə nə'vɑ:də/ **55**
**sieve** /sɪv/ **20**/2
**sightseeing** /'saɪtsi:ɪŋ/ **71**/9
**sign (verb)** /saɪn/ **43**/6
**sign** /saɪn/ **57**/9, 10
**signal tower** /'sɪgnəl taʊər/ **66**/1
**signal-box** /'sɪgnəl bɒks/ **66**/1
**signature** /'sɪgnətʃə(r)/ **43**/7
**signpost** /'saɪnpəʊst/ **60**/23
**sing (verb)** /sɪŋ/ **85**/6
**Singapore** /ˌsɪŋə'pɔ:(r)/ **54**
**singer** /'sɪŋə(r)/ **76**/9
**single lens reflex camera** /ˌsɪŋgl lenz 'ri:fleks ˌkæmərə/ **29**/16
**single room** /ˌsiŋgl 'ru:m, 'rʊm/ **71**/6
**singles match** /'sɪŋglz mætʃ/ **81**/1
**sink** /sɪŋk/ **17**/6, **19**/2
**Sioux Falls** /ˌsu: 'fɔ:lz/ **55**
**sister** /'sɪstə(r)/ **1**/11
**sister-in-law** /'sɪstər ɪn lɔ:/ **1**/13
**sit (verb)** /sɪt/ **84**/21
**six** /sɪks/ **33**/6
**sixteen** /ˌsɪks'ti:n/ **33**/16
**sixth** /sɪksθ/ **33**
**sixty** /'sɪkstɪ/ **33**/60
**skate (verb)** /skeɪt/ **77**/2
**skater** /'skeɪtə(r)/ **77**/3
**skeleton** /'skelɪtn/ **4**/10
**ski (verb)** /ski:/ **77**/7
**ski** /ski:/ **77**/9
**skiing** /'ski:ɪŋ/ **77**/6
**skip (verb)** /skɪp/ **82**/27
**skipping-rope** /'skɪpɪŋrəʊp/ **82**/26
**skirt** /skɜ:t/ **10**/11
**skull** /skʌl/ **4**/11
**sky** /skaɪ/ **60**/13
**skyline** /'skaɪlaɪn/ **60**/14
**skyscraper** /'skaɪskreɪpər/ **60**/12
**slate** /sleɪt/ **13**/2, 20
**sleep (verb)** /sli:p/ **84**/24
**sleeping-bag** /'sli:pɪŋ bæg/ **71**/21
**sleeve** /sli:v/ **11**/16
**slice** /slaɪs/ **27**/8
**slide** /slaɪd/ **29**/9, **46**/20
**slide projector** /'slaɪd prəˌdʒektə(r)/ **29**/8
**Sligo** /'slaɪgəʊ/ **56**
**sling** /slɪŋ/ **7**/11
**slip-road** /'slɪprəʊd/ **62**/2
**slipper** /'slɪpə(r)/ **11**/12
**slot** /slɒt/ **38**/25
**Slovakia** /sləʊ'vækɪə/ **54**
**Slovenia** /sləʊ'vi:nɪə/ **54**
**slow** /sləʊ/ **87**/24
**slow lane** /'sləʊ leɪn/ **62**/5, 15
**SLR camera** /ˌes el 'ɑ: ˌkæmərə/ **29**/16
**slug** /slʌg/ **92**/21
**small** /smɔ:l/ **87**/4
**smile (verb)** /smaɪl/ **84**/17
**smoke** /sməʊk/ **38**/7
**smoked salmon** /ˌsməʊkt 'sæmən/ **28**/3
**smokestack** /'sməʊkstæk/ **70**/10
**smooth** /smu:ð/ **88**/16
**snail** /sneɪl/ **92**/22
**snake** /sneɪk/ **91**/27
**sneaker** /sni:kər/ **12**/4
**snooker** /'snu:kə(r)/ **79**/4
**snorkel** /'snɔ:kl/ **77**/24
**snorkelling** (*US* **snorkeling**) /'snɔ:klɪŋ/ **77**/23
**snout** /snaʊt/ **91**/5
**snow (verb)** /snəʊ/ **51**/3
**snow** /snəʊ/ **51**/4
**snowy** /'snəʊɪ/ **51**/3
**soap** /səʊp/ **17**/8
**soccer** /'sɒkər/ **81**

**sock** /sɒk/ **11**/4
**socket** /ˈsɒkɪt/ **19**/21
**Socotra** /səˈkəʊtrə/ **54**
**soda** /ˈsəʊdə/ **27**/26
**sofa** /ˈsəʊfə/ **16**/17
**soft** /sɒft/ **88**/18
**soil** /sɔɪl/ **61**/19, **83**/7
**solar system** /ˈsəʊlə sɪstəm/ **50**
**soldier** /ˈsəʊldʒə(r)/ **39**/12
**solid** /ˈsɒlɪd/ **9**/16, **88**/22
**solid figure** /sɒlɪd ˈfɪgə(r); *US* ˈfɪgjər/ **47**/20
**Solomon Islands** /ˈsɒləmən ˌaɪləndz/ **54**
**Somalia** /səˈmɑːlɪə/ **54**
**Somerset** /ˈsʌməset/ **56**
**son** /sʌn/ **1**/16
**sore** /sɔː(r)/ **6**/8
**sound system** /ˈsaʊnd ˌsɪstəm/ **30**/13
**soup** /suːp/ **28**/5
**south** /saʊθ/ **56**
**South Africa** /ˌsaʊθ ˈæfrɪkə/ **54**
**South America** /ˌsaʊθ əˈmerɪkə/ **53**/2
**South Atlantic** /ˌsaʊθ ətˈlæntɪk/ **53**/10
**South Carolina** /ˌsaʊθ kærəˈlaɪnə/ **55**
**South China Sea** /ˌsaʊθ ˌtʃaɪnə ˈsiː/ **54**/33
**South Dakota** /ˌsaʊθ dəˈkəʊtə/ **55**
**South Georgia** /ˌsaʊθ ˈdʒɔːrdʒə/ **53**
**South Glamorgan** /ˌsaʊθ gləˈmɔːgən/ **56**
**South Korea** /ˌsaʊθ kəˈrɪə/ **54**
**South Pacific** /ˌsaʊθ pəˈsɪfɪk/ **53**/13
**South Yorkshire** /ˌsaʊθ ˈjɔːkʃə(r)/ **56**
**Southampton** /saʊθˈæmptən/ **56**
**space** /speɪs/ **50**
**space shuttle** /ˈspeɪs ʃʌtl/ **50**/11
**spacesuit** /ˈspeɪssuːt/ **50**/7
**spade** /speɪd/ **22**/19, **74**/34
**Spain** /speɪn/ **54**
**spanner** /ˈspænə(r)/ **21**/27
**sparrow** /ˈspærəʊ/ **93**/15
**spatula** /ˈspætʃʊlə/ **46**/10
**speak (verb)** /spiːk/ **85**/5
**speaker** /ˈspiːkə(r)/ **30**/10
**Special Delivery** /speʃl dɪˈlɪvərɪ/ **32**/24
**spectator** /spekˈteɪtə(r); *US* ˈspek-/ **80**/18
**speed limit** /ˈspiːd lɪmɪt/ **61**/6
**speedometer** /spiːˈdɒmɪtə(r)/ **64**/24
**spider** /ˈspaɪdə(r)/ **92**/11
**spine** /spaɪn/ **4**/14
**spiral** /ˈspaɪərəl/ **47**/28
**spirit-level** /ˈspɪrɪtlevl/ **21**/7
**spoke** /spəʊk/ **65**/7
**sponge** /spʌndʒ/ **17**/12
**spool** /spuːl/ **74**/11
**spoon** /spuːn/ **15**/11
**sport** /spɔːt/ **77–81**
**sports car** /ˈspɔːts kɑː(r)/ **63**/11
**sports centre** /ˈspɔːts sentə(r)/ **42**/19
**sprain (verb)** /spreɪn/ **6**/14
**spring** /sprɪŋ/ **52**/9
**spring balance** /ˌsprɪŋ ˈbæləns/ **46**/24
**square** /skweə(r)/ **47**/9
**squash** /skwɒʃ/ **42**/21, **78**/22
**squid** /skwɪd/ **91**/14
**squirrel** /ˈskwɪrəl/ **89**/6
**Sri Lanka** /ˌʃriː ˈlæŋkə/ **54**
**St Lawrence** /seɪnt ˈlɒrəns/ **55**
**St Louis** /seɪnt ˈluːɪs/ **55**
**St Paul** /seɪnt ˈpɔːl/ **55**
**stack** /stæk/ **24**/22
**Staffordshire** /ˈstæfədʃə(r)/ **56**
**stage** /steɪdʒ/ **46**/19, **76**/15
**stair** /steə(r)/ **18**/22
**staircase** /ˈsteəkeɪs/ **18**/25
**stall** /stɔːl/ **23**/1
**stalls** /stɔːlz/ **76**/20
**stamp** /stæmp/ **31**/19
**stamp album** /ˈstæmp ælbəm/ **74**/5
**stamp collecting** /ˈstæmp kəˌlektɪŋ/ **74**/4
**stamp machine** /ˈstæmp məˌʃiːn/ **31**/17
**stand (verb)** /stænd/ **84**/22
**stand** /stænd/ **23**/1, **81**/24
**staple (verb)** /ˈsteɪpl/ **43**/4
**stapler** /ˈsteɪplə(r)/ **44**/12
**star** /stɑː(r)/ **50**/26
**starfish** /ˈstɑːfɪʃ/ **91**/20
**start (verb)** /stɑːt/ **42**/15
**starter** /ˈstɑːtə(r)/ **28**
**starting-block** /ˈstɑːtɪŋ blɒk/ **80**/22
**starting-gate** /ˈstɑːtɪŋ geɪt/ **80**/27
**state line** /ˌsteɪt ˈlaɪn/ **55**
**station** /ˈsteɪʃn/ **66**
**station wagon** /ˈsteɪʃn ˌwægən/ **63**/14
**stationery** /ˈsteɪʃənrɪ; *US*–nerɪ/ **26**
**steak** /steɪk/ **28**/18
**steering-wheel** /ˈstɪərɪŋ wiːl; *US also* hwiːl/ **64**/22
**stem** /stem/ **25**/19
**step** /step/ **18**/22, **57**/11, 13
**stereo** /ˈsterɪəʊ/ **30**/13
**stereo system** /ˈsterɪəʊ ˌsɪstəm/ **30**/13
**stern** /stɜːn/ **69**/17
**stethoscope** /ˈsteθəskəʊp/ **7**/20
**steward** /ˈstjʊəd/ **67**/13
**stick** /stɪk/ **78**/18
**(sticking-)plaster** /ˈstɪkɪŋplɑːstə(r)/ **7**/3
**sting** /stɪŋ/ **92**/24
**stir (verb)** /stɜː(r)/ **83**/12
**stirrup** /ˈstɪrəp/ **80**/13
**stockings** /ˈstɒkɪŋz/ **11**/6
**Stoke-on-Trent** /ˌstəʊk ɒn ˈtrent/ **56**
**stomach** /ˈstʌmək/ **3**/25, **4**/8
**stomach-ache** /ˈstʌməkeɪk/ **6**/5
**stone** /stəʊn/ **13**/17
**stone wall** /ˌstəʊn ˈwɔːl/ **14**/18
**stool** /stuːl/ **45**/19
**stop** /stɒp/ **61**/2
**stop clock** /ˈstɒp klɒk/ **46**/16
**stopper** /ˈstɒpə(r)/ **17**/7, **46**/4
**store** /stɔːr/ **29, 59**/12
**stormy** /ˈstɔːmɪ/ **51**/9
**Strabane** /strəˈbæn/ **56**
**straight** /streɪt/ **5**/8, 9, **47**/26, **87**/1
**strainer** /ˈstreɪnər/ **20**/2
**Strait of Dover** /ˌstreɪt əv ˈdəʊvə(r)/ **56**
**strap** /stræp/ **29**/22
**Stratford-upon-Avon** /ˌstrætfəd əpɒn ˈeɪvən/ **56**
**Strathclyde** /ˌstræθˈklaɪd/ **56**
**strawberry** /ˈstrɔːbrɪ; *US* ˈstrɔːberɪ/ **24**/2
**stream** /striːm/ **73**/7
**street** /striːt/ **59**/10
**street corner** /ˌstriːt ˈkɔːnə(r)/ **59**/11
**street sign** /ˈstriːt saɪn/ **60**/10
**stretch (verb)** /stretʃ/ **82**/19
**stretcher** /ˈstretʃə(r)/ **38**/16
**string** /strɪŋ/ **26**/2
**string bean** /ˌstrɪŋ ˈbiːn/ **28**/23
**strings** /strɪŋz/ **75**
**striped** /straɪpt/ **9**/17
**stroller** /ˈstrəʊlər/ **60**/4
**strong** /strɒŋ/ **87**/22
**student** /ˈstuːdnt/ **49**/2
**stuffed olives** /ˌstʌft ˈɒlɪvz/ **27**/23
**stumps** /stʌmps/ **81**/19
**suburbs** /sʌˈbɜːbz/ **60**
**subway** /sʌbweɪ/ **66**
**Sudan** /suːˈdɑːn; *US* suːˈdæn/ **54**
**Suffolk** /ˈsʌfək/ **56**
**suit** /suːt/ **10**/18
**suitcase** /ˈsuːtkeɪs/ **66**/14, **86**/13–16
**summer** /ˈsʌmə(r)/ **52**/10
**Sun** /sʌn/ **50**/14
**sun-glasses** /ˈsʌnglɑːsɪz; *US* -glæsɪz/ **12**/18
**sunbather** /ˈsʌnbeɪðə(r)/ **72**/8
**sunbed** /ˈsʌnbed/ **72**/7
**sunburn** /ˈsʌnbɜːn/ **6**/16
**Sunday** /ˈsʌndɪ/ **33**
**sunny** /ˈsʌnɪ/ **51**/1
**sunshade** /ˈsʌnʃeɪd/ **72**/9
**surf (verb)** /sɜːf/ **77**/15
**surfboard** /ˈsɜːfbɔːd/ **77**/17
**surfer** /ˈsɜːfə(r)/ **77**/16
**surfing** /ˈsɜːfɪŋ/ **77**/13
**surgeon** /ˈsɜːdʒən/ **7**/18
**Surinam** /ˌsʊərɪˈnæm/ **53**
**Surrey** /ˈsʌrɪ/ **56**
**swallow** /ˈswɒləʊ/ **93**/21
**swan** /swɒn/ **93**/31
**Swansea** /ˈswɒnzɪ/ **56**
**Swaziland** /ˈswɑːzɪlænd/ **54**
**sweater** /ˈswetə(r)/ **10**/6
**sweatshirt** /ˈswetʃɜːt/ **12**/14
**Sweden** /ˈswiːdn/ **54**
**sweep (verb)** /swiːp/ **83**/5
**sweet corn** /ˈswiːt kɔːn/ **28**/20
**sweets** /swiːts/ **26**/10, 14, 15, 18
**swim (verb)** /swɪm/ **77**/26
**swimmer** /ˈswɪmə(r)/ **77**/27
**swimming** /ˈswɪmɪŋ/ **77**/25
**swimming-pool** /ˈswɪmɪŋ puːl/ **77**/28
**swimming-trunks** /ˈswɪmɪŋ trʌŋks/ **11**/1
**swimsuit** /ˈswɪmsuːt/ **11**/2
**swing (verb)** /swɪŋ/ **82**/11
**swing** /swɪŋ/ **22**/2
**Switzerland** /ˈswɪtsəlænd/ **54**
**synthesizer** /ˈsɪnθəsaɪzə(r)/ **76**/13
**Syracuse** /ˈsɪrəkjuːs/ **55**
**Syria** /ˈsɪrɪə/ **54**
**syringe** /sɪrɪndʒ/ **45**/16

**T-shirt** /ˈtiːʃɜːt/ **10**/5
**table** /ˈteɪbl/ **57**/8, **58**/4, 5, 6, **79**/6
**table tennis** /ˈteɪbl tenɪs/ **78**/26
**table-cloth** /ˈteɪblklɒθ/ **15**/8
**tablet** /ˈtæblɪt/ **7**/7
**tackle (verb)** /ˈtækl/ **78**/15
**tail** /teɪl/ **68**/18, **89**/17, **91**/2
**taillight** /ˈteɪllaɪt/ **64**/8
**Taiwan** /taɪˈwɑːn/ **54**
**Tajikistan** /tæˈdʒiːkɪstɑːn/ **54**
**take (verb)** /teɪk/ **41**/7, **85**/10
**take-off** /ˈteɪkɒf/ **68**/6
**talc** /tælk/ **17**/28
**talcum powder** /ˈtælkəm paʊdə(r)/ **17**/28
**talk (verb)** /tɔːk/ **85**/5
**tall** /tɔːl/ **5**/18
**tambourine** /ˌtæmbəˈriːn/ **75**/18

**Tampa** /'tæmpə/ **55**
**tank top** /'tæŋk tɒp/ **12**/10
**tanker** /'tæŋkə(r)/ **63**/3
**Tanzania** /ˌtænzə'nɪə/ **54**
**tape** /teɪp/ **32**/2
**tape deck** /'teɪp dek/ **30**/18
**tape-measure** /'teɪpˌmeʒə(r)/ **74**/13
**tartan** /'tɑ:tn/ **9**/20
**Tasman Sea** /ˌtæzmən 'si:/ **54**/31
**taxi** /'tæksɪ/ **60**/6
**Tayside** /'teɪsaɪd/ **56**
**tea** /ti:/ **83**/12
**tea towel** /'ti: taʊəl/ **20**/7
**teacher** /'ti:tʃə(r)/ **49**/16
**teapot** /'ti:pɒt/ **16**/11, **58**/16, 17, **83**/11
**tear (verb)** /teə(r)/ **86**/18
**teaspoon** /'ti:spu:n/ **16**/15
**teenage** /'ti:neɪdʒ/ **5**/3
**teenager** /'ti:neɪdʒə(r)/ **5**/3
**(tele)phone booth** /'telɪfəʊn bu:θ/ **38**/22
**(tele)phone box** /'telɪfəʊn bɒks/ **38**/22
**(tele)phone number** /'telɪfəʊn nʌmbə(r)/ **38**/21
**telescope** /'telɪskəʊp/ **29**/5
**television** /'telɪvɪʒn/ **16**/23, **42**/23, **58**/18
**teller** /'telər/ **34**/9
**temperature** /'temprətʃə(r); *US* 'tempərtʃʊər/ **6**/10, **52**
**ten** /ten/ **33**/10
**Tennessee** /ˌtenə'si:/ **55**
**tennis** /'tenɪs/ **81**
**tennis-court** /'tenɪsˌkɔ:t/ **81**/10
**tent** /tent/ **71**/19
**tentacle** /'tentəkl/ **91**/13
**tenth** /tenθ/ **33**
**terminal** /'tɜ:mɪnl/ **67**
**terraced house** /'terəst ˌhaʊs/ **13**/1
**test-tube** /'test tju:b; *US* 'test tu:b/ **45**/2
**Texas** /'teksəs/ **55**
**textbook** /'tekstbʊk/ **49**/3
**Thailand** /'taɪlænd/ **54**
**thatch** /θætʃ/ **13**/21
**thatched roof** /ˌθætʃt 'ru:f/ **14**/14
**The Gulf** /ðə 'gʌlf/ **54**/28
**theatre (*US* theater)** /'θɪətə(r)/ **76**
**thermometer** /θə'mɒmɪtə(r)/ **45**/21
**thick** /θɪk/ **87**/13
**thimble** /'θɪmbl/ **74**/17
**thin** /θɪn/ **5**/20, **87**/14
**third** /θɜ:d/ **33**, **48**/20
**thirsty** /'θɜ:stɪ/ **6**/1
**thirteen** /ˌθɜ:'ti:n/ **33**/13
**thirteenth** /ˌθɜ:'ti:nθ/ **33**
**thirtieth** /'θɜ:tɪəθ/ **33**
**thirty** /'θɜ:tɪ/ **33**/30
**thirty-first** /ˌθɜ:tɪ'fɜ:st/ **33**
**thousand** /'θaʊzənd/ **33**/1000
**thread** /θred/ **74**/11, 20
**three** /θri:/ **33**/3
**three quarters** /ˌθi: 'kwɔ:təz/ **48**/22
**throat** /θrəʊt/ **3**/27, **6**/8
**throttle** /'θrɒtl/ **65**/26
**through** /θru:/ **57**/3
**throw (verb)** /θrəʊ/ **57**/4, 5, **78**/13, **82**/9
**thumb** /θʌm/ **3**/21
**thunderstorm** /'θʌndəstɔ:m/ **51**/10
**Thursday** /'θɜ:zdɪ/ **33**
**ticket counter** /'tɪkɪt kaʊntər/ **66**/10
**ticket office** /'tɪkɪt ɒfɪs/ **66**/10
**ticket taker** /'tɪkɪt teɪkər/ **66**/19
**ticket-collector** /ˌtɪkɪtkə'lektə(r)/ **66**/19
**tidy** /'taɪdɪ/ **88**/7
**tie** /taɪ/ **10**/20
**tie up (verb)** /ˌtaɪ 'ʌp/ **83**/6
**tiger** /'taɪgə(r)/ **90**/17
**tight** /taɪt/ **88**/23
**tights** /taɪts/ **11**/7
**tile** /taɪl/ **13**/19, **17**/2
**(tiled) floor** /ˌtaɪld 'flɔ:(r)/ **49**/9
**tiled roof** /ˌtaɪld 'ru:f/ **14**/23
**time** /taɪm/ **37**
**timer** /'taɪmər/ **46**/16
**times** /taɪmz/ **48**/13
**timetable** /'taɪmteɪbl/ **66**/15
**tin** /tɪn/ **27**/6
**tin-opener** /'tɪn əʊpənə(r)/ **20**/10
**Tipp-Ex** /'tɪpeks/ **44**/9
**Tipperary** /ˌtɪpə'reərɪ/ **56**
**tired** /'taɪəd/ **6**/3
**tissues** /'tɪʃu:z/ **18**/9
**to** /tu:, tʊ/ **37**/10, 11, 12, **57**/6
**toast** /təʊst/ **28**/4
**toaster** /'təʊstə(r)/ **20**/17
**toe** /təʊ/ **3**/14
**Togo** /'təʊgəʊ/ **54**
**toilet** /'tɔɪlɪt/ **17**/17
**toilet paper** /'tɔɪlɪt ˌpeɪpə(r)/ **17**/18
**Toledo** /tə'li:dəʊ/ **55**
**tomato** /tə'mɑ:təʊ; *US* te'meɪtəʊ/ **23**/19
**tongs** /tɒŋz/ **45**/13
**tongue** /tʌŋ/ **4**/22
**tool** /tu:l/ **21**
**tool-box** /'tu:lbɒks/ **21**/1
**tooth** /tu:θ/ **8**/8
**toothache** /'tu:θeɪk/ **6**/4
**toothbrush** /'tu:θbrʌʃ/ **17**/4
**toothpaste** /'tu:θpeɪst/ **17**/3
**top box** /'tɒp bɒks/ **65**/24
**top case** /'tɒp keɪs/ **65**/24
**top floor** /ˌtɒp 'flɔ:(r)/ **13**/11
**Topeka** /tə'pi:kə/ **55**
**torch** /tɔ:tʃ/ **19**/17
**tortoise** /'tɔ:təs/ **91**/25
**total** /'təʊtl/ **35**/15
**tour guide** /'tʊə gaɪd; *Brit also* 'tɔ:/ **71**/10
**tourist** /'tʊərɪst; *Brit also* 'tɔ:rɪst/ **71**/12
**toward** /tɔ:rd/ **57**/10
**towards** /tə'wɔ:dz/ **57**/10
**towel rack** /'taʊəl ræk/ **17**/9
**towel-rail** /'taʊəlreɪl/ **17**/9
**tower block** /'taʊə blɒk/ **60**/12
**town** /taʊn/ **55**/**56**
**town house** /'taʊn haʊs/ **13**/1
**trachea** /trə'kɪə; *US* 'treɪkɪə/ **4**/2
**track** /træk/ **80**/17, **66**/7
**track and field** /træk ənd fi:ld/ **80**/15
**track number** /'træk ˌnʌmbər/ **66**/18
**track suit** /'træk su:t/ **12**/3
**tractor** /'træktə(r)/ **73**/28
**traffic** /'træfɪk/ **59**/13
**traffic circle** /'træfɪk sɜ:rkl/ **60**/26
**traffic-lights** /'træfɪklaɪts/ **60**/19
**trailer** /'treɪlə(r)/ **63**/9, **68**/3, **71**/27
**trailer camp** /'treɪlər kæmp/ **71**/26
**train** /treɪn/ **42**/13, **66**/8
**trainer** /'treɪnə(r)/ **12**/4
**tramline** /'træmlaɪn/ **81**/6
**trampoline** /'træmpəli:n/ **82**/6
**trampolining** /ˌtræmpə'li:nɪŋ/ **82**/4
**transporter** /træn'spɔ:tə(r)/ **63**/1
**trash can** /'træʃ kæn/ **57**/4, **59**/14
**travel agent** /'trævl eɪdʒənt/ **40**/3
**traveller's cheque (*US* traveler's check)** /'trævləz tʃek/ **34**/10, 11
**tray** /treɪ/ **16**/12
**tree** /tri:/ **22**/4, **25**/1, **57**/3
**triangle** /'traɪæŋgl/ **47**/13, **49**/6
**tricycle** /'traɪsɪkl/ **65**/17
**Trinidad and Tobago** /ˌtrɪnɪdæd ənd tə'beɪgəʊ/ **53**
**triple-pack** /'trɪplpæk/ **26**/13
**tripod** /'traɪpɒd/ **29**/4, **45**/26
**trolley** /'trɒlɪ/ **28**/6, **46**/15, **67**/18, **86**/21
**trombone** /trɒm'bəʊn/ **75**/8
**tropic of Cancer** /ˌtrɒpɪk əv 'kænsə(r)/ **53**/**54**
**tropic of Capricorn** /ˌtrɒpɪk əv 'kæprɪkɔ:n/ **53**/**54**
**trousers** /'traʊzəz/ **10**/4
**trout** /traʊt/ **28**/17, **91**/8
**trowel** /'traʊəl/ **22**/12
**truck** /trʌk/ **63**/4
**truck driver** /'trʌk draɪvər/ **40**/2
**trumpet** /'trʌmpɪt/ **75**/7
**trunk** /trʌŋk/ **25**/2, **64**/9, **90**/26
**tub** /tʌb/ **27**/20
**tuba** /'tju:bə; *US* 'tu:bə/ **75**/9
**tube** /tju:b; *US* tu:b/ **17**/3
**Tucson** /'tu:sɒn/ **55**
**Tuesday** /'tju:zdɪ/ **33**
**tulip** /'tju:lɪp; *US* 'tu:lɪp/ **25**/25
**Tulsa** /'tʌlsə/ **55**
**tuna** /'tju:nə; *US* 'tu:nə/ **27**/6, 18
**Tunisia** /tju:'nɪzɪə; *US* tu:'nɪʒə/ **54**
**tunnel** /'tʌnl/ **66**/9
**Turkey** /'tɜ:kɪ/ **54**
**turkey** /'tɜ:kɪ/ **93**/6
**Turkmenistan** /tɜ:k'mi:nɪstɑ:n/ **54**
**turn right** /ˌtɜ:n 'raɪt/ **61**/12
**turn signal** /'tɜ:rn ˌsɪgnəl/ **64**/3
**turnip** /'tɜ:nɪp/ **23**/18
**turntable** /'tɜ:nteɪbl/ **30**/14
**turquoise** /'tɜ:kwɔɪz/ **9**/8
**turtle** /'tɜ:tl/ **91**/24
**tusk** /tʌsk/ **90**/25
**TV** /ˌti: 'vi:/ **16**/23, **42**/23
**TV aerial** /ˌti: 'vi: eərɪəl/ **14**/20
**twelfth** /twelfθ/ **33**
**twelve** /twelv/ **33**/12
**twentieth** /'twentɪəθ/ **33**
**twenty** /'twentɪ/ **33**/20
**twenty-first** /ˌtwentɪ'fɜ:st/ **33**
**twenty-one** /ˌtwentɪ'wʌn/ **33**/21
**twenty-second** /ˌtwentɪ'sekənd/ **33**
**twenty-third** /ˌtwentɪ'θɜ:d/ **33**
**twin beds** /ˌtwɪn 'bedz/ **71**/8
**Twin Falls** /ˌtwɪn 'fɔ:lz/ **55**
**twin room** /ˌtwɪn 'ru:m, 'rʊm/ **71**/8
**twin-pack** /'twɪnˌpæk/ **26**/12
**two** /tu:/ **33**/2
**two-family house** /'tu:ˌfæməlɪ ˌhaʊs/ **14**/6
**two-way traffic** /ˌtu:weɪ 'træfɪk/ **61**/4
**Tyne and Wear** /ˌtaɪn ənd 'wɪə(r)/ **56**
**type (verb)** /taɪp/ **43**/3
**typewriter** /'taɪpraɪtə(r)/ **44**/27
**tyre (*US* tire)** /'taɪə(r)/ **65**/27

**U-tube** /'ju:tju:b; *US* 'ju:tu:b/ **45**/18

**Uganda** /juːˈɡændə/ **54**
**UK** /ˌjuːˈkeɪ/ **56**
**Ukraine** /juːˈkreɪn/ **54**
**umbrella** /ʌmˈbrelə/ **10**/16
**umpire** /ˈʌmpaɪə(r)/ **81**/11, 20
**uncle** /ˈʌŋkl/ **1**/4
**under** /ˈʌndə(r)/ **58**/5
**underground** /ˈʌndəɡraʊnd/ **66**
**underneath** /ʌndəˈniːθ/ **58**/5
**underpants** /ˈʌndəpænts/ **11**/10
**underpass** /ˈʌndəpɑːs; *US* -pæs/ **62**/21
**underwear** /ˈʌndəweə(r)/ **11**/3
**unhappy** /ʌnˈhæpɪ/ **88**/2
**United Arab Emirates** /juːˌnaɪtɪd ˌærəb ˈemɪrəts/ **54**
**United Kingdom** /juːˌnaɪtɪd ˈkɪŋdəm/ **56**
**United States of America** /juːˌnaɪtɪd ˌsteɪts əʌ əˈmerɪkə/ **55**
**untidy** /ʌnˈtaɪdɪ/ **88**/8
**up** /ʌp/ **57**/11
**upstairs** /ˌʌpˈsteəz/ **18**/24
**Uranus** /ˈjʊrənəs/ **50**/17
**Uruguay** /ˈjʊərəɡwaɪ; *US* ˈjʊərəɡweɪ/ **53**
**US** /ˌjuː ˈes/ **55**
**USA** /ˌjuː es ˈeɪ/ **55**
**usher** /ˈʌʃə(r)/ **76**/25, 26
**usherette** /ʌʃəˈret/ **76**/26
**Utah** /ˈjuːtɔː/ **55**
**utility room** /juːˈtɪlətɪ ˌruːm, ˌrʊm/ **19**
**Uzbekistan** /ʊzˈbekɪstɑːn/ **54**

**vacation** /veɪˈkeɪʃn/ **71/72**
**vacuum cleaner** /ˈvækjuːm ˌkliːnə(r)/ **19**/7
**valley** /ˈvælɪ/ **73**/3
**valve** /vælv/ **65**/11
**van** /væn/ **31**/7, **63**/5
**Vanuatu** /ˌvænʊˈɑːtuː/ **54**
**vase** /vɑːz; *US* veɪs, veɪz/ **15**/20
**vault (verb)** /vɔːlt/ **82**/16
**vaulting-horse** /ˈvɔːltɪŋhɔːs/ **82**/18
**VCR** /ˌviː siː ˈɑː(r)/ **16**/24
**vegetable** /ˈvedʒtəbl/ **23, 28**
**vehicle** /ˈvɪəkl; *US* ˈviːhɪkl/ **63**
**venetian blind** /vəˌniːʃn ˈblaɪnd/ **44**/17
**Venezuela** /ˌvenɪzˈweɪlə/ **53**
**Venus** /ˈviːnəs/ **50**/22
**verb** /vɜːb/ **43, 83–86**
**Vermont** /vərˈmɒnt/ **55**
**vest** /vest/ **12**/10
**vet** /vet/ **40**/6
**vice** (*US* **vise**) /vaɪs/ **21**/11
**video cassette recorder** /ˌvɪdɪəʊ kəˈset rɪˌkɔːdə(r)/ **16**/24
**(video)tape** /ˈvɪdɪəʊteɪp/ **30**/4
**Vietnam** /ˌvjetˈnæm; *US* ˌvjetˈnɑːm/ **54**
**viewfinder** /ˈvjuːˌfaɪndə(r) /**30**/3
**village** /ˈvɪlɪdʒ/ **71**/15
**viola** /vɪˈəʊlə/ **75**/1
**violin** /ˌvaɪəˈlɪn/ **75**/4
**Virginia** /vərˌdʒɪnjə/ **55**
**vocalist** /ˈvəʊkəlɪst/ **76**/9
**volleyball** /ˈvɒlɪbɔːl/ **78**/20

**waist** /weɪst/ **3**/24
**waiter** /ˈweɪtə(r)/ **28**/14
**waiting area** /ˈweɪtɪŋ eərɪə/ **67**/12
**wake up (verb)** /ˌweɪk ˈʌp/ **41**/1
**Wales** /weɪlz/ **56**
**walk (verb)** /wɔːk/ **57**/2, 9–11, 13, **82**/1
**walk** /wɔːk/ **83**/5
**Walkman** /ˈwɔːkmən/ **30**/11
**wall** /wɔːl/ **15**/2, **22**/25, **57**/12
**wall bars** /ˈwɔːl bɑːz/ **82**/14
**wall unit** /ˈwɔːl juːnɪt/ **16**/21
**wallet** /ˈwɒlɪt/ **11**/21, 22
**wardrobe** /ˈwɔːdrəʊb/ **18**/17
**warehouse** /ˈweəhaʊs/ **70**/3
**warm** /wɔːm/ **52**/4
**Warwickshire** /ˈwɒrɪkʃə(r)/ **56**
**wash (verb)** /wɒʃ/ **84**/13
**wash-basin** /ˈwɒʃbeɪsn/ **17**/6
**washcloth** /ˈwɔːʃklɔːθ/ **17**/13
**washer** /ˈwɒʃər; *US* ˈwɔːʃər/ **21**/26
**washing-machine** /ˈwɒʃɪŋməˌʃiːn; *US* ˈwɔːʃɪŋməˌʃiːn/ **19**/3
**washing-up liquid** /wɒʃɪŋˈʌp lɪkwɪd/ **20**/5
**Washington** /ˈwɒʃɪŋtən/ **55**
**Washington DC** /ˌwɒʃɪŋtən ˌdiː ˈsiː/ **55**
**wasp** /wɒsp/ **92**/3
**waste-paper basket** /ˌweɪstˈpeɪpə bɑːskɪt; *US* ˌweɪstˈpeɪpər bæskɪt/ **16**/16
**watch (verb)** /wɒtʃ/ **42**/23
**watch** /wɒtʃ/ **12**/15
**water** /ˈwɔːtə(r)/ **38**/6, **83**/10, 11
**water-ski (verb)** /ˈwɔːtəskiː/ **77**/11
**water-skier** /ˈwɔːtəskiːə(r)/ **77**/12
**water-skiing** /ˈwɔːtəskiːɪŋ/ **77**/10
**watercress** /ˈwɔːtəkres/ **23**/13
**waterfall** /ˈwɔːtəfɔːl/ **73**/6
**Waterford** /ˈwɔːtəfəd/ **56**
**watering-can** /ˈwɔːtərɪŋkæn/ **22**/6
**wave (verb)** /weɪv/ **85**/4
**wave** /weɪv/ **77**/14
**wavy** /ˈweɪvɪ/ **5**/11
**weak** /wiːk/ **87**/21
**weather** /ˈweðə(r)/ **51**
**webbed foot** /ˌwebd ˈfʊt/ **93**/29
**Wednesday** /ˈwenzdɪ/ **33**
**week** /wiːk/ **37**
**weight** /weɪt/ **46**/13, **48**/23
**welder** /ˈweldə(r)/ **40**/9
**west** /west/ **56**
**West Glamorgan** /ˌwest ɡləˈmɔːɡən/ **56**
**West Indies** /ˌwest ˈɪndɪz/ **53**
**West Meath** /west ˈmiːθ/ **56**
**West Midlands** /ˌwest ˈmɪdləndz/ **56**
**West Sussex** /ˌwest ˈsʌsɪks/ **56**
**West Virginia** /ˌwest vərˈdʒɪnjə/ **55**
**West Yorkshire** /ˌwest ˈjɔːkʃə(r)/ **56**
**Western Isles** /ˈwestən ˈaɪls/ **56**
**wet** /wet/ **88**/10
**Wexford** /ˈweksfəd/ **56**
**whale** /weɪl; *US also* hweɪl/ **90**/30
**wheel** /wiːl; *US also* hwiːl/ **65**/20
**wheelbarrow** /ˈwiːlbærəʊ; *US also* ˈhwiːlbærəʊ/ **22**/17
**wheelchair** /ˈwiːltʃeə(r); *US also* ˈhwiːltʃeər/ **7**/15
**whisker** /ˈwɪskər; *US also* ˈhwɪskər/ **89**/19
**whistle** /ˈwɪsl; *US also* ˈhwɪsl/ **82**/24
**white** /waɪt; *US also* hwaɪt/ **9**/14
**Wichita** /ˈwɪtʃɪtɔː/ **55**
**wicket** /ˈwɪkɪt/ **81**/19
**wicket-keeper** /ˈwɪkɪtkiːpə(r)/ **81**/13
**Wicklow** /ˈwɪkləʊ/ **56**
**wide** /waɪd/ **87**/15
**width** /wɪdθ, wɪtθ/ **48**/3
**wife** /waɪf/ **1**/12
**Wiltshire** /ˈwɪltʃə(r)/ **56**
**wind up (verb)** /ˌwaɪnd ˈʌp/ **83**/8
**window** /ˈwɪndəʊ/ **14**/8, **31**/5, **57**/1, **58**/1, **66**/11, **83**/3
**window-box** /ˈwɪndəʊbɒks/ **13**/3
**window-ledge** /ˈwɪndəʊledʒ/ **14**/9
**window-sill** /ˈwɪndəʊsɪl/ **14**/9
**windpipe** /ˈwɪndpaɪp/ **4**/2
**windscreen** /ˈwɪndskriːn/ **64**/19
**windscreen wiper** /ˈwɪndskriːn ˌwaɪpə(r)/ **64**/10
**windshield** /ˈwɪndʃiːld/ **64**/19
**windshield wiper** /ˈwɪndʃiːld ˌwaɪpər/ **64**/10
**windsurfer** /ˈwɪndsɜːfə(r)/ **77**/19
**windsurfing** /ˈwɪndsɜːfɪŋ/ **77**/18
**windy** /ˈwɪndɪ/ **51**/5
**wing** /wɪŋ/ **68**/16, **93**/17
**wing mirror** /ˈwɪŋ mɪrə(r)/ **64**/2
**wings** /wɪŋz/ **76**/18
**winter** /ˈwɪntə(r)/ **52**/12
**wire** /ˈwaɪə(r)/ **46**/5
**wire mesh screen** /ˌwaɪər ˈmeʃ skriːn/ **45**/25
**Wisconsin** /wɪsˈkɒnsɪn/ **55**
**witch** /wɪtʃ/ **12**/16
**withdraw (verb)** /wɪðˈdrɔː/ **34**/15
**withdrawal slip** /wɪðˈdrɔːəl slɪp/ **34**/19
**wolf** /wʊlf/ **90**/3
**woman** /ˈwʊmən/ **5**/4
**wood** /wʊd/ **13**/22, **73**/19
**wooden gate** /ˌwʊdn ˈɡeɪt/ **14**/17
**woodwind** /ˈwʊdwɪnd/ **75**
**wool** /wʊl/ **74**/22
**work** /wɜːk/ **42**/15, 18
**work surface** /ˈwɜːk ˌsɜːfɪs/ **20**/13
**workbench** /ˈwɜːkbentʃ/ **21**/5
**worm** /wɜːm/ **92**/20
**wrapping paper** /ˈræpɪŋ ˌpeɪpə(r)/ **26**/6
**wrench** /rentʃ/ **21**/19, 27
**wrestle (verb)** /ˈresl/ **79**/24
**wrestling** /ˈreslɪŋ/ **79**/23
**wrist** /rɪst/ **3**/23
**writing-paper** /ˈraɪtɪŋˌpeɪpə(r)/ **26**/4
**Wyoming** /waɪˈəʊmɪŋ/ **55**

**X-ray** (*also* **x-ray**) /ˈeksreɪ/ **8**/10
**X-ray scanner** /ˈeksreɪ ˌskænə(r)/ **67**/9

**yacht** /jɒt/ **69**/12
**year** /jɪə(r), *also* jɜː(r)/ **37**
**yellow** /ˈjeləʊ/ **9**/5
**Yellow Sea** /ˌjeləʊ ˈsiː/ **54**/35
**Yemen Republic** /ˌjemən rɪˈpʌblɪk/ **54**
**yield** /jiːld/ **61**/1
**yoghurt** /ˈjɒɡət/ **27**/19, 27
**yogurt** /ˈjəʊɡərt/ **27**/19, 27
**York** /jɔːk/ **56**
**young** /jʌŋ/ **5**/2
**Yugoslavia** /ˌjuːɡəʊˈslɑːvɪə/ **54**

**Zambia** /ˈzæmbɪə/ **54**
**zebra** /ˈzebrə, ˈziːbrə/ **90**/15
**zero** /ˈzɪərəʊ/ **52**/8
**Zimbabwe** /zɪmˈbɑːbwɪ/ **54**
**zip** /zɪp/ **74**/12
**zip code** /ˈzɪp kəʊd/ **32**/16
**zipper** /ˈzɪpər/ **74**/12
**zoom lens** /ˈzuːm lenz/ **29**/15
**zucchini** /zʊˈkiːnɪ/ **23**/12

a 57/6
a lo largo 57/12
a rayas 9/17
a través 57/3
abajo 18/23
abeja 92/2
abeto 25/1
abierto 87/9
abrazar 85/3
abrelatas 20/10
abrigo 10/17
abril 52
abrir 85/11
abuela 1/1
abuelo 1/2, 21
acampada 71/18
acantilado 73/11
accidente 6
accidente de coche 38/13
aceituna 27/23
acelerador 64/28, 65/26
acera 59/6
acomodador 76/25
acomodadora 76/26
acordeón 75/23
actor 76/16
actriz 76/17
adjetivos opuestos 87/88
administrativo 44/20
adolescente 5/3
aduana 67/19
adulta 5/4
adulto 5/5
aerodeslizador 70/8
aeropuerto 67/68
Afganistán 65
Africa 53/3
Africa del Sur 54
aftershave 17/21
afueras 60
agalla 91/4
agarrar 86/15
agenda 44/21
agente de viajes 40/3
agosto 52
agricultor 39/9
agricultora 39/9
agua 38/6, 83/9, 11
agua mineral 27/25
aguacate 24/13
aguijón 92/24
águila 93/8
aguja 74/19
aguja de punto 74/23
agujero 79/16
ahumado 28/3
ajedrez 74/29
ajo 23/2
al 57/5
ala 68/16, 93/17
ala delta 72/23
Albania 54
albañil 40/12
álbum de fotos 29/12
álbum de sellos 74/5
aldaba 13/4
alejarse 57/9
Alemania 54
aleta 90/28, 91/3
alfarería 74/3
alféizar 14/9
alfiler 74/16
alfombra 16/6
algodón 7/4
alicates 21/6
almacén 70/3
almendra 28/17
almohada 18/12
almohadón 18/7
alpinismo 72/24
alpinista 72/25
alrededor 58/2
altavoz 30/10
alto 5/18, 88/3, 87/17
altura 48/2
alumna 49/2
amarillo 9/5
amarre 69/15
ambulancia 38/14
América del Norte 53/1
América del Sur 53/2
americana 10/3
americano 32/33
amigo 42/20
amortiguadores 65/29
amplificador 30/16
ancho 87/15
anchura 48/3
anciano 5/6
ancla 70/16
andar 82/1
andén 66/6
Angola 54
anguila 91/11
ángulo 48/5
ángulo agudo 47/19
ángulo obtuso 47/18
ángulo recto 47/15
anillo 12/24
animal 89/90
animal doméstico 89
Antártica 53/7
Antártico 53/11
antena 14/20, 92/10
anuncio 59/20
año 37
Apalaches 55
aparador 15/18
aparato de la tensión 7/23
aparcamiento 13/15
apio 23/16
aplaudir 85/8
apretado 88/23
apuntar 79/3
Arabia Saudita 54
arado 73/29
arandela 21/26
araña 92/11
arañazo 6/17
árbitro 79/25
árbol 22/4, 57/3
arbusto 22/9, 58/1
arcén 62/4, 14
archivador 44/14
archivar 43/9
archivo 44/15
arco 14/10, 47/7, 75/2
arco iris 51/12
ardilla 89/6
área de servicio 61/11
arena 73/16
arenque 91/6
Argelia 54
Argentina 53
armario 18/17, 20/20
armario de baño 17/1
Armenia 54
armónica 75/25
arquitecta 40/1
arquitecto 40/1
arriba 18/24
arrodillarse 82/21
arroyo 59/8
Artico 53/8
artista 39/1
as de espadas 74/34
asa 30/9
asado 23/24, 27/o, 28/16
ascensionismo 72/20
Asia 53/5
asiento 57/3, 67/13
áspero 88/15
aspiradora 19/7
astronauta 50/6
atar 83/6
aterrizaje 68/8
Atlántico Norte 53/9
Atlántico Sur 53/10
atleta 80/20
atletismo 80/15
atún 27/6, 18
auricular 38/23
auriculares 30/12
Australia 53/6
Austria 54
autobús 63/2
autobús de dos pisos 60/25
automovilismo 80/5
autopista 62/1, 11
auxiliar del dentista 8/6
ave 93
avestruz 93/22
avión 68/12
avispa 92/3
azafata 67/14
Azerbaiyán 54
azucena 256/26
azul 9/7
azul marino 9/9

babosa 92/21
backgammon 74/24
badminton 78/24
Bahamas 53
bahía 53
Bahía de Bengala 54/30
Bahía de Hudson 53/17
Bahrain 54
bailar 85/7
bajar 41/3, 57/13
bajo 5/19, 52/8, 75/5, 87/18, 88/4
balanza 31/2, 46/23
balanza de tensión 46/24
balanza electrónica 46/27
balcón 13/12
baloncesto 78/8

baldosa 17/2
ballena 90/30
banco 22/14, 34
banco de carpintero 21/5
bandeja 16/12
bandeja de entrada 44/3
bandeja de salida 44/4
bandera 59/19
Bangladesh 54
bañador 11/1
bañera 17/15
baqueta 75/19
baraja 74/30
barato 87/7
barba 4/24
barbacoa 22/16
barbilla 3/28
barca de remos 69/7
barcaza 69/9
barco 60/11, 70/5
barco de pesca 69/14
barco de vela 69/1
barra de labios 12/21
barrer 83/5
barrera 66/22
báscula 17/14
base 47/16
bastidores 76/18
bastón 77/8
bata 11/13, 46/1
bateador 78/3, 81/14
batería 46/14, 76/10, 11
batidora 20/8
batuta 76/5
bebé 5/1
béisbol 78/1
Belice 53
Benin 54
berbiquí 21/15
berenjena 23/20
berlina 63/12
Bermudas 53
berro 23/13
besar 85/2
biblioteca 57/6, 7
bici 65/1
bicicleta 65/1
biela 65/5
Bielorrusia 54
bigote 4/21, 89/19
billar 79/4
billete 35/36
billete de avión 67/2
Birmania 54
blanco 9/14
blando 88/18
bloc de anillas 44/16
bloque de pisos 13/10
bloquear 78/15
blusa 10/9
bobina de hilo 74/11
boca 3/29
bol 15/13, 20/3
boleador 81/17
bolera 79/9
bolígrafo 49/22
Bolivia 53
bollo 27/4
bolos 79/8, 10
bolsa 24/12, 26/10, 66/13, 83/6, 90/9
bolsa de papel 23/22
bolsillo 11/18
bolso 10/10
bomba 64/3
bombero 38/10
bombilla 19/15
bombona de aire 77/22
bombones 26/9
bongos 75/20
bonsai 25/12
boquilla 64/13
bordado 74/18
borde 48/4
bordillo 59/9
Bosnia-Herzegovina 54
bosque 73/5, 19
bota 10/13
botar 82/8
bote salvavidas 69/18
botella 27/25
botón 74/15
botones 71/2
Botswana 54
boxeador 12/9
boxeo 79/17
bragas 11/10
Brasil 53
brazo 3/7
británico 32/33
broche 12/22
brócoli 23/17
bruja 12/16
Brunei 54
bucear 77/23
bueno 88/5
búfalo 90/19
bufanda 10/14
buhardilla 14/15
búho 93/12
bulbo 25/13
Bulgaria 54
bureta 46/25
Burkina 54
burro 89/11
Burundi 54
Bután 54
buzón 13/5, 31/11, 14, 59/3

caballete 49/13
caballo 89/13
caballo de carreras 80/25
cabecera 18/13
cabestrillo 7/11
cabeza 3/1, 6/6
cabina 69/5
cabina de la tripulación 68/14
cabina de teléfonos 38/22
cable 19/11, 46/5, 65/15, 69/6
cabra 89/8
cacahuete 24/5
cachorro 89/23
cactus 25/21
caddy 79/12
cadena 12/25, 65/8
cadena de sonido 30/13
caer 6/11, 82/5
caerse 57/8
café 42/16
cafetera 15/21
cafetería 59/4
caja 18/9, 21/1, 24/2, 26/5, 9, 27/1, 21
caja de pinturas 49/15
caja registradora 29/3
cajero 34/9
cajero automático 34/16
cajón 15/19, 58/3
calabacín 23/12
calamar 91/14
calcetín 11/4
calculadora 49/5
calendario 44/2
calle 59/10, 79/13, 80/19
calle de sentido único 61/10
calle lateral 60/5
calle para peatones y bicicletas 61/9
calor 52/4
calva 5/7
calzoncillos 11/10
cama 18/3, 42/24
cama elástica 82/4, 6
cámara compacta de 35 mm 29/19
cámara de vídeo 30/1
cámara polaroid 29/23
cámara réflex 29/16
camarero 28/14
camarón 91/17
cambiar 34/10, 12
cambio 35/16
Camboya 54
camello 90/10
Camerún 54
camilla 7/22, 38/16
caminar 57/10
camino 22/23, 26, 83/5
camión 63/4
camión cisterna 63/3
camionera 40/2
camionero 40/2
camioneta 63/7
camisa 10/19, 83/1
camiseta 10/5, 12/10
camisón 11/11
camping para caravanas 71/26
campo 71/16, 73/24, 80/16, 81/22
campo de cereal 73/26
Campuchea 54
canal 14/22, 72/12
Canal de la Mancha 56
Canal de San Jorge 56
canario 93/18
candado 65/6
cangrejo 91/18
canguro 90/8
canoa 69/19
cansado 6/3
cantante 76/9
cantar 85/6
caña de pescar 72/15
capacidad 48/26
caparazón 91/26
capital 56
capó 64/14
cápsula 7/6
cápsula de Petri 46/9
capullo 25/27, 92/7
cara 4/17
caracol 92/22

# Indice Alfabético 

caravana 63/9, 71/27
cardenal 6/15
carga 70/4
carne 27/7, 8
carnicera 39/8
carnicero 39/8
caro 87/8
carpintera 40/8
carpintero 40/8
carreras de caballos 80/23
carrete de fotos 29/11
carretera 61/62, 62/24
carretera en obras 61/13
carretilla 22/17
carretilla elevadora 63/8
carril central 62/6, 16
carril de la derecha 62/7, 15
carril de la izquierda 62/5, 17
carrito 28/6, 46/15
carro 68/3, 67/18, 86/21, 22
carta 32/5, 43/1, 3, 4, 6, 10
cartera 11/21
cartero 31/8
casa 41/10
casa adosada 13/1, 14/6
casa de campo 14/13
casa de la granja 73/21
casa unifamiliar 14/1
cascada 73/6
casco 12/2, 89/12
casco de bateador 78/2
casete 30/6, 58/3
castaño 5/9
castillo 71/13
Cataratas del Niágara 55
catarro 6/7
catorce 33/14
cavar 83/7
cazo 20/11, 26
cazuela 20/1
cebolla 23/11
cebra 90/15
ceda el paso 61/1
ceja 4/26
celo 26/1
cenar 42/22
centavo 35
centímetro 48/30
centro 25/10, 47/4
centro turístico 72/2
cepillarse 84/16
cepillo 19/5, 18, 21/8
cepillo de dientes 17/4
cepillo de uñas 17/5
cepillo del pelo 18/8
cereal 27/1
cero 52/8
cerrado 87/10
cerradura 18/26
césped 22/3
cesta 24/22, 25/6, 58/2
cesta de ropa 17/16
Chad 54
chalé 14/19
champiñón 28/21
champú 17/26
chándal 12/3
chaqueta 12/7
chaquetón 10/8
charcutería 27
cheque 43/4
cheque de viajero 34/10, 11
chica adolescente 5/3
chico 5/2
Chile 53
chimenea 14/7, 16/3, 58/6, 7, 70/10
China 54
Chipre 54
chocolate 26/11, 17, 28/13, 86/20
chuleta 28/19
cicatriz 6/21
ciclismo 80/3
ciclista 60/20
cielo 60/13
cien 33/100
ciervo 90/1
cilindro 47/24
Cimbaue 54/
cinco 33/5
cinco puertas 63/15
cincuenta 33/50
cine 76
cinta 32/2, 59/2, 74/14
cinta de vídeo 30/4
cintura 3/24
cinturón 12/11
circuito de carreras 80/6
círculo 47/1
circunferencia 47/2
ciruela 24/20
cirujano 7/18
cisne 93/31
cita 43/8
ciudad 55, 59/60
clarinete 75/14
claro 9/11
clase 49
clavel 25/24
clavo 21/23
cliente 29/1
clip 44/10
club deportivo 42/19
cobrar un cheque 34/14
coche 60/24, 64
coche de bomberos 38/4
coche de carreras 80/7
coche de policía 38/2
cochecito de niño 60/3
cocida 27/7, 28 26
cocina 20, 20/27
coco 24/7
cocodrilo 91/29
código postal 32/13, 16
codo 3/8
coger 41/6, 42/13, 92/10, 85/10
cohete 50/10
cojín 16/11
col 23/21
col de Bruselas 23/15
cola 66/12, 68/18, 89/17, 91/2
colador 20/9
colcha 18/4
colchón 18/11
colchoneta 82/17
coleta 5/13
colgador 19/6
colibrí 93/16
coliflor 23/4
colina 73/12
colirio 8/21
collar 12/26
colmillo 90/25
Colombia 53
color 9
columna vertebral 4/14
columpiarse 82/11
columpio 22/2
coma 48/16
comba 82/26
combinación 11/5
comedor 15
comer 42/17
comida 83/2
comisaría 38/1
cómoda 18/19
compás 49/19
comprar 41/11
condado 56
condensador 45/23
conejo 89/26
conga 75/22
congelador 20/15
Congo 54
cono 47/22, 61/17
constelación 50/25
consulta del médico 7
contestador automático 44/5
continente 53
contra 58/4
contraventana 14/5
control de enfoque 46/18
control de pasaportes 67/5
controlador aéreo 68/5
copia 43/11
corazón 4/4
corbata 10/20
cordero 28/19, 89/10
cordón de zapato 11/23
Corea del Norte 54
Corea del Sur 54
cornamenta 90/2
corno francés 75/6
Cornualles 56
correa 29/22
corredor 82/3
correo 31/10, 41/6
correo aéreo 32/17
correo certificado 32/20, 21
correo de primera clase 32/11, 14
correo de segunda clase 32/15
correr 80/21, 24, 82/2
corriente 73/7
cortacésped 22/5
cortar 86/17
corte 6/18
corteza 25/8
cortina 16/20
corto 5/8-11
cosechadora 73/25
coser 83/4
costa 71/1
Costa de Marfil 54
Costa Rica 53
costilla 4/13
costura 74/9
cráneo 4/11
crecer 57/3, 12

crema **9**/6
cremallera **74**/12
crin **89**/16
criquet **81**
crisantemo **25**/15
crisol **46**/26
cristal **13**/23
Croacia **54**
cronómetro **46**/16
cruce **60**/21
crucero **72**/6
cruzar **57**/2
cuaderno **49**/4
cuadrado **47**/9
cuadro **15**/25, **58**/10, **54**/4
cuadros **9**/19
cuarenta **33**/40
cuarto **37**/8, **48**/19
cuarto creciente **50**/1
cuarto de baño **17**
cuarto de estar **16**
cuarto de plancha **19**
cuarto menguante **50**/4
cuatro **33**/4
Cuba **53**
cubierta **69**/4
cubilete **74**/27
cubo **19**/6, **47**/21, **54**/12
cubo de la basura **22**/20
cucaracha **92**/16
cuchara **15**/11
cucharilla **16**/15
cuchilla de afeitar **17**/24
cuchillo **15**/10
cuello **3**/5, **11**/15
cuentagotas **46**/11
cuerda **26**/2, **75**, **79**/20, **82**/12
cuerno **90**/20
cuerpo humano **3**/4
cuerpo sólido **47**/20
cuervo **93**/11
cuidado de la salud **7/8**
culata del cilindro **64**/17
cuneta **62**/23
cuñada **1**/10, 13
curva **47**/27
curva peligrosa a la derecha **61**/8

dados **74**/28
damas **74**/26
daño **6**/12
dar **78**/28, **85**/9
dar vueltas **83**/12
dardos **79**/1
darse la mano **85**/1
de **57**/7-9
de cuadros **9**/19
de lunares **9**/18
de pie **84**/22
debajo de **58**/5, 16
débil **87**/21
décimo **33**
décimo segundo **33**
décimo tercero **33**
decorado **76**/14
dedal **74**/17
dedo **3**/20
dedo del pie **3**/14
dejar **86**/16
delante de **58**/18
delfín **90**/29
delgado **5**/20, **87**/14
dentista **8**/1
dependiente **29**/6
deporte **77-81**
deportivo **63**/11
derecho **87**/1
desayunar **41**/9
descapotable **63**/13
describir **9**
descripción **5**
desde **57**/14
desgraciado **88**/2
desierto **73**/15
desordenado **88**/8
despacho de billetes **66**/10
despedirse **85**/4
despegue **68**/6
despejado **51**/13
despertador **18**/14
despertarse **41**/1
destornillador **21**/21
detector de metales **67**/8
detergente **19**/1
detrás de **58**/19
día **37**
diagonal **47**/12
diámetro **47**/5
diana **79**/2
diapositiva **29**/9
dibujo **74**/2
diciembre **52**
dictáfono **43**/2
dictar **43**/1
diecinueve **33**/19
dieciocho **33**/18
dieciséis **33**/16
diecisiete **33**/17
diente **8**/8, 11
diez **33**/10
difícil **87**/12
Dinamarca **54**
dinero **34**/12
dinero americano **35**
dinero británico **36**
dique **72**/4
dirección **32**/10
dirección del remitente **32**/18, 19
dirección prohibida **61**/3
director **76**/4
disc jockey **39**/3
disco **30**/5
disco compacto **30**/7
disco flexible **44**/23
diseño **9**
disfrazarse **12**
distrito **56**
Distrito de Columbia **55**
doblar **86**/19
doblarse hacia atrás **82**/20
doble línea amarilla **60**/22
doce **33**/12
docena **27**/13
dólar **35**
doler **6**/4-6, 8
domingo **33**
dormido **84**/24
dormitorio **18**
dos **33**/2
Dublín **56**
ducha **17**/20
ducharse **41**/7
dulces **26**/10, 14, 15, 18
duna de arena **73**/17
duro **88**/17

echar **83**/11
Ecuador **53**
ecuador **53**
ecualizador gráfico **30**/17
edad **5**
edificio **13**/14, **60**/1
Edimburgo **56**
EEUU **55**
Egipto **54**
El Salvador **53**
electricista **40**/7
electrodo **46**/6
elefante **90**/24
embarcadero **60**/16
embarque **68**/1
émbolo **45**/15
embrague **64**/26
embudo **45**/10
Emiratos Arabes Unidos **54**
empaste **8**/9
empedrado **22**/11
empezar **42**/15
empleada **31**/4
empujar **86**/21
en **58**/3, 7, 9
en el centro de **58**/13
en la parte alta de **58**/12
en la parte inferior de **58**/14
enagua **11**/8
encender **86**/23
encendido **64**/25
enchufe **19**/12, 21
encía **8**/7
encima de **58**/11, 15
encimera **20**/13
encontrarse **42**/20
enero **52**
enfermera **7**/12
enrollar **83**/8
ensalada **28**/22
entrada **66**/21
entre **48**/14, **58**/8
entrega urgente **32**/24, 25
equipaje **67**/17
equitación **72**/16, **80**/9
erizo **89**/5
escala **53-56**
escalera **18**/25, **38**/5, **57**/11, 13
escalón **13**/6, **18**/22
escama **91**/7
escarabajo **92**/13
escayola **7**/13
escenario **76**/15
escoba **22**/13
escocés **9**/20
Escocia **56**
escorpión **92**/23
escuadra **49**/6
escuchar **41**/12
esfera del reloj **37**/2
Eslovaquia **54**

Eslovenia **54**
espacio **50**
espacio exterior **50**
espalda **3**/9
espalderas **82**/14
España **54**
esparadrapo **7**/10
espárrago **23**/5
espátula **46**/10
espectadores **80**/18
espejo **15**/1
espejo retrovisor **64**/2
espiral **47**/28
esponja **17**/12
esposa **1**/12
espuma de afeitar **17**/25
esqueleto **4**/10
esquí **77**/6, 9
esquí acuático **77**/10
esquiador acuático **77**/12
esquiar **77**/7
esquina **59**/11
estación **66**
estaciones **52**
estado de cuenta **34**/5
Estados Unidos de América **55**
estampado **9**/21
estanque **73**/23
estante **20**/23
estantería **16**/21, **58**/11-14
estar cansada **6**/3
este **56**
esternón **4**/12
estetoscopio **7**/20
estirarse **82**/19
estómago **3**/25, **4**/8, **6**/5
Estonia **54**
estrecho **87**/16
Estrecho de Dover **56**
estrella **50**/26
estrella de cine **76**/24
estrella de mar **91**/20
estribos **80**/13
estropajo **20**/6
Etiopía **54**
Europa **53**/4
examen de la vista **8**/14
excavadora **61**/18
excursionismo **71**/23
excursionista **71**/24
extintor de incendios **38**/9

fábrica **59**/23
fácil **87**/11
facturación **67**/1
fagot **75**/15
faisán **93**/7
falda **10**/11
fallar **81**/29
familia **1**
familiar **63**/14
famaceútica **39**/6
faro **64**/4, **70**/12
farola **60**/7
fax **43**/10
febrero **52**
fecha **33**
Federación Rusa **54**
feliz **88**/1
felpudo **18**/21
Fermanagh **56**
ferrocarril **66**
ferry **70**/9
fichero **44**/8
Fidji **54**
fiebre **6**/10
figura **58**/11
filatelia **74**/4
filete **28**/18
Filipinas **54**
filtro de papel **45**/11
filtro del aire **64**/16
Finlandia **54**
firma **43**/7
firmar **43**/6
física **5**
flamenco **93**/25
flash **29**/18
flash incorporado **29**/20
flauta **75**/12
flauta de pico **75**/11
flautín **75**/10
flequillo **5**/14
flexiones **82**/22
flojo **88**/24
flor **57**/12
flor seca **25**/9, 10, **58**/7
Florida **55**
floristería **25**
foca **90**/27
fondo **48**/8
fontanera **40**/10
forma **47**
formón **21**/14
foso de la orquesta **76**/19
foto en blanco y negro **29**/14
foto en color **29**/13
fotógrafa **40**/4
fotógrafo **40**/4
fracción **48**/18
frambuesa **28**/10
Francia **54**
fregadero **19**/2
fregona **19**/8
freno de pie **64**/27
frente **4**/18, **48**/7
fresa **8**/2, **24**/2
fresco **52**/5
fresia **25**/20
frío **52**/6
frío helador **52**/7
frita **28**/26
frontera **56**
frontera interacional **56**
frontera nacional **56**
fruncir el ceño **84**/19
fruta **24, 28**/7
fruto seco **24**/12
fuego **16**/4, **38**/8
fuera **58**/1
fuerte **87**/22
funda de cámara **29**/21
funda de gafas **8**/19
furgoneta **63**/5
furgoneta de correos **31**/7
fuselaje **68**/17
fútbol **81**
fútbol americano **78**/11
gabardina **10**/22
Gabón **54**
gafas **8**/15
gafas de sol **12**/18
gafas protectoras **45**/1
galaxia **50**/24
Gales **56**
galleta **27**/15, 16
gallina **93**/2
gallo **93**/4
Gambia **54**
ganso **93**/27
garaje **14**/2
garganta **3**/27, **6**/8
garita de señales **66**/1
garra **89**/24
gasa **7**/9
gasolinera **64**/1
gatito **89**/21
gato **89**/18
gaviota **93**/30
Georgia **54**
Ghana **54**
gimnasia **80**/1
gimnasio **82**/15
gimnasta **80**/2
giro obligatorio a la derecha **61**/12
giro postal **32**/22, 23
gitana **12**/5
globo **72**/21
globo terráqueo **49**/11
gol **81**/28
golf **79**/11
golfo **53**
Golfo de Alaska **53**/16
Golfo de Guinea **54**/24
Golfo de México **53**/18
Golfo Pérsico **54**/28
golondrina **93**/21
golosinas **26**
golpear **79**/22
goma **49**/26
gordo **5**/21, **87**/13
gorila **90**/14
gorra **10**/2
gorrión **93**/15
grados Celsius **52**/2
grados centígrados **52**/2
grados Fahrenheit **52**/1
gramo **48**/24
Gran Bretaña **56**
grande **87**/3
grandes almacenes **59**/18
granero **73**/22
granja **73**/20
grano **73**/27
grapadora **44**/12
grapar **43**/4
Grecia **54**
green **79**/14
grifo de agua caliente **19**/20
grifo de agua fría **19**/19
grillo **92**/18
gris **9**/15
Groenlandia **53**
grúa **70**/2
grupo de turistas **71**/11
grupo pop **76**/7
guante **10**/15

guante de béisbol 78/4
guante de boxeo 79/21
guante del horno 20/21
guardabarros 65/22
guardameta 81/13
guarniciones 72/26
Guatemala 53
Guayana Francesa 53
guía 71/10
guinda 28/1
Guinea 54
Guinea Ecuatorial 54
Guinea-Bissau 54
guisante 22/23
guisar 83/2
guitarra eléctrica 76/8
gusano 92/8
Guyana 53

habitación de dos camas 71/8
habitación de hospital 7
habitación doble 71/7
habitación individual 71/6
hablar 85/5
hacer ciclismo 80/4
hacer el pino 82/25
hacer esquí acuático 77/11
hacer flexiones 82/22
hacer lucha 79/24
hacer surf 77/15
hacerse daño 6/12
hacha 21/17
hacia 57/10
Haití 53
halcón 93/10
hambre 6/2
hámster 89/25
hebilla 11/19
helado 28/10
helecho 25/5
hélice 68/10, 15
helicóptero 68/9
hermana 1/11
herramienta 21
hervidora 20/19, 83/9
hervir 83/10
hidrante 38/11
hidroala 70/7
hierba 22/3
hígado 4/6
hija 1/17
hijo 1/16, 19
hilera 26/7
hilo 74/20
hipódromo 80/28
hipopótamo 90/22
hipotenusa 47/17
hobby 74
hockey sobre hierba 78/16
hoja 25/11
hoja de música 76/6
Holanda 54
hombre 5/5, 6
hombre herido 38/15
hombro 3/6
Honduras 53
hora 37
horario 37/4, 66/15
hormiga 92/15
hormigón 13/18
hormigonera 63/6
hornillo 71/22
horno 20/22
horquilla 22/18
hueco 88/21
hueso de la cadera 4/15
huésped 71/3
huevo 27/13, 14
humo 38/7
Hungría 54

igual a 48/15
imán 46/8
impresión 44/18
impreso 43/5
impresora 44/19
imprimir 43/11
India 54
Indiana 55
Indias Occidentales 53
indicador 60/23
indicador de combustible 64/23
Indico 53/12
Indonesia 54
Inglaterra 56
ingresar dinero 34/17
insecto 92
instructor 82/7
instrumento musical 75
intermitente 64/3
interruptor 18/27
intersección 62/25
intestino 4/9
invierno 52/12
inyección 7/21
ir 57/6
ir a correr 41/4
ir en coche 42/19
Irak 65
Irán 54
iris 4/29
Irlanda del Norte 56
irse 41/10, 42/24
isla 55
Isla de Man 56
Isla de Wight 56
Islandia 54
Islas Británicas 56
Islas Canarias 54
Islas de Scilly 56
Islas Faroe 54
Islas Galápagos 53
Islas Hawai 55
Islas Malvinas 53
Islas Occidentales 56
Islas Orkney 56
Islas Salomón 54
Islas Shetland 56
Israel 54
Italia 54

J de tréboles 74/31
Jamaica 53
Japón 54
jardín 22
jardín delantero 22/21
jardín trasero 22/1
jardinera 13/3, 39/2
jardinero 39/2
jarra 15/17
jarrón 15/20
jeep 63/10
jeringa 45/16
jersey 10/6
jinete 80/11
jirafa 90/23
jockey 80/26
Jordania 54
joroba 90/11
joyas 12
judía verde 28/23
judo 79/26
juego de modelismo 74/7
jueves 33
juez 81/11, 20
jugador de hockey 78/17
jugar 42/21
julio 52
junio 52
junto 58/6, 17
Júpiter 50/19

Kampuchea 54
karate 79/27
Kazakistán 54
Kenia 54
kilogramo 48/25
kiosco 59/15
Kirguizistán 54
kiwi 24/18
Kuwait 54

labio 4/23
laboratorio de ciencias 45/46
lado 47/10, 48/9
ladrillo 13/16
lagarto 91/28
lago 55, 73/4
Lago Erie 55
Lago Hurón 55
Lago Michigan 55
Lago Ontario 55
Lago Superior 55
lámpara 15/22
lana 74/22
lancha inflable 70/14
lancha motora 69/11
langosta 91/16
lanzador 81/17
lanzar 78/13, 81/18, 82/9
Laos 54
lápiz 49/20
largo 5/12, 15
lata 27/6, 26
lata de galletas 16/10
lavabo 8/5, 17/6
lavadero 19
lavadora 19/3
lavarse 84/13
lavavajillas 20/5
leche 27/24
lechuga 23/7
leer 42/14, 85/12
lengua 4/22
lente 8/16, 29/17, 46/21
lentes de contacto 8/20

# Indice Alfabético 


**lento 87**/24
**leño 16**/5
**león 90**/16
**leopardo 90**/18
**Lesotho 54**
**levantar 86**/13
**levantarse 41**/2
**Letonia 54**
**Líbano 54**
**libélula 92**/5
**Liberia 54**
**Libia 54**
**libra 36**
**libreta 44**/13
**librillo de sellos 31**/20
**libro 58**/4, 14, 15, **85**/12
**libro de cocina 20**/4
**libro de texto 49**/3
**lichi 24**/15
**ligero 88**/13
**lima 21**/13, **24**/17
**límite de velocidad 61**/6
**limón 24**/6
**limpiador 8**/22
**limpiaparabrisas trasero 64**/10
**limpiar 83**/3
**limpio 88**/19
**línea 47**
**línea de estado 55**
**línea de fondo 81**/4
**línea de saque 81**/5
**línea perpendicular 47**/29
**línea recta 47**/26
**líneas laterales 81**/6
**linier 81**/25
**linterna 19**/17
**líquido corrector 44**/9
**lirio 25**/28
**liso 5**/8, 9, **9**/16
**litro 48**/28
**Lituania 54**
**llama 45**/3, **90**/12
**llave 44**/11
**llave de la habitación 71**/5
**llave fija 21**/17
**llave inglesa 21**/19
**llenar 83**/9
**lleno 88**/11
**llevar 86**/14
**llorar 84**/20
**lloviendo 51**/2
**lobo 90**/3
**locomotora 66**/3
**locutor 39**/4
**locutora 39**/4
**lombriz 92**/20
**loncha 27**/8
**Londres 56**
**longitud 48**/6
**loro 93**/19
**lucha 79**/23
**luna llena 50**/3
**lunares 9**/18
**lunes 33**
**lupa 45**/14
**luz 18**/16

**Macedonia 54**
**macedonia de frutas 28**/11
**maceta 22**/10
**macizo 88**/22
**macizo de flores 22**/24
**Madagascar 54**
**madera 13**/22
**madre 1**/5
**Maine 55**
**maíz 28**/20
**Malasia 54**
**Malawi 54**
**maleta 66**/14, **86**/13-16
**maletero 64**/9
**maletín 10**/12
**Mali 54**
**malo 88**/6
**mandar 43**/10
**mandibula 3**/4
**mando a distancia 16**/9
**manga 11**/16
**mango 24**/19
**manguera 38**/12, **64**/12, **83**/8
**manillar 65**/19
**mano 3**/19
**mano de mortero 45**/7
**mansión 71**/14
**manta 18**/5
**mantel 15**/8
**manteniéndose en forma 82**
**mantequilla 27**/29
**mantis religiosa 92**/19
**manzana 24**/4, **28**/8
**mañana 37**/15
**mapa 49**/18
**maqueta 74**/8
**maquillaje 12**/20
**máquina de coser 74**/10
**máquina de escribir 44**/27
**máquina de sellos 31**/17
**maquinilla de afeitar 17**/23
**maquinilla eléctrica 17**/22
**mar 73**/8
**Mar Amarillo 54**/35
**Mar Báltico 54**/22
**Mar Caribe 53**/19
**Mar Caspio 54**/27
**Mar de Arabia 54**/29
**Mar de Barents 54**/41
**Mar de Beaufort 53**/15
**Mar de Bering 54**/38
**Mar de Irlanda 56**
**Mar de Japón 54**/36
**Mar de Kara 54**/39
**Mar de la China Este 54**/34
**Mar de la China Sur 54**/33
**Mar de Laptev 54**/39
**Mar de Noruega 54**/20
**Mar de Okhotsk 54**/37
**Mar de Tasmania 54**/31
**Mar del Coral 54**/32
**Mar del Norte 54**/21
**Mar Mediterráneo 54**/23
**Mar Negro 54**/26
**Mar Rojo 54**/25
**marcar 81**/26
**marcar un gol 81**/23
**marco 15**/24
**margarina 27**/20, 28
**margarita 25**/23
**marido 1**/18
**marinero 39**/11
**mariposa 92**/6, 9
**mariquita 92**/14
**marrón 9**/4
**Marruecos 54**
**Marte 50**/20
**martes 33**
**martillo 21**/16
**marzo 52**
**más 48**/11
**mascarilla 7**/17
**mástil 69**/2
**matasellos 32**/12
**material de construcción 13**
**matraz cónico 45**/17
**matraz de fondo plano 45**/9
**matraz de fondo redondo 45**/22
**matrícula 64**/5
**matriz 34**/2
**Mauricio 54**
**Mauritania 54**
**mayo 52**
**mazo 21**/2
**mecánica 40**/11
**mecánico 40**/11
**mecanografiar 43**/3
**media 37**/9, 11
**media docena 27**/14
**media luna 50**/2
**mediana 62**/8, 18
**medianoche 37**/13
**medias 11**/6
**medicamento 7**/1
**médico 7**/19
**medida 48**
**medio 48**/21
**medio ambiente 73**
**mediodía 37**/13
**medusa 91**/15
**mejilla 4**/19
**mejillón 91**/23
**melocotón 24**/11
**melón 24**/1, **28**/2
**Memphis 55**
**menos 48**/12
**mensajero 31**/16
**menú 28**/15
**mercado 23/24**
**Mercurio 50**/23
**merienda 71**/17
**mermelada 27**/5, 17
**mes 52**
**mesa 44**/6, **57**/8, **58**/4-6, **79**/6
**mesa de café 16**/i
**meseta 73**/18
**mesilla 18**/10
**metálico 35**
**metro 66, 74**/13
**México 53**
**micrófono 30**/2
**microscopio 46**/17
**miércoles 33**
**mil 33**/1000
**mililitro 48**/27
**milímetro 29, 48**/29
**millón 33**/1000000
**minutero 37**/3
**mirar 57**/1, 14
**mochila 49**/8, **66**/16, **71**/25

modelismo 74/6
módulo lunar 50/5
mojado 88/10
Moldavia 54
moneda 35/36
moneda extranjera 34/13
monedero 11/22
Mongolia 54
mono 90/13
monstruo12/13
Montana 55
montaña 55, 73/1
Montañas Rocosas 55
montar 80/10
montura 8/18
moqueta 16/7
morado 9/10
moreno 5/8
morro 68/13, 91/5
mortero 45/8
mosca 92/1
mosquito 92/4
mostrador 31/3
mostrador de facturación 67/4
motocicleta 65/21, 25
motor 64/15, 64/28
motor a reacción 68/19
motor fueraborda 70/15
Mozambique 54
mucha niebla 51/7
mucho calor 52/3
muela 6/4, 8/12
muelle 70/1
mujer 5/4
muleta 7/14
multitud 78/7
mundo 53/54
muñeca 3/23
mural 49/17
murciélago 89/4
muro 22/25
muro de hormigón 14/12
muro de piedra 14/18
música 41/12, 76
músico 76/2
Myanmar 54

nabo 23/18
nadador 77/27
nadar 77/26
nalgas 3/11
Namibia 54
naranja 9/3, 24/9
narciso 25/14
nariz 4/20
nata 28/12
natación 77/25
navaja 21/4
negativo 29/10
negro 9/13
Nepal 54
Neptuno 50/16
neumático 65/27
nevar 51/3
nevera 20/14
Nicaragua 53
nido 93/13
niebla 51/6
nieta 1/23
nieto 1/22
nieve 51/4
Níger 54
Nigeria 54
niña 85/2-4
niño 5/2
nivel 21/7
noche 37/18
norte 56
Noruega 54
noveno 33
noventa 33/90
noviembre 52
nublado 51/8
Nueva Caledonia 54
Nueva Zelanda 54
nueve 33/9
nuevo 87/6
Nuevo México 55
número 33
número de cuenta 34/7
número de vía 66/18

oboe 75/13
océano 53
ochenta 33/80
ocho 33/8
octavo 33
octubre 52
oeste 56
oficial de aduanas 67/20
oficial de policía 38/3
oficina 43/44
oficina de correos 31/1
ojo 4/25
ojo morado 6/20
ola 77/14
Omán 54
once 33/11
ondulado 5/11
operación 7
óptico 8/13
órbita 50/13
ordenado 88/7
ordenador personal 44/25
oreja 3/3
órgano interno 4/1
orilla 60/18
orquesta 76/1
orquídea 25/18
oscuro 9/12, 51/14
oso 90/4
oso polar 90/6
ostra 91/21
otoño 52/11
óvalo 47/8
oveja 89/9

paciente 8/3
Pacífico Norte 53/14
Pacífico Sur 53/13
padre 1/6, 20
pagar 35
país 53
paja 13/21
Pakistán 54
pala 22/19
palanca de cambio 64/21, 65/13
palanca de freno 65/16
palma 3/22
palmera 25/16
palo 79/15
palo de hockey 78/18
paloma 93/14
palos 81/19
pan de molde 27/2
panadera 39/7
panadero 39/7
Panamá 53
panda 90/7
pandereta 75/18
pantalla 15/23, 44/26, 76/23
pantalla de salidas 66/17
pantalones 10/4
pantalones cortos 12/12
pantano 73/13
pantis 11/7
paño de cocina 20/7
pañuelo 12/6, 10/21
pañuelos de papel 18/9
papaya 24/14
papel 57/4, 5, 8, 86/17-19
papel de carta 26/4
papel de lija 21/3
papel de regalo 26/6
papel higiénico 17/18
papelera 16/16, 59/14, 57/4
papelería 26
Papúa Nueva Guinea 54
paquete 26/3, 26/15, 16, 27/16, 32/1
paquete doble 26/12
paquete triple 26/13
par 8/15
parabrisas 64/19
paracaídas 72/19
paracaidismo 72/18
parachoques 64/7
parada de autobús 59/21, 21
paraguas 10/16
Paraguay 53
paramédico 38/17
pared 15/2, 57/12
pared de ladrillo 13/7
parentesco 1/2
párpado 4/27
parque 60/2
parrilla del radiador 64/18
parte trasera 48/10
partido de criquet 18/22
partido de dobles 81/8
partido individual 81/1
partir 79/28, 86/20
pasajero 66/20, 68/2
pasaporte 67/6
pasarela peatonal 62/22
paseo 72/5
pasillo 76/27
paso a nivel 66/2
paso de peatones 59/24
paso elevado 62/10, 20
paso inferior 62/21
pasta de dientes 17/3
pastel 27/11, 12, 28/9
pastilla 7/7
pastilla de jabón 17/8
pata palmípeda 93/29
patata 23/9, 25, 27

patatas fritas **26**/16, 19, **28**/27
paté **28**/4
patín **77**/4
patinadora **77**/3
patinaje sobre hielo **77**/1
patinar **77**/2
patio **57**/2
patio de butacas **76**/20
pato **93**/28
pavo **93**/6
pavo real **93**/24
peatón **60**/8
pecho **3**/26
pedal **65**/9
pegamento **49**/23
peinarse **84**/15
peine **17**/27
pelo **3**/2, 5, **84**/13, 14, 16
pelota de badminton **78**/25
pelota de fútbol **78**/12
pelota de hockey **78**/19
peluquera **39**/5
peluquero **39**/5
pelvis **4**/15
pendiente **12**/27
penique **36**
Pensilvania **55**
pepino **23**/10
pequeño **87**/4
pera **24**/16
percha **18**/18
percusión **75**
perfil urbano **60**/14
perforador **44**/7
perfume **67**/11
periódico **26**/8, **41**/11, **42**/14, **59**/16
periquito **93**/20
perla **91**/22
perno **21**/24
perro **89**/22
persiana **17**/19, **44**/17
Perú **53**
pesa **46**/13
pesado **88**/14
pesca **72**/13
pescador **72**/14, **39**/10
peso **48**/23
pestaña **4**/28
pétalo **25**/4
petrolero **70**/6
pez **91**
piano **76**/3
picador de billetes **66**/19
pico **73**/2, **93**/9, 26
pie **3**/13, **84**/22
piedra **13**/17
piel **89**/20
pierna **3**/12, **6**/12, 13
pieza **27**/7
pijama **11**/14
pila **24**/22, **26**/8
pilar **14**/4
piloto **68**/11, **80**/8
piloto de carreras **12**/1
piloto trasero **64**/8
pimienta **15**/16
pimiento verde **23**/3
pincel **49**/14
ping-pong **78**/26
pingüino **93**/23
pinta **27**/24
pintura **74**/1
pinza **19**/10, **46**/7, **91**/19
pinzas **45**/13
piña **24**/8, **25**/22
pipeta **46**/12
pirámide **47**/23
piscina **77**/28
pista **68**/7, **80**/17, **81**/16
pista de hielo **77**/5
pista de tenis **81**/10
pito **82**/24
pizarra **13**/20, **49**/1
placa de la calle **60**/10
plancha **19**/13
planchar **83**/1
planeta **50**
planta **16**/19, **58**/11
planta baja **13**/14
plataforma de lanzamiento **50**/12
plátano **24**/3
platija **91**/10
platillo **75**/21
platito **16**/13
plato **15**/9, **30**/14, **58**/13, 15, 17, **65**/10
playa **72**/3, **73**/10
pletina **30**/18
pliego de sellos **31**/18
plinto **82**/18
pluma **93**/5
Plutón **50**/15
poco profundo **87**/20
policía **38, 59**/5
pollito **93**/3
pollo **27**/9, 10, **93**/1
Polonia **54**
polvos de talco **17**/28
pomada **7**/8
pomelo **24**/21
poni **89**/15
Poole **56**
popa **69**/17
por **48**/13, **57**/1
por ciento **48**/17
porche **14**/16
portaequipajes **65**/24
portaobjectos **46**/19
portero **81**/30
Portugal **54**
poste **81**/27
póster **18**/15
postre **28**
potro **89**/14
prefijo del país **38**/19
prefijo internacional **38**/18
prefijo local **38**/21
prefijo nacional **38**/20
preparación **46**/20
preposición **57/58**
presa **73**/14
prima **1**/9
primavera **52**/9
primer piso **13**/13, **76**/21
primer plato **28**
primero **33**
primo **1**/9
prisma **45**/12
prismáticos **29**/7
proa **69**/16
probeta **46**/3
profesora **49**/16
profundidad **48**/1
profundo **87**/19
programador de ordenadores **40**/5
programadora de ordenadores **40**/5
prohibido girar a la izquierda **61**/7
prohibido girar en U **61**/5
proyector de diapositivas **29**/8
público **76**/28, **78**/7
pueblo **71**/15
puente **8**/17, **60**/15
puerta **22**/22, **67**/15
puerta de madera **14**/17
puerta de salida **80**/27
puerta principal **14**/3
puerto **69/70**
puerto deportivo **69**/10
Puerto Rico **53**
puesto **23**/1
pulgar **3**/21
pulmón **4**/3
pulpo **91**/12
pulsera **12**/23
punto **74**/21
puño **3**/10, **11**/17
pupila **4**/30

Qatar **54**
quemador de Bunsen **45**/5
quemadura del sol **6**/16
quemarse **86**/24
queso **27**/22, **28**/9
quince **33**/15
quinto **33**
quirófano **7**/16

rábano **23**/6
racimo **24**/3, 10
radiador **14**/4
radio **30**/15, **47**/3
radiocasete **30**/8
radios **65**/7
raíz **25**/3
rama **25**/7
ramo **25**/9
rampa de acceso **62**/2, 12
rana **92**/25
ranura **38**/25
rápido **87**/23
raqueta **78**/23
rascacielos **60**/12
rasgar **86**/18
rastrillo **22**/6
raya **5**/16
rayas **9**/17
rayo **51**/11
rayos X **8**/10, **67**/9
recepción del hotel **71**/1
recepcionista **71**/4
receta **7**/5
recibo **29**/21, **35**/14
recibo de depósito **34**/18
recibo de reintegro **34**/19
recogedor **19**/4
recogepelotas **81**/9
recogida **31**/6

recogida de equipajes **67**/16
rectángulo **47**/11
red **78**/9, **81**/7
reflector **65**/14
refresco **27**/26
regadera **22**/6
regalo **85**/9-11
región **56**
regla **49**/21
reina de corazones **74**/32
Reino Unido **56**
reírse **84**/6
rellena **27**/23
rellenar **43**/5
reloj **12**/15, **15**/16, **58**/8
remo **69**/8, 20
remolacha **23**/8
reparto **31**/12
reparto por mensajero **31**/15
repisa de la chimenea **16**/2, **58**/9, 10
reproductor de disco compacto **30**/19
reptil **91**
República Centroafricana **54**
República Checa **54**
República de Irlanda **56**
República del Yemen **54**
República Domincana **53**
restaurante **28**
retrete **17**/17
Reunión **54**
revista **26**/7, **58**/18, 19
rey de diamantes **74**/33
riendas **80**/14
rincón **79**/18
ring **79**/19
rinoceronte **90**/21
riñón **4**/7
río **60**/17
Río Grande **55**
río principal **55**
rizado **5**/10
robot de cocina **20**/25
roca **70**/13, **73**/9
rodilla **3**/18
rodilleras **81**/15
rodillo **20**/12
rojo **5**/12, **9**/1
rollo **26**/1, 2, 6
romperse **6**/13
ropa **9**/11
ropa de cama **18**/2
ropa interior **11**/3
rosa **9**/2, **25**/17
rotonda **60**/26
rótula **4**/16
rotulador **26**/5
rótulo **32**/3
Ruanda **54**
rubio **5**/15
rueda **65**/20
rugby **78**/14
Rumania **54**
Rusia **54**
rutina diaria **41**

sábado **33**
sábana **18**/6
saca de correos **31**/9
sacapuntas **49**/25
sacar **81**/2
sacar dinero **34**/15
saco de dormir **71**/21
saco postal **31**/13
safari **72**/17
sal **15**/15
sala de embarque **67**/12
saldo de cuenta **34**/6
salmón **28**/3, **91**/9
salpicadero **64**/20
saltador **77**/30
saltamontes **92**/17
saltar **77**/29, **78**/21, **82**/4, 16
saltar a la comba **82**/27
sandalia **12**/8
sandwich **27**/3
sangre **6**/19
sartén **20**/24
satélite **50**/9
Saturno **50**/18
saxofón **75**/16
secador **18**/20
secarse **84**/14
seco **88**/9
secretaria **44**/20
sector **47**/6
sed **6**/1
segundero **37**/5
segundo **33**
segundo piso **76**/22
segundo plato **28**
seguridad **67**/7
seis **33**/6
sello **31**/19
semáforo **60**/19
semana **37**
Senegal **54**
sentado **84**/21
señal **59**/1
señal de aparcamiento **59**/2
señal de salida **66**/5
señal de tráfico **61/62**
septiembre **52**
séptimo **33**
serpiente **91**/27
serrucho **21**/12
servicio **81**/3
servicio de ambulancia **38**
servicio de correos **31/32**
servicio de urgencias **38**
servidor **81**/21
servilleta **15**/7
sesenta **33**/60
setenta **33**/70
seto **22**/27
sexto **33**
sierra de pelo **21**/20
sierra eléctrica **21**/9
Sierra Leona **54**
Sierra Nevada **55**
siete **33**/7
siglo **37**
silla **49**/10, **80**/12
silla de ruedas **7**/15
sillín **65**/2, 23
sillita de niño **60**/4
sillón **16**/22
sillón de dentista **8**/4
Singapur **54**
sintetizador **76**/13
Sioux Falls **55**
Siria **54**
sistema solar **50**
sobre **26**/3, **32**/6, **58**/10
sobrina **1**/14
sobrino **1**/15
Socotra **54**
sofá **16**/17
Sol **50**/14
sol **51**/1
solapa **32**/7
soldado **39**/12
soldador **40**/9
soldadora **40**/9
Somalia **54**
sombrero **12**/17
sombrilla **72**/9
sonreír **84**/17
sopa **28**/5
sopera **15**/6
soporte **45**/6
soporte con abrazadera **45**/20
squash **42**/21, **78**/22
Sri Lanka **54**
stop **61**/2
suave **88**/16
subir **57**/11
submarinismo **77**/21
sucio **88**/20
Sudán **54**
sudadera **12**/14
Suecia **54**
suegra **1**/8
suegro **1**/7
suelo **57**/5, **86**/16
suelo de baldosas **49**/9
Suiza **54**
sujetador **11**/9
sur **56**
surco **73**/30
surf **77**/13
surfista **77**/16
Surinam **53**
surtidor de gasolina **64**/11
Swazilandia **54**

tabla de cortar **20**/18
tabla de planchar **19**/9
tabla de surf **77**/17
tabla de wind-surf **77**/20
tablero **74**/25
tableta **7**/7, **26**/11, **86**/20
tablón **57**/9, 10
tablón de anuncios **44**/1
taburete **45**/19
taco **79**/5
taco de salida **80**/22
tacón **11**/20
Tailandia **54**
Taiwán **54**
Tajikistán **54**
taladro **21**/18
taladro eléctrico **21**/10
taladro neumático **61**/16
tallo **25**/19
talón **3**/15
talonario de cheques **34**/1
tamiz **20**/2

Tanzania **54**
tapa **15**/5
tapa de registro **59**/7
tapón **17**/7, **46**/4
tarde **37**/16, 17
tarjeta de crédito **34**/4
tarjeta de embarque **67**/3
tarjeta de felicitación **32**/4
tarjeta de garantía de cheques **34**/3
tarjeta de telefóno **38**/24
tarjeta postal **32**/8
tarro **27**/5
tarta **28**/8, 13
taxi **60**/6
taza **16**/14, **20**/16, **42**/16, **58**/5, 16
té **83**/12
teatro **76**
techo **16**/1
tecla **75**/24
teclado **38**/26, **44**/22
teclista **76**/12
teja **13**/19
tejado de paja **14**/14
tejado de pizarra **13**/2
tejado de tejas **14**/23
Tejas **55**
tela de araña **29**/15
tela impermeable **71**/20
tela metálica **45**/25
teleobjetivo **29**/15
telescopio **29**/5
televisión **16**/23, **42**/23, **58**/18, 19
temperatura **52**
tendedero **19**/22
tenedor **15**/12
tener fiebre **6**/10
tener hambre **6**/2
tener sed **6**/1
tener tos **6**/9
tener un catarro **6**/7
tenis **81**
Tennessee **55**
tentáculo **91**/13
tercero **33**
tercio **48**/20
terminal **67**
terminar **42**/18
termómetro **45**/21
ternera **28**/16
ternero **89**/2
terraplén **62**/3, 13
terraza **57**/14
terrina **27**/20
tetera **16**/11, **58**/16, 17, **83**/11
texto **32**/9
tía **1**/3
tiburón **91**/1
tiempo **51**
tienda **59**/12, **71**/19
tienda de fotografía **29**
tienda de periódicos **26**
tienda de sonido **30**
tienda libre de impuestos **67**/10
Tierra **50**/21
tierra **61**/19, **83**/7
tigre **90**/17
tijeras **49**/12
tijeras de jardín **22**/8
timbal **75**/17
timbre **65**/18
tío **1**/4
tipo de cambio **34**/8
Tipp-Ex **44**/9
tirar **57**/4, 5, **78**/10, **86**/22
tirita **7**/3
tiza **49**/24
toalla de baño **17**/11
toalla de cara **17**/13
toalla de manos **17**/10
toallero **17**/9
tobillo **3**/16, **6**/14
tocador **18**/1
tocar el pito **82**/23
Togo **54**
tomar nota **43**/8
tomarse **42**/16
tomate **23**/19, **28**/5
torcerse **6**/14
torcido **87**/2
tormenta **51**/9, 10
tornillo **21**/22
torno **21**/11
toro **89**/3
torre de control **68**/4
tortuga **91**/24, 25
tos **6**/9
tostada **28**/4
tostador **20**/17
total **35**/15
trabajador de la construcción **61**/15
trabajar **42**/15, 18
trabajo **39/40**
tractor **73**/28
tráfico **59**/13
tráfico de doble sentido **61**/4
traje **10**/18
traje de baño **11**/2
traje espacial **50**/7
transatlántico **70**/11
transbordador espacial **50**/11
transplantador **22**/12
transportador **49**/7
transporte **63**/1
trapo del polvo **19**/14
tráquea **4**/2
trece **33**/13
treinta **33**/30
tren **42**/13, **66**/8
trenza **5**/17
trepar **82**/13
tres **33**/3
tres puertas **63**/15
triángulo **47**/13
tribuna **81**/24
triciclo **64**/17
trigésimo **33**
Trinidad y Tobago **53**
trípode **29**/4, **45**/26
triste **88**/2
trombón **75**/8
trompa **90**/26
trompeta **75**/7
tronco **25**/2
tronera **79**/7
trópico de Cancer **53/54**
trópico de Capricornio **53/54**
trozo **27**/10, 12, **49**/24, **86**/17-19
trucha **28**/17, **91**/8
tuba **75**/9
tubería **14**/21
tubo **17**/3
tubo de bucear **77**/24
tubo de ensayo **45**/2
tubo de escape **64**/6
tubo de goma **45**/4
tubo en U **45**/18
tuerca **21**/25
tulipán **25**/25
tumbado **84**/23
tumbona **72**/7
túnel **66**/9
Túnez **54**
turista **71**/12
Turkmenistán **54**
turquesa **9**/8
Turquía **54**

Ucrania **54**
Uganda **54**
último piso **13**/11
undécimo **33**
unidad de disco **44**/24
uniforme escolar **10**/1
uno **33**/1
uña **3**/17
Urano **50**/17
Uruguay **53**
uva **24**/10
Uzbekistán **54**

vaca **89**/1
vacaciones en barco **72**/11
vacío **88**/12
vagón **66**/4
valla **22**/15
valla de seguridad **62**/9, 19
valle **73**/3
válvula **65**/11
Vanuatu **54**
vaqueros **10**/7
varilla de vidrio **46**/2
vaso **15**/14, **27**/19
vaso de precipitación **45**/24
vehículo **63**
vehículo lunar **50**/8
veinte **33**/20
veintiuno **33**/21
vela **15**/3, **58**/8, 9, **69**/3, **72**/10, **86**/23, 24
velero **69**/12
velocímetro **64**/24
venda **7**/2
vendedor de periódicos **59**/17
Venezuela **53**
venir **57**/7
ventana **14**/8, **57**/1, **58**/1, **83**/3
ventana de guillotina **13**/8
ventana del sótano **13**/9
ventana en saledizo **14**/11
ventanilla **31**/5, **66**/11
Venus **50**/22
ver **42**/23
veraneante **72**/8
verano **52**/10
verbo **43, 83-86**
verde **9**/11, 12
verduras **23, 28**

verja **60**/9
vértice **47**/14
vesícula biliar **4**/5
vestido **12**/19
vestirse **41**/8
veterinaria **40**/6
veterinario **40**/6
vías **66**/7
vídeo **16**/24
viejo **5**/6, **87**/5
viento **51**/5
viento-madera **75**
viento-metal **75**
viernes **33**
Vietnam **54**
vigésimo **33**
viola **75**/1
violín **75**/4
violoncelo **75**/3
visita a monumentos **71**/9
visor **30**/3, **46**/22
vocalista **76**/9
volante **64**/22
voleibol **78**/20
volquete **61**/14
volver **41**/5
vuelo delta **72**/22

Walkman **30**/11
wind-surf **77**/18
windsurfista **77**/19

yate **69**/13
Yibuti **54**
yogur **27**/19, 27
Yugoslavia **54**

Zambia **54**
zanahoria **23**/14
zapatilla **11**/12
zapatilla de deporte **12**/4
zapato **10**/23
zarpa **90**/5
zorro **89**/7
zumo de naranja **27**/21

# People and Health Pages 1-8

## 1 Who's who?

Read the sentences about this family and then write the names in the family tree.

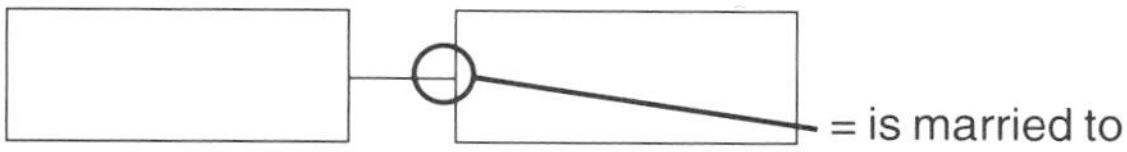


Peter is married to Ann and they have a daughter called Laura.
Peter's parents are Jack and Rosy.
Ann's sister, Sarah, has a son called Leo.

Linda is Ann's sister-in-law.
Alan's mother-in-law is called Joan.
Jamie is Leo's cousin.
Bill has got two grandsons and one granddaughter.

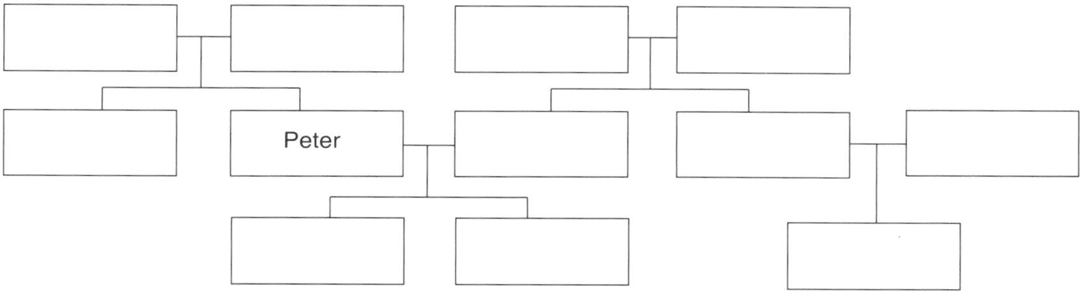


## 2 The Human Body

There are sixteen parts of the body hidden in this square. Can you find them all?

thumb

______ ______ ______
______ ______ ______
______ ______ ______
______ ______ ______
______ ______ ______

| | | | | | | | | | | |
|---|---|---|---|---|---|---|---|---|---|---|
| e | i | b | h | e | a | d | e | n | o | x |
| o | y | u | e | a | m | o | o | a | t | s |
| t | o | e | o | u | b | i | f | i | s | t |
| a | e | z | o | m | e | f | i | l | o | o |
| n | c | a | u | e | c | a | n | g | e | m |
| k | e | h | i | e | a | h | g | i | i | a |
| l | t | e | i | o | u | e | e | i | o | c |
| e | e | a | o | n | a | i | r | s | e | h |
| u | l | u | o | e | t | x | u | e | t | e |
| a | i | b | a | c | k | a | e | e | i | e |
| e | p | a | i | k | n | e | e | t | e | k |

## 3 What's the matter?

Match what the patient says to the doctor's advice.

Patient

a I have dreadful earache.
b I've got a sore throat and a temperature.
c I've fallen over and hurt my arm.
d I've got a small scratch on my leg.
e I've got terrible toothache.

a 3 b ___ c ___ d ___ e ___

Doctor

1 Take two of these tablets and go straight to bed.
2 You probably need a filling.
3 Put two drops in each ear twice a day.
4 We'll need to put it in a sling.
5 Put some of this ointment on it and then cover it with a plaster.

# Exercises page 125

## Clothes Pages 9-12

**1 Test your memory!**

Look carefully at page 10.

Fill in the missing words in the sentences below. Use words from the box.

**a** The woman is wearing a ________________ blouse and a ________________ blue jacket.

**b** The boy is wearing a ________________ blazer and ________________ trousers.

**c** The man is wearing a red and white ________________ tie and he is carrying a raincoat.

**d** The girl is wearing a ________________ coat and a ________________ scarf.

polka-dot tartan pink grey striped plain patterned

■ *Language note*

The man in the picture is **wearing** a suit and he is **carrying** a raincoat.

**2 What other things are people carrying in the picture? Write some sentences.**

________________________________________

________________________________________

________________________________________

________________________________________

________________________________________

**3 Match each of these words with the right part of the body.**

| | |
|---|---|
| trainer | head |
| belt | hand |
| watch | neck |
| glove | waist |
| tights | foot |
| helmet | legs |
| tie | wrist |

**4 Find the words from the mixed-up letters. They are all things that people wear or carry. When you have finished, read down the box to find the mystery word.**

1 FRIEHCEKHDAN
2 FRASC
3 LABRUMEL
4 ERUPS
5 RECIFEABS
6 RENGIRA
7 LACKENCE
8 NABAHGD
9 GIRN
10 LOSECAHE
11 LAWLET
12 GESSNALUSS

# At Home Pages 15-22 and 58

**1 Find the word in each group that is different from the others.**

**a** mug cup freezer saucer teapot

**b** scales aftershave soap shampoo toothpaste

**c** wardrobe sideboard vase wall unit chest of drawers

**d** duster brush scourer oven mop

**e** rake watering-can shears lawnmower bush

**2 Write in the words.**

**a** ____________

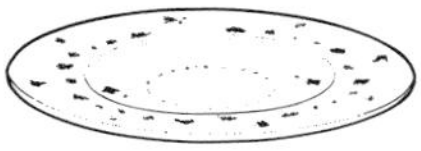

**b** ____________

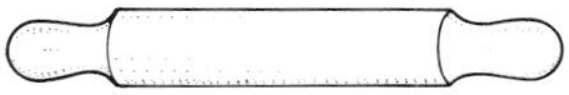

**c** ____________

**d** ____________

**e** ____________

**f** ____________

**g** ____________

**h** ____________

**3 Test your memory!**

Look at page 18 for two minutes, then read these sentences about the picture. Decide if they are true or false.

**a** The box of tissues is in the bedside cabinet.
**b** There's a poster over the bed.
**c** There's a hair-drier on the dressing table.
**d** The dressing table is in front of the chest of drawers.
**e** The blanket is under the bedspread.
**f** There's a coat-hanger betweeen the light and the alarm clock.

If the sentences are false, write them correctly.

____________________________________________

____________________________________________

____________________________________________

____________________________________________

# Exercises page 127

## Shopping and Food Pages 23-28

**1 Match a word in A with the right word in B.**

| A | B |
|---|---|
| a tube of | chocolate |
| a loaf of | cereal |
| a bar of | toothpaste |
| a bottle of | margarine |
| a jar of | jam |
| a packet of | bread |
| a tub of | biscuits |
| a box of | mineral water |

**2 Complete these dialogues using words from the box. Use each word only once.**

1 a Can I help you?
b Yes, please. How much are the ________________?
a They're 70p a bunch.
b And the strawberries?
a 85p a ________________.

2 a I'd like some ________________ for my wife's birthday.
b Certainly, sir. Any particular kind?
a Well, yes, she likes these blue ones.
b Oh, you mean ________________.

3 a I'm looking for a ________________ of chocolates. Have you got any?
b They're up on the top ________________.
a They're a present for somebody so I'll need a roll of ________________ and a ________________ of Sellotape too, please.

4 a Are you ready to order? Here comes the ________________.
b No, I haven't decided yet. Are you going to have a ________________?
a Yes, I think I'll have the melon.

| flowers | bananas | starter | shelf | punnet | waiter | wrapping paper | irises | box | reel |
|---|---|---|---|---|---|---|---|---|---|

**3 Where do each of the conversations in exercise 2 take place?**

1 ________________ 3 ________________

2 ________________ 4 ________________

# Dates and Times Pages 33 and 37

**1 Look at the clocks, then find two ways of saying each time, using the expressions in the box.**

18:30

1 c, ______ 2 ______

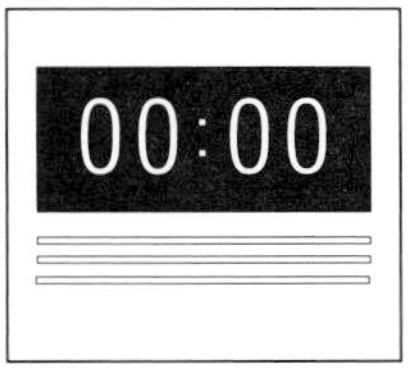
00:00

3 ______ 4 ______

14:45

5 ______ 6 ______

- a midnight
- b ten to five
- c eleven fifty-five
- d four fifty
- e a quarter to three in the afternoon
- f six thirty pm
- g seven minutes past four
- h two forty-five pm
- i half past six in the evening
- j twelve o'clock at night
- k five to twelve
- l four o seven

**2 Dates**

John always forgets important dates so he writes them down at the beginning of the year in a special page in his diary.

Look at the page, then answer the questions by writing the dates **in words**.

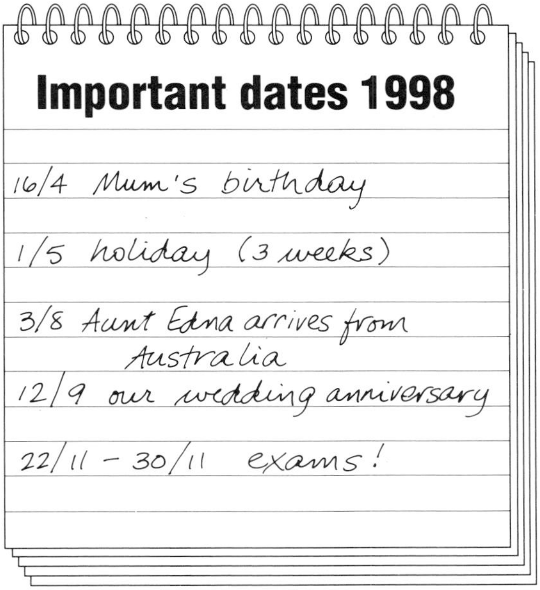
Important dates 1998
16/4 Mum's birthday
1/5 holiday (3 weeks)
3/8 Aunt Edna arrives from Australia
12/9 our wedding anniversary
22/11 – 30/11 exams!

**a** When is John's mother's birthday?

______

**b** When does John's holiday begin?

______

**c** On what date does Aunt Edna arrive?

______

**d** When is John's wedding anniversary?

______

**e** On what date do his exams finish?

______

# Exercises page 129

## At Work Pages 39-40 and 43-44

**1 What do we call someone who...**

...reads the news aloud on the radio or TV?

______________________

...arranges people's holidays for them?

______________________

...works with wood?

______________________

... makes bread and cakes?

______________________

...treats sick animals?

______________________

...repairs cars?

______________________

**2 Read these job advertisements and decide what job is being offered in each one.**

**a** Ladies' and gentlemen's ***** needed for modern salon. Experience of cutting all types of hair necessary.

**b** ***** for long-distance deliveries. Must have licence.

**c** WANTED! Qualified ***** for small chemist's. Duties to include dispensing prescriptions plus general shop work.

**d** EXPERIENCE IN RADIO? Love all kinds of music? 'Joy FM' is looking for a *****.

a ______________________

b ______________________

c ______________________

d ______________________

**3 Office wordsearch**

There are thirteen words connected with the office in this square. Can you find them all?

| | | | | | | | | | | |
|---|---|---|---|---|---|---|---|---|---|---|
| e | a | n | d | i | s | k | a | i | l | s |
| i | o | c | h | e | q | u | e | o | e | i |
| u | b | o | i | e | s | y | f | u | t | w |
| f | c | t | t | a | i | k | d | n | t | a |
| t | i | e | y | u | n | r | i | g | e | a |
| e | u | l | p | e | e | r | a | c | r | i |
| i | e | i | e | l | p | u | r | d | x | x |
| n | g | r | p | i | u | o | y | a | e | u |
| e | c | a | o | o | i | e | f | m | i | o |
| s | t | e | o | x | p | u | u | o | y | e |
| s | n | o | t | e | b | o | o | k | a | e |

cheque

______________________

# Describing Things Pages 47-49 and 87-88

**1 Write the names of these shapes.**

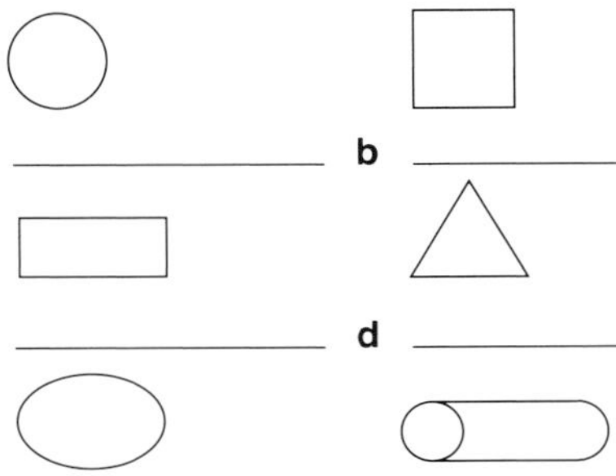

a ____________ b ____________

c ____________ d ____________

e ____________ f ____________

■ *Language note*

We say: This page is **rectangular**.
(Not: **a rectangle.**)
*Rectangular* is an adjective.

| *Noun* | *Adjective* |
|---|---|
| rectangle | rectangular |
| triangle | triangular |
| circle | circular |
| oval | oval |
| square | square |
| cylinder | cylindrical |

**2 Match these questions and answers by writing the correct number next to the questions.**

| *Question* | | *Answer* |
|---|---|---|
| a What shape is it? | ☐ | 1 It's used for measuring things and for drawing straight lines. |
| b How much does it weigh? | ☐ | 2 This one is made of plastic but they are also made of wood. |
| c How big is it? | ☐ | 3 It's rectangular. |
| d What's it made of? | ☐ | 4 About 10g. |
| e What's it used for? | ☐ | 5 It's about 15 cm long, 3 cm wide and 0.2 cm thick. |

**What is it? It's on page 49 of this dictionary.** ____________

**3 Find the opposites of these adjectives and write them in the puzzle.**

1 crooked
2 thin
3 light
4 tight
5 empty
6 hollow
7 dry

**Now read down the box to find another adjective!**

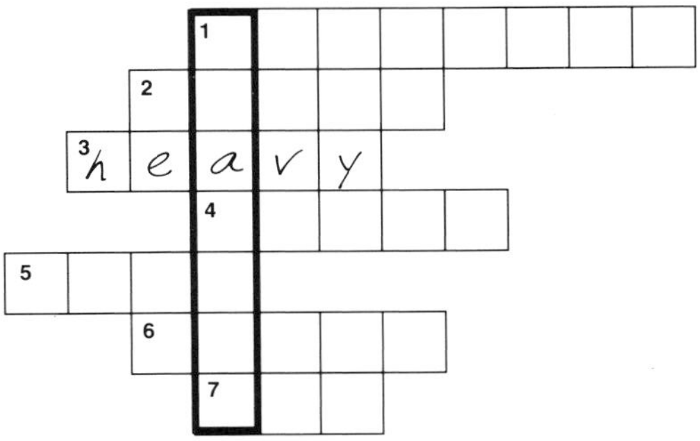

# Exercises page 131

## The Weather Pages 51-52 and 56

**1 Look at the weather map of the British Isles below. Find a symbol for each of the words in the box and draw it.**

| | | |
|---|---|---|
| sun | cloud | rain |
| wind | fog | snow |

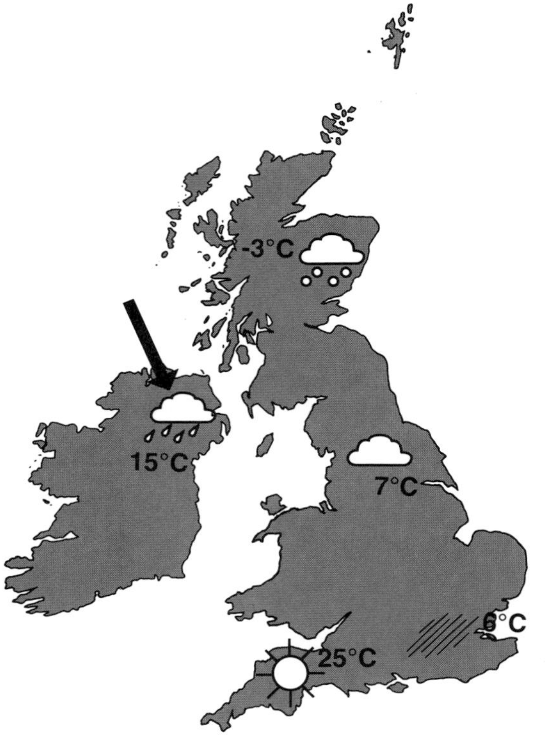


■ *Language note*

The adjective from { **cloud** is **cloudy**. / **sun** is **sunny**. }

Make adjectives from the other words in the box. (If you are not sure about the spelling, check on page 51.)

wind ____________________

snow ____________________

fog ____________________

rain ____________________

**2 Look at the weather map and write in the missing information below.**

*Tomorrow's Weather*

The South-East will start the day quite (1)____________________ and (2)____________________, but in the South-West it's going to be rather (3)____________________ and (4)____________________. Further north it will be (5) ____________________ all day with a maximum (6)____________________ of 7°C.

Over in Northern Ireland it will be (7) ____________________ with some (8)____________________ during the morning and it will be very (9) ____________________ on the coast. Up in Scotland the temperature will fall to (10) ____________________ 3°C and there may be some (11)____________________.

# The City Pages 57 and 59-60

## 1 Letter-box or mailbox?

These are six things that you can find in a city street. Complete the table by writing the British or American words.

| *British* | *American* |
|---|---|
| letter-box | |
| | sidewalk |
| crossroads | |
| | traffic circle |
| | trash can |
| pedestrian crossing | |

## 2 Look at the pictures and complete the sentences using words from the box.

a

b

c

d

e

bus stop, building, pavement, across, away from, into, road sign, towards, along, road

a She is walking ______________________________ the ______________________________.

b He is going ______________________________ the ______________________________.

c She is going ______________________________ the ______________________________.

d They are walking ______________________________ the ______________________________.

e He is running ______________________________ the ______________________________.

# Exercises page 133

## Travelling Pages 63-68

1 **Label these pictures.**

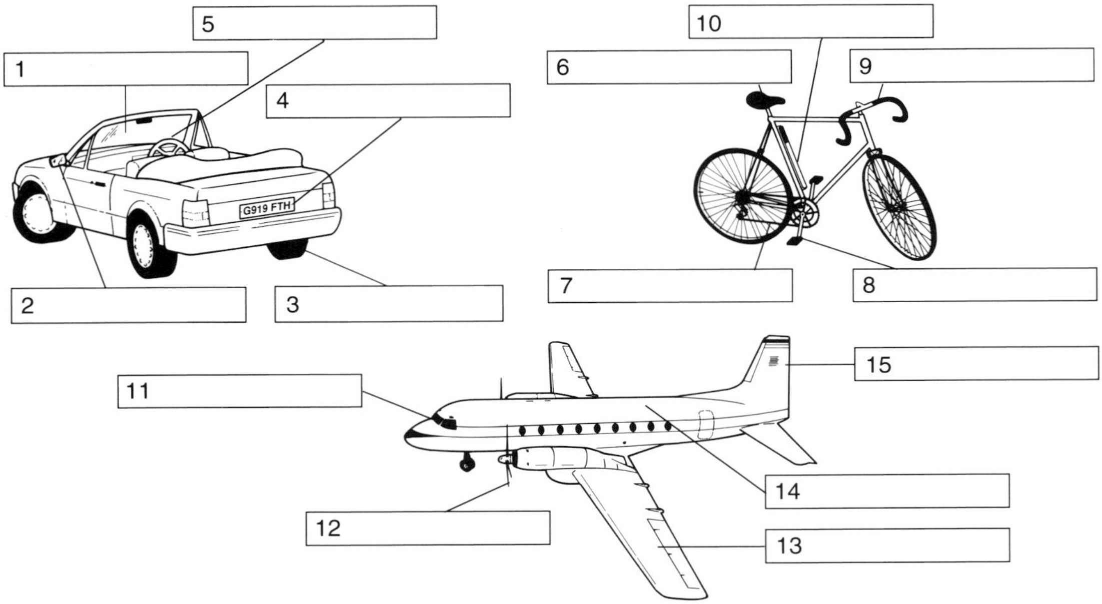


2 **Airport crossword**

*Across*

1 ____ pass

5

6 ____ desk
(where you go to collect your *1 across*)

7

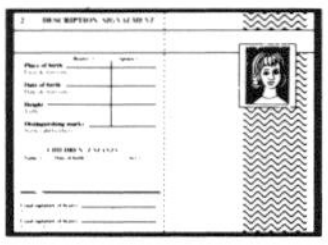

8 departure ____

10 You sit on this.

*Down*

2 ____ ticket

3 The part of the plane where the passengers are.

4 You can find an X-ray scanner here.

9 'Your flight is now boarding at ____ six.'

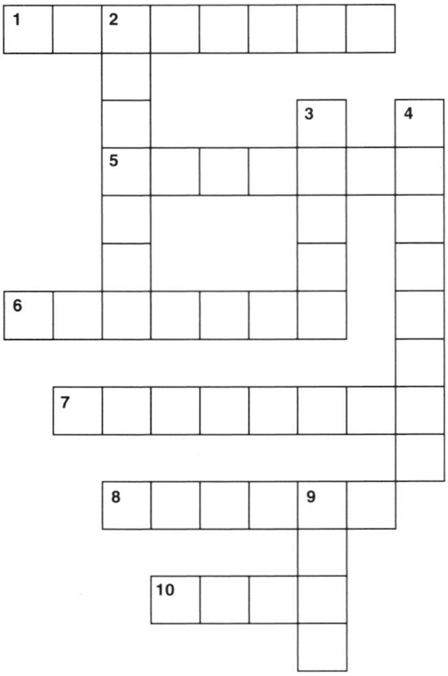

# On Holiday Pages 71-73

**Read the hotel information, look at the pictures, and fill in the missing words.**

## Sunnyview Hotel - information

*Please leave your 1 ____ ____ ____ ____ ____ ____ ____ at the hotel reception when you go out.*

*Thank you.*

### Activities

Dalton Lake is only half a mile from the hotel. There you can go 2 ________________ or 3 ________________.

Northend-by-the-sea is a pretty holiday resort. Go 4 ____________ along the cliffs or just sit on the 5 __________ and enjoy the sun!

If you want to do something really exciting, why not try 6 ______________________ or even 7 ________ - ________________?

### SIGHTSEEING

Monday: Visit to Longleat, a historic 8 ________________ ____________ in Wiltshire.

Wednesday: A tour of the local countryside. A 9 ______________ is provided.

Friday: Coach trip to a beautiful 10 ______________________.

Bring your camera!

1

2

3

4

5

6

7

8

9

10

# Exercises page 135

## Music and Theatre Pages 75-76

1 **Write the names of these instruments. The words are in the box, but the letters of each word have been mixed up.**

**a**

**b**

**c**

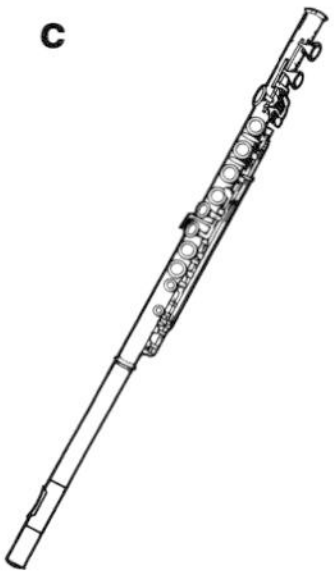

**d**

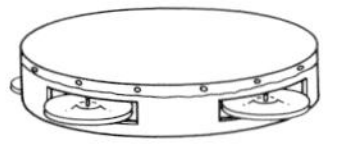

**e**

**f**

| | |
|---|---|
| tufel | olcel |
| phosanoex | bornmote |
| beamotunir | slycbam |

2 **What's the word?**

a You walk along this to get to your seat in a cinema or a theatre.

— — — — —

b He or she helps you to find your seat.

— — — — —

c Somebody who plays a large percussion instrument.

— — — — — — —

d Where the orchestra sits.

— — —

e The American word for a 'balcony' in a cinema or a theatre.

— — — — — — — — —

f Actors and actresses wait here before they go on stage.

— — — — —

g A word that means 'singer'.

— — — — — — — —

h Things on the stage of a theatre that make it look like a real place.

— — — — — — —

Now take the first letter of each of the words you found for **a**, **b** and **c**, the second letter of **d** and **e** and the third letter of **f**, **g** and **h**. You will then have the word for a group of people who are watching a film or a play!

____________________

# Sports Pages 77-81

1 **Fill in the table using words from the box.
Use each word only once.**

| Sport | Person | Place | Equipment |
|---|---|---|---|
| | | *court* | |
| | *caddy* | | |
| *cricket* | | | |
| | | *track* | |
| | | | *starting-gate* |

racket athlete jockey club horse-racing stumps starting-block golf field racecourse batsman tennis athletics umpire fairway

2 **Sports Quiz**

**a** Name three sports in which players **tackle** each other.

______________________________

**b** What is the other name for **ping-pong**?

______________________________

**c** Name three objects that you need for playing baseball.

______________________________

**d** In which sport do players use **sticks**?

______________________________

**e** Name a sport that takes place under water.

______________________________

**f** Name three sports that need a **net**.

______________________________

# Exercises page 137

## Verbs Pages 83-86

**1 What shall I do now?**

Bob never knows what to do. Give him some advice by writing the correct numbers by the letters.

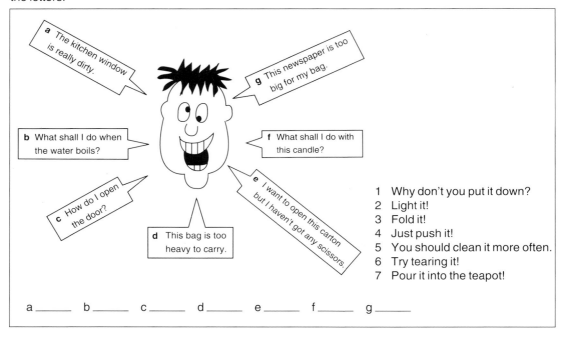

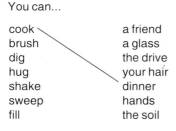

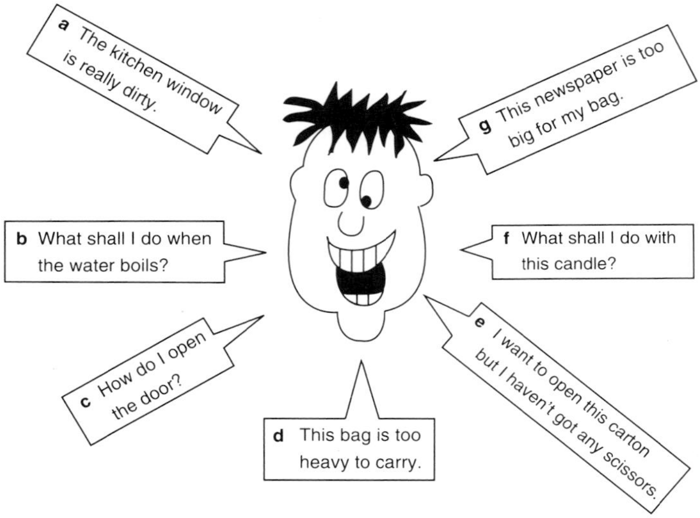

a The kitchen window is really dirty.
g This newspaper is too big for my bag.
b What shall I do when the water boils?
f What shall I do with this candle?
c How do I open the door?
d This bag is too heavy to carry.
e I want to open this carton but I haven't got any scissors.


1 Why don't you put it down?
2 Light it!
3 Fold it!
4 Just push it!
5 You should clean it more often.
6 Try tearing it!
7 Pour it into the teapot!

a ______ b ______ c ______ d ______ e ______ f ______ g ______

**2 Match these verbs to the right thing or person.**

You can...

| | |
|---|---|
| cook | a friend |
| brush | a glass |
| dig | the drive |
| hug | your hair |
| shake | dinner |
| sweep | hands |
| fill | the soil |

# Animals

Pages 89-93

**Wordsnake**
Complete the puzzle with the first letter of each word at the correct number. Every answer except the first begins with the last letter of the word before it.

1 An insect with hard wings.
2 A large grey animal with a trunk.
3 A wild animal with yellow fur and black stripes.
4 It's got a horn on its nose.
5 This small animal has got a big tail and lives in trees.
6 A reptile with a long body usually seen in hot, dry places.
7 A young one of these is called a puppy.
8 It has a very long neck.
9 It looks like a snake and lives in water.
10 A young sheep.
11 A large black animal with horns found mainly in Asia and Africa.
12 It has got eight 'arms'.
13 We get wool from these.
14 A large animal with black and white fur.
15 A very small insect.

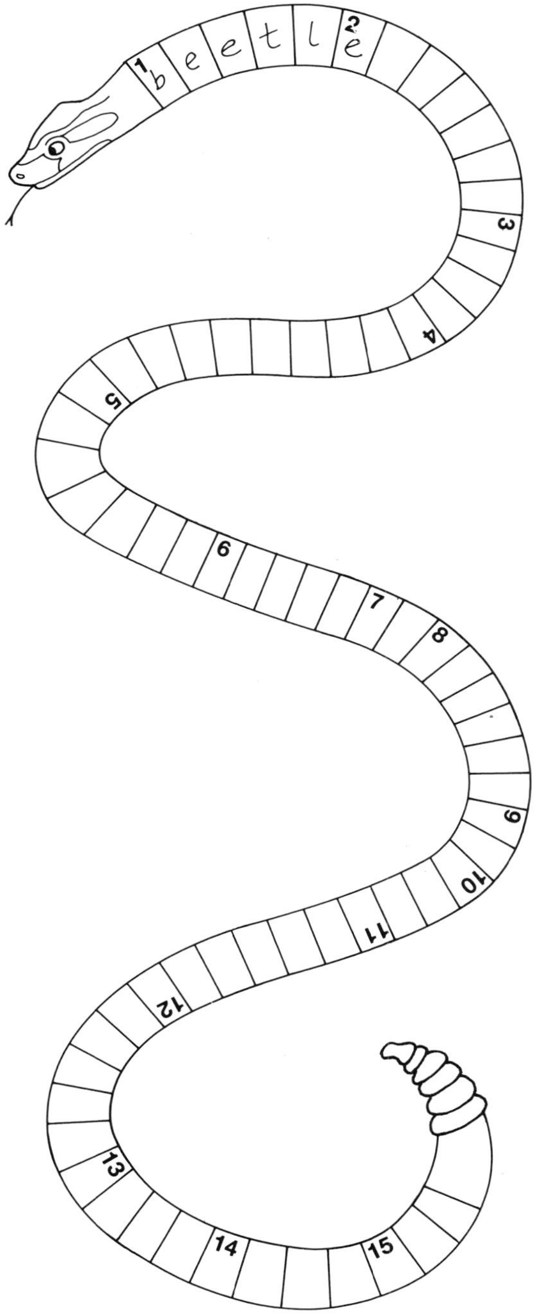

# Key to exercises 

## **People and Health** page 124

1 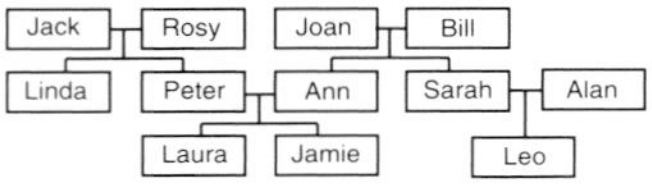


2 ankle, back, cheek, chest, chin, eye, finger, fist, head, knee, lip, nail, neck, stomach, toe

3 **b** 1 **c** 4 **d** 5 **e** 2

## **Clothes** page 125

1 **a** patterned, plain **b** striped, grey **c** polka-dot **d** pink, tartan

2 The girl is carrying an umbrella.
The woman is carrying a handbag and a briefcase.
The man is carrying a sweater.

3 belt - waist, watch - wrist, glove - hand, tights - legs, helmet - head, tie - neck

4 2. scarf 3. umbrella 4. purse 5. briefcase 6. earring 7. necklace 8. handbag 9. ring 10. shoelace 11. wallet 12. sun-glasses
**dressing gown**

## **At Home** page 126

1 **a** freezer **b** scales **c** vase **d** oven **e** bush

2 **a** frying-pan **b** plate **c** rolling-pin **d** fork **e** ladle **f** kettle **g** jug **h** toaster

3 **a** *false.* The box of tissues is on the bedside cabinet. **b** *true.* **c** *false.* There's a hair-drier on the chest of drawers. **d** *false.* The dressing table is next to the chest of drawers. **e** *true.* **f** *false.* There's a poster between the light and the alarm clock.

## **Shopping and Food** page 127

1 loaf of bread, bar of chocolate, bottle of mineral water, jar of jam, packet of biscuits, tub of margarine, box of cereal

2 1. bananas, punnet 2. flowers, irises 3. box, shelf, wrapping paper, reel 4. waiter, starter

3 1. market 2. florist's 3. newsagent's 4. restaurant

## **Dates and Times** page 128

1 1. c, k 2. f, i 3. g, l 4. a, j 5. b, d 6. e, h

2 **a** On the sixteenth of April/ April the sixteenth. **b** On the first of May/ May the first. **c** On the third of August/ August the third. **d** On the twelfth of September/ September the twelfth. **e** On the thirtieth of November/ November the thirtieth.

## **At Work** page 129

1 newsreader, travel agent, carpenter, baker, vet, mechanic

2 **a** hairdresser **b** lorry driver **c** pharmacist **d** disc jockey

3 desk, diary, disk, fax, file, letter, notebook, pen, print, screen, stapler, type

## **Describing Things** page 130

1 **a** circle **b** square **c** rectangle **d** triangle **e** oval **f** cylinder

2 **a** 3 **b** 4 **c** 5 **d** 2 **e** 1 It's a **ruler**.

3 1. straight 2. thick 4. loose 5. full 6. solid 7. wet **shallow**

## **The Weather** page 131

1 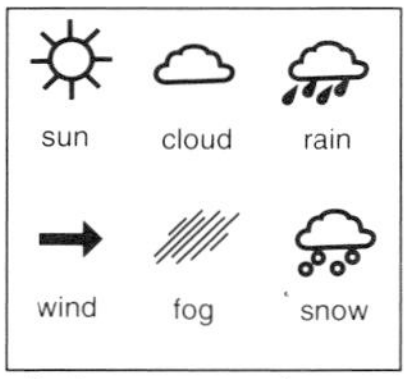


windy snowy foggy rainy

2 1. cold 2. foggy 3. warm 4. sunny 5. cloudy 6. temperature 7. cool 8. rain 9. windy 10. minus 11. snow

## **The City** page 132

1 mailbox, pavement, intersection, roundabout, litter-bin, crosswalk

2 **a** away from, road sign **b** across, road **c** into, building **d** along, pavement **e** towards, bus stop

## **Travelling** page 133

1 1. windscreen 2. wing mirror 3. tyre 4. number-plate 5. steering-wheel 6. saddle 7. chain 8. pedal 9. handlebar 10. pump 11. cockpit 12. propeller 13. wing 14. fuselage 15. tail

2 1. boarding 2. airline 3. cabin 4. security 5. luggage 6. check-in 7. passport 8. lounge 9. gate 10. seat

## **On Holiday** page 134

1. room key 2. sailing 3. fishing 4. hiking 5. beach 6. ballooning 7. hang-gliding 8. country house 9. picnic 10. waterfall

## **Music and Theatre** page 135

1 **a** cello **b** trombone **c** flute **d** tambourine **e** saxophone **f** cymbals

2 **a** aisle **b** usher **c** drummer **d** pit **e** mezzanine **f** wings **g** vocalist **h** scenery **audience**

## **Sports** page 136

1

| *Sport* | *Person* | *Place* | *Equipment* |
|---|---|---|---|
| tennis | umpire | court | racket |
| golf | caddy | fairway | club |
| cricket | batsman | field | stumps |
| athletics | athlete | track | starting-block |
| horse-racing | jockey | racecourse | starting-gate |

2 **a** rugby, hockey, football
**b** table tennis
**c** batting helmet, baseball glove/mitt, face mask/catcher's mask
**d** hockey **e** scuba-diving
**f** basketball, volleyball, badminton, *or* tennis

## **Verbs** page 137

1 **a** 5 **b** 7 **c** 4 **d** 1 **e** 6 **f** 2 **g** 3

2 brush your hair, dig the soil, hug a friend, shake hands, sweep the drive, fill a glass

## **Animals** page 138

1. beetle 2. elephant 3. tiger 4. rhinoceros 5. squirrel 6. lizard 7. dog 8. giraffe 9. eel 10. lamb 11. buffalo 12. octopus 13. sheep 14. panda 15. ant